THE UNION BLOCKADE
— IN THE —
AMERICAN CIVIL WAR

THE UNION BLOCKADE
— IN THE —
AMERICAN CIVIL WAR

A REASSESSMENT

Michael Brem Bonner and Peter McCord

THE UNIVERSITY OF TENNESSEE PRESS | KNOXVILLE

Frontispiece: "Maffit on bridge," original art by
Joseph E. Baker (1837–1914). Rosanna Blake Library of
Civil War History, Special Collections, Marshall University.

Library of Congress Cataloging-in-Publication Data
Names: Bonner, Michael Brem, 1970- author. | McCord, Peter, author.
Title: The Union blockade in the American Civil War : a reassessment /
Michael Brem Bonner and Peter McCord.
Description: First edition. | Knoxville : University of Tennessee Press, 2021. |
Includes bibliographical references and index. | Summary: "This book
re-examines multiple aspects of the Union blockade during the American Civil
War. Michael Bonner and Peter McCord scrutinize the blockade's operation
under international maritime law, its psychological effect on citizens of southern
port cities, and the truth about blockade runners often masked by Confederate
lore. This deep examination of the blockade critiques the widely accepted notion
that the blockade was, by and large, extremely effective"—Provided by publisher.
Identifiers: LCCN 2020056876 (print) | LCCN 2020056877 (ebook) |
ISBN 9781621906704 (hardcover) | ISBN 9781621906711 (Adobe PDF)
Subjects: LCSH: War, Maritime (International law) | United States—History—
Civil War, 1861–1865—Blockades. | United States—History—Civil War,
1861–1865—Blockades—Psychological aspects. | Great Britain—Foreign
relations—United States. | United States—Foreign relations—Great Britain.
Classification: LCC E600 .B69 2021 (print) | LCC E600 (ebook) |
DDC 973.7/3—dc23
LC record available at https://lccn.loc.gov/2020056876
LC ebook record available at https://lccn.loc.gov/2020056877

CONTENTS

ACKNOWLEDGMENTS

THE AUTHORS WOULD LIKE TO THANK several individuals and institutions for their generous support. First, this project would have never taken shape had the authors not met in graduate school at the University of California Riverside and worked under the direction of emeritus professor of history Roger Ransom. Many years ago, Professor Ransom planted the seed of compiling a comprehensive statistical study of blockade-running, which had yet to be compiled. Being a cliometrician, he foresaw that a fresh statistical interpretation of the blockade's effectiveness was overdue. Professor Ransom also knew exactly where to find the data, and thus he sent two young—at the time—graduate students off to seek the answers he knew were still to be mined from the extant data. Roger, we hope you are pleased with the final result! At the time, it seemed like a laborious task, but we came to realize that our combined knowledge of the blockade and blockade-running was enough to combine our efforts on a larger work. Year after year passed, and no matter how great the temptation, we simply could not drop this project. Indeed, we took long breaks from analyzing the blockade to work on other historical scholarship and fulfill the requirements of careers in history, but we could never shake the desire to bring this project to fruition. As friends and as scholars we have been both blessed and cursed by this book, but in the end, writing it has been a fulfilling experience.

Many people and institutions have assisted along the way. We apologize if we forgot anyone—it is not intentional. Salvatore Mercogliano, history professor at Campbell University, has been a constant source of expertise in maritime history for over two decades. Sal was always willing to help track down obscure sources. Jack Dickinson at the Rosanna Blake Library of Confederate History in Marshall University's Special Collections Department provided crucial primary source materials, but more importantly, he was willing to talk about Civil War topics and the blockade on a weekly basis. The Rosanna Blake Collection is one of the best kept secrets in Civil War archives. Special thanks are also due to Annie Miller and the *North Carolina Historical Review* for allowing us to use portions of a 2011 article for this work.

A generous research grants from the University of South Carolina Lancaster allowed us to travel to London in 2014 and conduct research in the British National Archives at Kew. We are very fortunate to have had the opportunity to do so, and the book is much stronger as a result. We hope that incorporating more primary materials from the British perspective will improve the overall understanding of the blockade on this side of the Atlantic. We would love to go back and uncover more!

Introduction

───────★───────

THE CIVIL WAR BLOCKADE and blockade-running continues to captivate our collective historical imagination. Cat-and-mouse competition between Union blockaders and blockade-runners provides historians with wonderful stories of swashbuckling adventure, and the personalities involved in this contest are among the most colorful of the Civil War era. This romantic, even nostalgic, view of maritime Civil War history enhances the more important topic of the blockade's influence on the outcome of the Civil War.

One could argue that most war-related events from 1861 to 1865 were directly or indirectly affected by the blockade. There is no doubt that the blockade prevented mass importation of crucial industrial materials that could not be manufactured in the Confederacy. Items such as railroad locomotive engines, manufacturing machinery, and numerous other items had to be produced by ersatz methods. The blockade hampered full-scale industrial production in the rebellious states, despite a remarkably innovative Confederate industrial policy.

Blockade squadrons' inability to keep armaments out of Southern ports could influence major events. For example, in November 1861 the blockade-runner *Fingal* arrived from England via Bermuda carrying an extremely valuable cargo—over 11,500 rifles, some of which were state-of-the-art Enfields, in addition to other desperately needed munitions. On the outbound voyage, the *Fingal* transported James D. Bulloch, the Confederacy's overseas naval agent who was eventually responsible for developing the commerce raiders CSS *Florida* and CSS *Alabama*.

The matter is speculative, but how might the war have been different if the *Fingal* had been sunk or captured in November 1861? Bulloch's services would have been temporarily lost to the Confederacy and the building program of rebel commerce raiders would have suffered a serious setback, sparing numerous American merchant vessels. It is also impossible to calculate the number of Union soldiers killed or wounded by the 11,500 rifles

imported by the *Fingal*. These rifles were enough to outfit about fifteen
regiments of rebel infantry, which would have had time for extensive train-
ing before the spring campaigns of 1862. One can only speculate how many
Yankee soldiers suffered at Shiloh and in the Seven Days' Campaign because the *Fingal* got through the blockade.[1] The purpose of this question
is not to encourage additional "what-ifs" but to emphasize that every day
from April 1861 to April 1865, blockade squadrons and blockade-runners
engaged in an ongoing battle in which success or failure could have serious
ramifications. No other military campaign lasted as long as the blockade,
or had as many long-term consequences for the outcome of the Civil War.

The Union blockade of the Confederacy was a four-year military campaign, and the only Union strategy with continuity. It was also an important component of the Anaconda Plan that slowly constricted the Confederacy. Before either side incurred any battlefield casualties, the United
States Navy consistently applied a blockade that went unquestioned by the
Northern high command. President Lincoln never second-guessed the efficacy of the Union blockade, and he rarely worried about the blockaders'
performance. Much of the time these servicemen's duty was boring and un-
eventful. Union blockaders did not garner the same amount of newspaper
coverage compared to soldiers in large-scale land battles, but these sailors
served their country in a ceaseless four-year campaign that eventually assisted in Union military victory.

The task of blockading over three-thousand miles of Southern coastline proved Herculean. In reality, the Union navy only needed to close
off the main rebel ports of Norfolk, Wilmington, Charleston, Savannah,
Pensacola, Mobile, New Orleans, and Galveston in order to stifle maritime
trade. These ports were important due to their railroad links with the Confederate interior and their capacity for handling large cargoes. It was never
feasible for the Union navy to blockade every mile of the Southern coast.
After the blockade declaration in April 1861, the US Navy embarked on an
extensive shipbuilding program. By the end of 1861 over 260 vessels were
available for blockade service, and by the end of the war about 500 steamships were dedicated to blockading Southern ports. Crewing the blockade
squadrons required immense manpower. Over the course of the war about
one-hundred thousand sailors performed blockade duty—a force approximately the same size as the largest Union army.[2]

Although the blockade squadrons accounted for only 5 percent of overall Union military forces, the Union blockade was a vast undertaking that

required a massive investment of US naval resources. Blockaders required immense quantities of coal, food, and other supplies to stay on active duty. Unlike their army counterparts, Union blockade personnel rarely seized Southern commodities to supplement their food supplies. The allocation of resources, both human and material, necessary to conduct a four-year blockade was colossal. This resource outlay rivaled Union efforts for the land campaigns in the Eastern and Western Theaters. As historian Craig L. Symonds notes, "The hundreds of ships, thousands of men, and millions of dollars invested in the effort to close down the southern ports ranks as one of the greatest undertakings of the Federal government in its history."[3]

Union blockade squadrons and the numerous blockade-runners waged their own four-year high-stakes military campaign that helped to determine the war's outcome. For the embattled Confederacy, piercing the blockade was vital. Historian Stephen R. Wise does not exaggerate when he labels blockade-running the "lifeline of the Confederacy"; Southern states could not have waged war for as long as they did without the supplies brought through the blockade. Over four-hundred thousand modern rifles and other necessities like medicine, lead, and saltpeter were smuggled into the Confederacy. The number of steam-powered blockade-runners bringing these indispensable materials never exceeded three-hundred, but these vessels made about one-thousand passes through the Union cordon of ships.[4]

Even one successful run through the blockade made prodigious profits possible. The risks of blockade-running were ever present, but also somewhat limited. It was always in Union crews' pecuniary interest to capture blockade-runners intact instead of sinking them, because the value of confiscated contraband items was divided up among the crew in percentage shares at a prize court. Even if a blockade-runner foundered and was taken unharmed, the typical foreign crew from a neutral nation, like Great Britain, could not be held indefinitely in a Northern prison. Throughout the war, the promise of fabulous earnings continued to entice runners to test the Union blockade. Well-financed blockade-running operations introduced technologically advanced ships into the business because the profits were so high. The business of smuggling goods into the Confederacy was a four-year boom economy for those willing to take the risk.

Who won the four-year blockade campaign? This question has antagonized historians since the end of the war. Strong scholarly arguments support both the effectiveness and ineffectiveness of the Union blockade, and the answer depends on the specific question asked. The wounds of internal strife were still fresh when Civil War participants began to recount their stories of the blockade and to analyze its role in the conflict. Rear Adm. John A. Dahlgren, head of the South Atlantic Blockading Squadron from 1863 until the end of the war, applauded the efforts of the Union blockaders. On June 17, 1865, from his new flagship USS *Philadelphia*—his longest-serving flagship the USS *Harvest Moon* had been destroyed by a rebel mine on March 1st—Dahlgren congratulated the sailors under his command for a job well done. He declared, "Never was any service performed involving a more resolute struggle against the cold and the storms of winter, the heavy sea and the unsleeping enterprise of a vigilant enemy."

The rear admiral argued that proof of the blockade's effectiveness was evident, telling servicemen, "The desolate wrecks that strew the shores . . . make manifest that your labors were not in vain." Despite rebel arguments to the contrary, the rear admiral asserted, "The blockade was perfectly close until a few very fast steamers of trifling draught were built in England, expressly for the purpose of evading it . . . but even they could not pass with entire impunity." In summation, Dahlgren alluded to the overall contribution of the blockade squadrons: "In all these operations, and in others which I cannot here enumerate the [personnel] of this Squadron has manifested all that could be asked of the Navy, and if brilliant victory was not possible, the general results were not less useful directly to the great end."[5] His analysis praised the blockade's contributory nature to overall Union victory, and this has remained a powerful theme in blockade historiography.

Years after the war, former Confederate president Jefferson Davis decried the blockade as a "monstrous pretension" that was ineffective and illegal according to international law. Davis argued that foreign powers hypocritically observed this "paper blockade" even though it did not substantially deprive the Confederacy of critical supplies. He could not admit one of the blockade's lesser discussed achievements - that it did not anger foreign nations enough to cause Confederate recognition. As it turned out, foreign countries, especially Great Britain, were afraid to provoke the United States in order to trade openly with the Confederacy.[6]

The idea of a naval blockade was not a new strategy in 1861, but its goals and implementation during the Civil War distinguished it from previous examples. As historian Stephen R. Wise points out, "This was to be the first modern blockade."[7] How did the Union blockade differ from the British blockades of the Napoleonic Wars and the War of 1812? According to historians Lance E. Davis and Stanley Engerman these earlier cases were examples of a "defensive blockade." The main goal of these British efforts was containment of enemies. Davis and Engerman note that "the English defended their county by deploying their fleets off French ports to prevent that country's naval vessels from putting to sea and attacking the British coast and its colonies."[8]

Likewise, the British launched a defensive blockade of America's coast in the War of 1812. In addition to seriously disrupting the commerce of the American merchant marine, the British successfully suppressed the most powerful ships of the US Navy. As Davis and Engerman point out, "The navy's four frigates, the *Constitution*, the *United States*, and the *President* were effectively bottled up in Atlantic ports."[9] Thus, in a defensive blockade strategy, commerce suppression is a secondary aim. The main goal is to prevent the enemy's capital ships from attacking the home territory or colonial possessions. Since the Confederacy did not have a high-seas navy to threaten American territory, Union blockade strategists did not need to pursue a defensive strategy, but instead could pursue an offensive strategy focused on rebel commerce.[10]

Union blockade squadrons' tactics also differed from their predecessors'. The primary naval interdiction method prior to 1861 was the cabinet blockade, in which squadrons patrolled coastal areas and the high seas searching for enemy vessels. In the age of sail this made perfect sense, but the widespread use of steam power changed blockading tactics. The typical strategy for Union blockading steamships would be to sit for long periods outside Southern ports. Squadrons were resupplied with coal, food, fresh water, and other items while remaining on duty.

Blockade strategies that directly interdict enemy ports are called "close blockades."[11] Steam power allowed for close blockades without necessarily using widespread cabinet blockade-style cruising tactics, although eventually the Union navy used both. In the age of steamships close blockades could be perpetually maintained so long as serious naval threats did not materialize and supplies and repairs could be effectively managed. It was embarrassing when blockade-runners successfully exited a Southern port, but it was much more important to catch them coming into port laden with valuable cargo. Union blockaders made this interdiction, or close blockade, strategy their main mission, and they developed tactics consistent with this goal.

On several occasions the Confederate navy attempted to break the Union's close blockade of Southern ports. Four important episodes highlight rebel efforts: the CSS *Virginia*'s attack at Hampton Roads in March 1862, the strike by the CSS *Palmetto State* and CSS *Chicora* outside Charleston on

January 30,1863, the CSS *Atlanta*'s foray from Savannah in June 1863, and the first successful submarine attack by the CSS *Hunley* in February 1864. However, for the most part, the Union blockade was virtually impervious to Confederate naval power. As it turned out, rebel military victories against the blockade were only temporary, and if anything, they caused the US Navy to redouble its efforts after each episode. In the end, vast naval superiority allowed Union strategists to maintain a continual close blockade of Southern ports.

Before the Civil War, interdiction was typically a secondary goal of blockades, taking a back seat to suppression of the enemy fleet.[12] But the Union blockade was designed to comprehensively interdict resources coming into and out of the Confederacy. In fact, it was the first blockade to be fully equipped and backed by an industrialized nation that set its main mission as the interdiction of supplies instead of giving primacy to military targets. This strategy was part of a larger vision, and was the one constant in Union military strategy from 1861 to 1865.

This book will cover several fundamental themes and questions surrounding the blockade. How did the existence of a Union blockade influence the mind-set of participants in the Civil War? The blockade's psychological effects on Southern morale will be explored as well as the way in which historians have treated the topic. This focus will help us better understand the blockade from the viewpoint of contemporaries in the 1860s and those who study the era. The Union blockade was a very important component of the United States' involvement in international law. How did it fit established legal definitions and transform the war into a transatlantic diplomatic test for the Union and Confederacy?

The amount of resources dedicated to the blockade towered over any previous American naval commitment, but thanks to the staggering profits they stood to gain, plenty of crews were willing to attempt blockade-running. The Confederacy had an insatiable demand for supplies. A consortium of self-interested parties such as foreign investors, private trading firms, individual Southern states, and the Confederate government undertook the business of blockade-running with varying levels of success. One of the great enduring controversies of Civil War scholarship is the effectiveness of the Union's naval interdiction. A new perspective based on statistics will analyze whether the blockade's effectiveness increased over time, as many historians suggest. This foray into a few diverse questions and themes about the Union blockade will hopefully serve as a starting point for an assortment of deeper studies of the topic.

The goal of this book is not to establish a new paradigm or to revise previous historical analysis of the blockade. Instead, this book hopes only to spark additional questions and create new avenues of exploration. As historian David Surdam proves in his impressive economic study of the blockade, fresh approaches to the topic are possible and bring additional insight to Civil War scholarship. The outstanding work of Robert M. Browning Jr. initiated an ongoing process of asking deeper questions about the blockade's importance to the Union war effort. Likewise, Marcus Price and particularly Stephen Wise laid the groundwork for studies of blockade-running. These scholars have produced works that stand the test of time. The authors of this study do not expect to supplant, or even rival, any of this excellent scholarship, but we hope to contribute some new insights into the continuing evolution of blockade scholarship.

One obstacle to a greater understanding of the blockade has been that some Civil War historians treat it as a sideshow - an important but ancillary aspect of the war – thus they fail to integrate the blockade into a more comprehensive analysis. We hope to augment the process by which the blockade is discussed not as a subsection of general histories about the Civil War, but as a critical component of Union strategy that deserves greater detailed inquiry. Our goal is to ask probing questions about the Union blockade and blockade-running and to add several analytical layers to this vital chapter of Civil War history.

CHAPTER 1

---- ★ ----

Great Britain, International Law, and Blockade Diplomacy

GREAT BRITAIN WAS THE primary diplomatic factor in Union blockade policy. A long-running disagreement about neutral shipping rights formed the backdrop for the nation's potentially hostile relationship with the United States. Britain's refusal to respect America's claims to neutral shipping rights was one of the causes of the War of 1812. Later in the 1800s Britain and the US maneuvered for control of places like the Oregon Territory and Central America, but they resolved these disputes diplomatically. By the 1850s imperial ventures had established the United States as a legitimate rival to Great Britain. Throughout the nineteenth century the two powers constantly competed for commercial and imperial supremacy in the Western Hemisphere. However, despite claims in the Monroe Doctrine, the United States needed to be cautious when it challenged British dominance. British leaders understood that although the Civil War had temporarily hampered America's imperial momentum, a victorious United States would renew expansion in the postbellum years—which it did.

Background and Precedents up to 1861

From the 1790s until the Civil War, the issue of neutral shipping rights tainted the relationship between the United States and Europe's naval powers. Trade with Europe formed the backbone of the American economy, and US merchant fleets were constantly entangled in the Anglo-French wars of the Napoleonic era. In the 1790s both France and Great Britain sought to deny American products to their enemies, and both nations attacked American ships. Britain issued Orders in Council in the 1790s, and up to 1812 it tried to prevent neutral ships from resupplying France. Likewise, France harassed neutral vessels it suspected of supplying Britain. In 1807 Napoleon issued the Milan Decree, which allowed French ships to interdict neutral ones. The United States complained both sides were violating neutral shipping rights, and this became an important foreign policy issue during the early republic era.

The administrations of Washington, Adams, and Jefferson confronted the intractable problem of neutral rights without going to war. Each president wanted to remain independent. Federalist policy under Washington and Adams favored Great Britain, whereas Republican policy under Jefferson and Madison favored France. Proof of partisan inclinations can be found in Federalist support of the Jay Treaty and the Quasi-War against France, and later in the Republicans' passage of the Embargo Act and declaration of war against Britain in 1812. This is an oversimplification of twenty years of American foreign policy, but the main point remains—the issue of neutral shipping rights between the United States, Great Britain, and France had a long history of mutual recrimination.

Up to 1861 the United States tried to protect neutral shipping rights in the midst of foreign conflicts. However, during the Civil War, it was Great Britain's turn to worry about the matter. The nation's leaders feared that both the Union and Confederate navies would attack the British merchant fleet in an attempt to deny supplies to their enemies. In an ironic turn of events, Great Britain now became the defender of neutral shipping rights during an American war. In addition to the issue of neutral shipping rights, Great Britain and the United States also had some experience with blockade policy.

By 1861 blockades were a well-established part of naval strategy. Increased international codification of blockade law occurred throughout the nineteenth century, and the Civil War served as another important evolutionary moment. The two most important prewar- Anglo-American experiences with blockades occurred in the War of 1812 (1812–15) and the Mexican War (1846–48).

Leading up to the War of 1812, maritime nations roughly agreed on a set of blockade principles. Neutrals had to be warned to stay away from blockaded ports in a timely fashion, and blockading squadrons were expected to position enough ships off of enemy ports to actually impede trade. In 1806 the US missed an opportunity to agree with Great Britain on these conditions in the aborted Monroe-Pinkney Treaty. In this void Great Britain set the international legal standards for blockades. In fact, one of the casus belli leading up to the War of 1812 was the argument that Great Britain's Orders in Council amounted to an illegal blockade.

In 1812 and 1813 the British navy blockaded America's southern and Middle Atlantic states. The New England states were eventually blockaded in 1814. It is unclear how many vessels were captured, sunk, or interdicted, but the economic results for the US economy were ruinous. As historian Donald R. Hickey notes, "The tonnage of American ships engaged in foreign trade dropped from 948,000 in 1811 to 60,000 in 1814."[1] The British navy accomplished all of these feats while burdened with other duties in Europe. By the end of the war, Great Britain could boast of successfully interdicting American trade, but part of Britain's blockade strategy in the War of 1812 was defensive, or aimed at suppressing the US Navy's frigates. After the close of the Napoleonic Wars and the War of 1812, there was little doubt that Great Britain would dominate international blockade law, and use that influence to its advantage at every opportunity.

In the Mexican War, the United States Navy declared a blockade on May 14, 1846. American strategists created blockade plans in 1845, thus contingent orders were implemented immediately after the declaration of war. Secretary of the Navy George Bancroft understood that a legal blockade must effectively prevent the coming and going of enemy ships. Bancroft also desired to maintain neutral shipping rights, and US vessels allowed British ships to leave Mexican waters unmolested. A pitifully small number of ships were available for blockade duty along Mexico's eastern coast, and an even smaller number were available for Pacific Coast duty. Historian K. Jack Bauer notes this paucity of blockading resources: "To blockade the Mexican coast all the way from the Rio Grande to Yucatan, [Cmdre. David E.] Conner had two sloops and three brigs, and of the latter the *Perry*, had been blown ashore . . . by a hurricane."[2]

America's Pacific fleet also experienced chronic shortages of vessels and supplies. The primary scene of naval action was in Alta California in conjunction with American land forces. Baja California and the western coast of Mexico simply could not be blockaded. On August 19, 1846, Cmdre. Robert F. Stockton declared a blockade of Mexico's Pacific coast, but Secretary of the Navy John Y. Mason rescinded the declaration due to lack of enforcement and thus illegality.[3] In fact there were periods when no American vessels were stationed in the Gulf of California or outside major ports like Mazatlan. As a result, Great Britain instantly recognized the US blockade in the Gulf of Mexico, but not in the Pacific.[4] The US Navy implemented an offensive blockade against Mexico, but since Mexico had few capital ships to suppress, the blockaders focused on interdicting trade and supporting land forces. For US blockade strategists, the Mexican War was an opportunity to learn about the logistical problems of mobilizing enough resources to effectively blockade an enemy's ports. But the US naval experience in the Civil War dwarfed the scale of the US Navy's blockade in the war with Mexico.[5]

The *Vixen* Affair

In 1836 the British navy was involved in a precedent-setting example of blockade legality. The experience of the British ship *Vixen* proved to be only one episode in a larger effort to protect Great Britain's economic interests in the Near East.[6] In particular, British foreign policy strategists hoped to buttress the Ottoman Empire against Russian expansion into the Middle East. David Urquhart, British diplomat to Turkey and an inveterate intriguer, unofficially assisted the Circassian rebels against Russia. The *Vixen* embarked for Circassia in the northeastern Black Sea laden with much-needed supplies for the Circassian rebels. However, after the vessel docked in a rebel port, Russian naval forces seized it. The *Vixen* affair caused an in-depth debate about international blockade law and previewed some of the legal arguments about the Union blockade in 1861.[7]

Important long-term legal issues were involved in the *Vixen* affair. British secretary of state for foreign affairs Lord Palmerston argued that Russia had every right to seize the *Vixen* under international law. Great Britain had recognized a treaty that endorsed Russian sovereignty over the region. Russia declared a blockade of Circassia although Russian forces were not in control of rebel ports. However, at the time of the *Vixen's* seizure in 1836, Russia had not yet *officially* proclaimed a blockade to British authorities.

After being lambasted by critics in the House of Commons about the failure to punish the Russians, Palmerston explained the government's position on legal blockades. He noted that Britain recognized other countries' blockades so long as they were implemented "according to the undoubted law of nations, which is, that the belligerents have the right to blockade, if that blockade be effective." Palmerston added "[A legal blockade] must not be a matter of paper, but there must be the presence of force; and I say that as a maritime nation, our power depending on our fleet, we are satisfied that not only our commercial, but our political existence is connected with this principle of maritime law." He also reminded his critics "There is a distinction to be drawn between measures which may be applied by one power to the ports and coasts of another power with which she may be at war, and a blockade maintained to enforce municipal regulations." One supporter of Palmerston's argument pointed out that it was "unnecessary to place a notification of the blockade in The Gazette [the official blockade register] if this territory belonged to Russia."[8]

The opposition countered with several points that cast doubt on Palmerston's legal analysis and foreshadowed a number of particulars about the Union's Civil War blockade. Lord Dudley Stuart did not deny Russia's right to blockade Circassia, but he argued "this was only an apparent blockade, and not a real one." He also noted that the Russians only controlled "two or three forts" in Circassia and thus could not claim municipal authority to close all ports to trade.[9] This position would be similar to British arguments in 1861 that, although it had every legal right to proclaim a blockade, the United States could not close Confederate ports to neutral ships because it did not control Confederate territory. However, Palmerston's argument and handling of the Vixen affair prevailed; Great Britain continued to interpret international blockade laws in accordance with his analysis. Ironically, Lord Palmerston argued a point in 1837 that US secretary of state William Seward used in 1861. American diplomats cited the Vixen affair as a legal precedent that Great Britain should also recognize the United States' right to close Southern ports. The Vixen's fate proved that even Britain had to respect the rules of international blockades. International law could be inconvenient to British foreign policy, as in the Vixen affair, but every nation's conformity to established blockade laws was far more valuable to the country's maritime dominance.

The Vixen affair was only one episode in the development of international blockade law in the decades before the Civil War. By the 1850s a coalition of nations including France, Turkey, and Great Britain prepared to wage war against Russia. A variety of factors, among them naval control of the Black Sea, caused the Crimean War (1854–56).[10] But the most important legacy of the Crimean War for the American Civil War was the Declaration of Paris, agreed to on April 16, 1856.

The Declaration of Paris

The Declaration of Paris (1856) became the international legal standard for blockades, and its signatories included Great Britain, France, Russia, Austria, Prussia, Sardinia, and Turkey. The United States did not sign the agreement because it was not represented at the negotiations ending the

Crimean War. However, all parties understood that America would acquiesce to the declaration's tenets if it expected reciprocal maritime rights. After 1856 all naval powers should heed the declaration's principles if they desired international recognition of a legal blockade.

The Declaration of Paris was premised on the idea that "maritime law in time of war has long been the subject of deplorable disputes." Prior to this agreement, "uncertainty of the law and . . . differences of opinion between neutrals and belligerents" had caused diplomatic problems, some of which led to outright war. The time had come to create "a uniform doctrine" to define international rules regarding maritime law. Delegates agreed to abolish privateering, protect neutral trade goods on enemy ships, and protect enemy trade goods on neutral ships except for contraband of war. The most important aspect of the agreement for the Civil War was the new definition of a legal blockade "Blockades, in order to be binding, must be effective—that is to say, maintained by a force sufficient really to prevent access to the coast of the enemy."[11]

The signatories hoped to make these rules comprehensive and agreed to "bring the present declaration to the knowledge of the States which [had] not taken part in the Congress of Paris, and to invite them to accede." Nations that had agreed to the declaration eventually extended this invitation to both the United States and the Confederate States of America. However, the decree's final clause stated "The present Declaration is not and shall not be binding, except between those Powers who have acceded, or shall accede, to it."[12] Neither the United States nor the Confederate States ever consented to or fully complied with the Declaration of Paris, but both nations understood that the agreement could be leveraged in the all-important game of international diplomacy. The pronouncement provided Great Britain with a powerful diplomatic tool. Second to the nation's naval power, the Declaration of Paris symbolized British maritime dominance, and it allowed British foreign policy strategists to navigate the treacherous waters of Civil War diplomacy with formidable legal standing.

Secession Crisis and Blockade Diplomacy

From the 1790s up to the American Civil War, the United States and Great Britain developed a complex mutual understanding of maritime law. The issue of neutral shipping rights was among the causes of the War of 1812, but on many maritime issues like the application of legal blockades, Britain and America conformed to similar standards. Some legal precedents were influenced by experiences like the *Vixen* affair (1836) and others, like the Declaration of Paris, resulted from misguided wars. By 1860 the evolution of maritime law approached widespread acceptance. It was in the interest of established naval powers like Great Britain and rising naval powers like the United States to observe international law so long as it benefited their naval strategies. But the Civil War temporarily ruptured this tenuous understanding. America could ill afford to obey maritime laws if doing so meant it might be defeated. In 1861 Great Britain held an unmatched position of prestige and influence over the outcome, and British diplomats used every weapon in their arsenal—legal, military, and economic—to pursue their country's geopolitical goals during the Civil War.

From December 1860 to February 1861, the Southern states seceded and created the Confederate States of America. British diplomats watched with interest to see how the Lincoln administration handled the crisis. Great Britain's main concern in the sectional dispute was the continued supply of cotton to its textile mills. Some British abolitionists immediately sided with the Union, but many leaders understood that the Civil War was a delicate situation in which Great Britain could neither completely give up supplies of Southern cotton, nor risk war with the United States. Cotton was the lifeblood of Britain's industrial economy. The great question for British diplomats was, Can Southern cotton be secured without implicitly recognizing Confederate nationhood and plunging Great Britain into a war with the United States? These diplomats hoped to use their nation's pivotal economic and military position to leverage both the North and the South into acceptable international behavior, and the Declaration of Paris was the definitive legal protection for Britain's neutral rights.

At the outset of the Civil War the British Foreign Service was among the most experienced and professional diplomatic corps in the world. Great Britain had good reason to send consuls and ambassadors to the remotest corners of the globe to protect its vast economic interests. Lord John Russell, the secretary of state for foreign affairs, headed the Foreign Service Department. He reported to the prime minister, and he oversaw the diplomatic and consular corps, which were separate entities under the British system. Ambassadors and consuls might work on similar issues, but class and professionalism differentiated the two agencies. Ambassadors in the diplomatic corps were assigned to foreign capitals and typically hailed from upper-class British society. These individuals were career envoys, widely traveled and well-versed in the protocols of international diplomacy. Britain's ambassador to the United States during the Civil War, Lord Richard Lyons, was an excellent example of the diplomatic corps' professionalism. In a twenty-two-year career before the Civil War, Lyons served in numerous posts in Greece, Italy, and Germany. The main difference between British and American diplomats was professionalism. British ambassadors were trained specifically for national service, whereas American ambassadors were selected for partisan political loyalty and with less regard for experience.[13]

The British consular corps was not under the ambassador's direct oversight. The diplomatic corps focused on political relations with the host country, while the consular corps primarily dealt with local economic issues. However, the two branches of the Foreign Service, the diplomatic and consular corps, often worked toward the same goals. In 1860 Great Britain operated fourteen consulates in the United States from Charleston to San Francisco, and the nation even had a consulate in Richmond. In addition, eleven vice-consulates served smaller port cities. Consuls and vice-consuls focused on localized trade problems regarding British merchants in America's port cities. In so doing, they accumulated valuable economic information about shipping, trade rules, and tariffs. After 1861, British envoys in the Southern states spent much of their time trying to protect the neutral rights of British citizens. Great Britain's consulates in Richmond, Charleston, Savannah, Mobile, New Orleans, and Galveston remained open during the war, but the United States did not recognize their authority. Confederate leaders viewed the consulates as a potential conduit for British recognition, but when this support did not materialize, Secretary of State Judah P. Benjamin kicked the British representatives out of the Confederacy in September 1863. Throughout the war Britain's Southern consuls were required to balance a delicate diplomatic situation.[14]

The wave of secession from December 1860 through May 1861 prompted much speculation about a Union blockade among leaders in the North, the South, and Great Britain. The main point of discussion was not whether the United States would use its navy to isolate the Confederacy. Instead, officials debated the nature of naval interdiction and its effect on transatlantic diplomacy.

Early in the secession crisis British foreign minister Lord Russell prompted his ambassador in the United States, Lord Lyons, to keep him informed about a possible blockade.

On January 10, 1861, Lord Lyons informed his superior about a conversation he had with Sen. William Seward. Seward had already accepted the secretary of state position in the Lincoln administration, so this conversation presaged later diplomatic arguments. Lyons and Seward discussed whether a foreign vessel should conform to the regulation of the de facto or the de jure government. The senator naturally argued that "the authority de jure in the Southern Ports still belonged to the United States." After Seward declared that hypothetically the US Navy could rightfully "make the Southern states feel uncomfortable . . . by intercepting their commerce," Lyons replied with a veiled threat: "If the United States determined to stop by force so important a commerce as that of Great Britain with the cotton growing states, I could not answer for what might happen."[15]

Seward then offered to supply cotton through Northern ports. Lyons, realizing this would not be sufficient, replied as follows: "Cotton, although by far the most important article of the trade, was not the only point to be considered. It was however a matter of the greatest consequence to England to procure cheap cotton. If a considerable rise were to take place in the price of cotton, and British ships were to be at the same time excluded from the Southern ports, an immense pressure would be put upon the Majesty's government to use all the means in their power to open those ports."[16] The British ambassador informed Seward that the "most simple, if not the only way [to procure cotton], would be to recognize the Southern Confederacy." Lyons remarked that "Seward listened with complacency" to his warning. As the two men discussed the differences between a legal blockade and the closing of ports, Lyons worried that the Lincoln administration would violate British shipping rights. The ambassador advised Lord Russell that the cotton trade could be severely interrupted, but he hoped that the threat of British recognition might prevent port closures. After speaking with the future secretary of state, Lyons informed the foreign minister that "[I am] afraid we must be prepared for" a total closure of Southern ports.[17]

Lord Russell attentively considered information provided by Lord Lyons and guided the ambassador on British policy. On February 16, 1861, the foreign minister admitted to Lyons "Events in the U.S. have been so astounding that I have been quite unable to know what to expect." If there was any doubt about British priorities as the fledgling Confederacy came into existence, Russell advised his envoy to "above all things endeavor to prevent a blockade of the Southern coast." After Lincoln's inauguration, Russell contemplated the possibilities of a Union blockade, and he told Lyons, "If

[Lincoln] blockades the southern ports we shall be in a difficulty—but according to all American doctrine it must be an actual blockade kept up by an effective force." Russell hoped the Lincoln administration would acknowledge the Declaration of Paris. But if the president tried to close the ports to all trade, Russell believed the only recourse would be recognition of the Confederacy.[18] Lyons responded on March 29 that the Lincoln administration appeared to be avoiding "any interference with foreign commerce." On April 6 Russell replied "I rely upon your wisdom, patience, and prudence to steer us through the dangers of this crisis. . . . If it can possibly be helped Mr. Seward must not be allowed to get us into a quarrel."[19] The difficult diplomatic process of British neutrality had begun, but Great Britain's policy always revolved around two goals—obtaining as much cotton as possible while avoiding war with the North.

Secretary of State William Seward probed British opinion about the denial of access to Southern ports. Britain's ambassador to the United States, Lord Lyons, carelessly replied on March 20 that a Union blockade might cause Great Britain to recognize the Confederacy. The next day at a public function Seward menaced the envoy in an intentionally bellicose manner, declaring that if Britain recognized the Confederacy, "the whole world [would be] be engulfed and revolution will be the harvest."[20] Seward's overt threat to spread unrest throughout the British Empire, in particular through an American incursion into Canada, startled Lyons. Eventually the diplomatic bluster from both sides subsided.

On March 25, 1861, ubiquitous *London Times* reporter William Howard Russell conversed with fellow correspondents in New York about a potential Union blockade. He witnessed a discussion over whether Lincoln would blockade or close rebel ports. "One of the gentlemen present" the journalist observed, "said that England might dispute the right of the United States Government to blockade the ports of her own States, to which she was entitled to access under treaty." These reporters apparently understood the importance of the Declaration of Paris. Another newspaperman argued that "the President could open and shut ports as he pleased; and that he might close the Southern ports by a proclamation in the nature of an Order in Council."[21] The legal distinction between blockade and port closure was a news item, not just a diplomatic point of conflict. Would the Lincoln administration follow international law and declare a blockade? Or would the president use the dubiously legal method of closing Southern ports?

The same day Confederates fired on Fort Sumter, Lyons informed

Russell "All [the Lincoln administration's] naval preparations look pain-fully like a blockade." On April 15, Lyons opined on how a blockade would affect British policy. The ambassador thought "a regular blockade would be less objectionable than any such measures as closing the Southern ports." And since "the rules of a blockade are to a great extent determined and known," he noted, indiscriminate seizure of British vessels would consti-tute "a Paper Blockade of the worst kind." According to Lyons, any Amer-ican seizure of neutral ships "would certainly justify Great Britain and France in recognizing the Southern Confederacy and sending their fleets to force the United States to treat British and French vessels as neutrals in conformity with the Law of Nations."[22]

Lyons further complained that the Lincoln administration's inexperi-ence, particularly that of the hotheaded Seward, might prompt a "fool-ish violent proceeding of the government with regard to Foreign Powers." The British ambassador noted, "Neither the President nor any man in the Cabinet has a knowledge of Foreign Affairs," and he offered the following professional opinion: "The best chance of keeping them within bounds will be to be very firm with them."[23] When Lincoln declared a blockade of Southern ports on April 18, 1861, the British diplomatic team was pre-pared to match Seward's bluster with international legal arguments. For the next four years Great Britain's blockade diplomacy sought to protect the nation's economic interests and force US acknowledgment of neutral shipping rights.

Blockade Diplomacy Begins

Confederate forces in Charleston, South Carolina attacked Union forces in Fort Sumter on April 12, 1861 igniting the Civil War. On April 15 Lincoln responded to the attack by issuing a call for seventy-five thousand volun-teers to forcibly put down the rebellion. The president now had to decide between blockade or port closure, and his cabinet debated the pros and cons of each approach. Secretary of State William Seward and Secretary of the Navy Gideon Welles took opposite sides of the argument. Welles supported closing Southern ports, thus avoiding the inconvenient legal limitations spelled out in the Declaration of Paris. However, the blockade argument won out and on April 18 Lincoln declared a blockade of the Confederacy.

British officials expected formal notice from Seward, but this was de-layed. Lord Lyons informed Russell on April 23, "The blockade has not yet

been officially announced to me . . . [but] I suppose it must be recognized."
When Lyons finally received official notification on April 27, he observed
"The blockade is less likely to be injurious or to raise awkward questions
than any of the irregular modes of closing the Southern ports." The ambassador hoped to cultivate "a tolerably liberal application of [the blockade's] rules," and he noted that Seward appeared to be "willing to adhere
to the declaration of . . . Paris abolishing privateering."[24] Lincoln's blockade
declaration meant Seward and Lyons – both of whom were determined to
subjectively interpret blockade law, could commence diplomatic arguments
over legality.

On May 7, *London Times* correspondent William Howard Russell
dined with Confederate secretary of state of Judah P. Benjamin and Sen.
Louis Wigfall in New Orleans. Russell remarked that conversation with
Benjamin was "agreeable and lively." The Southern statesman seemed
"certain that the English law authorities must advise the [British] Government that the blockade of the Southern ports [was] illegal so long as
. . . President [Lincoln claimed] them to be ports of the United States."
Benjamin touted King Cotton Diplomacy, the intentional withholding of
cotton from Britain, but seriously misjudged future results. Speaking of the
spring and summer of 1861, he told Russell, "[The Union's] paper blockade
does no harm; the season for shipping cotton is over; but in October next,
when the Mississippi is floating cotton by the thousands of bales, and all
our wharfs are full, it is inevitable that the Yankees must come to trouble
with this attempt to coerce us."[25]

In the end, many British leaders believed King Cotton Diplomacy was
a Confederate attempt to coerce Britain to intervene in the Civil War.
Russell remained in New Orleans through mid-June and commented about
the early effects of the blockade on the Crescent City. "The great commercial community of New Orleans," he noted, "which now feels the pressure
of the blockade, depends upon the interference of the European powers
next October."[26] The false hope of King Cotton Diplomacy undermined
Southern states' diplomacy and did not cause Great Britain to recognize
the Confederacy. By April 1862, New Orleans was under Union occupation, thereby depriving the Confederate States of the full economic and
diplomatic assets that King Cotton might have provided.

It is impossible to overestimate the importance of American cotton to
Great Britain's industrial economy in the nineteenth century. The expansion of Southern cotton production from 1820 to 1860 coincided with the

rapid growth of British textile manufacturing. Historian Gavin Wright notes that "American cotton accounted for more than 70 percent of the cotton imports of Great Britain, the world's largest producer of cotton textile goods."[27] Scholar Sven Beckert points out that Great Britain possessed "two-thirds of the world's mechanical spindles . . . [and] the livelihood of between one-fifth and one-fourth of the population was based on the industry." In addition, "close to one-half of all exports" from Great Britain, the global superpower of the nineteenth century, "consisted of cotton yarn and cloth." According to Beckert, by 1861 "whole regions of Europe and the United States had come to depend on a predictable supply of cheap cotton" that was grown in the newly established Confederate States.[28]

In navigating the labyrinth of Civil War diplomacy, British diplomats wanted to preserve the cotton supply coming from the Confederacy. On May 6, 1861, Lord Lyons analyzed how the war could cause problems for his country, "The injury inflicted on both [the North and the South] will be felt in England—but the consequences of the sudden failure of the supply of cotton from the South are appalling." Lyons understood that the Confederacy's overreliance on cotton was a major weakness that many Southern leaders had misinterpreted as a source of power. As he stated "There is on the part of the South an enormously exaggerated idea of its own strength and of its 'faut vivre' [reason to live] for the rest of the world." Although he respected the seceded states' determination, the ambassador prophetically noted that the Confederacy "was ill fitted for a . . . protracted contest," remarking "More especially will they lose heart when or if their anchor [cotton] fails them, and England and France permit the blockade for a year or more."[29] Maintaining Britain's cotton supply was only slightly less important than avoiding war with the United States, but in 1861 it remained to be seen whether Britain would risk war to maintain cotton imports.

In 1861 Southern leaders relied too heavily on King Cotton Diplomacy —or a self-imposed embargo on cotton exports—to force British intervention on the Confederacy's behalf. As historian Frank Owsley points out, "Timing was as important in this economic coercion-diplomacy as it was in a military campaign."[30] In the war's first year, when the Union blockade had yet to be fully implemented, the South's foolish policy kept its most valuable product from reaching foreign markets. King Cotton Diplomacy was a grievous self-inflicted economic wound to the Confederacy. Its untimeliness in 1861, when the blockade was porous and vast quantities of cotton were left to rot in Confederate ports, became all the more obvious in 1862 when the Union blockade was more fully implemented. In the meantime, while the Confederacy was carrying out its worst foreign policy decision of the war in 1861, the United States and Great Britain were fighting over the legal definition of a blockade.

That summer William Seward and Lord Lyons argued about how the Declaration of Paris and blockade law should be interpreted. The British envoy thought his opponent was "arrogant and reckless," and he distrusted Seward's verbal promises. However, Lyons remained hopeful that US ambassador to Great Britain Charles Francis Adams had been "instructed to make an offer which [could] be accepted respecting the adhesion of the United States to the Declaration of Paris."[31] Lord Russell would treat with Adams, so it was Lyons' task to clarify international law with Seward.

Lyons had several concerns. Would the United States completely abide by all the tenets in the Declaration of Paris? If not, would the Lincoln administration obey certain parts, and if so, which ones? Lyons speculated to the home office in London "We may take it for granted that this [US] government will admit without hesitation that the principles of the second and third articles [respecting neutral goods] of the Declaration of Paris are to be observed." He remained hopeful concerning another point: "Both governments will no doubt also be quite ready to declare in principle that a Blockade to be recognized must be effective."[32] Both the US and the Confederacy interpreted blockade effectiveness to support their own agendas. Great Britain consistently relied on its interpretation of the Declaration of Paris to counter one-sided claims by the Lincoln and Davis administrations.

Lord Lyons wanted agreement from Seward, and hopefully from the Confederacy, that privateers would not be unleashed on British ships. Article 1 in the Declaration of Paris abolished privateering. "The immediate question" Lyons pointed out to his superior, "is whether we shall admit the Southern privateers and their prizes into our ports." Since the North possessed an established navy it had little need for this naval strategy. But the Confederacy, lacking a navy, issued letters of marque on May 6, 1861, to encourage privateer attacks on the US merchant fleet. Lyons understood this would be a major point of dispute with the Lincoln administration. The ambassador told Lord Russell "Mr. Seward will be furious when he finds that his adherence to the Declaration of Paris will not stop the southern privateering."[33]

Great Britain officially opposed privateering, but some instances did occur. Rebel privateers gleefully informed Britain's Charleston consulate about the seizure of Union ships and property. The British Admiralty and Foreign Office gave strict orders not to assist with privateering, yet they collected data about successful privateering actions. It is unclear why this information was needed, but from the Confederate perspective, it was likely delivered to the British consulates to show rebel naval potency. Despite these examples, Lyons did not want to ask Southern leaders to stop the privateering. Instead, Lyons encouraged French ambassador Henri Mercier to persuade the Confederates to disallow the practice. The issue was resolved indirectly when, on June 1, 1861, the British government officially refused to accept captured vessels in its prize courts, thus denying the Confederacy this source of naval power.[34]

By mid-June Lyons seemed content with his diplomatic progress, informing Lord Russell that he had "been lucky to get through the beginning of the blockade with so few awkward questions." However, Lyons did not know that Seward was planning to close Southern ports in addition to creating a legal blockade. Regarding the effectiveness of the Union cordon, the ambassador noted, "The blockade is by no means regularly carried on—but as yet I hardly think any British vessel has practically suffered an injury or experienced treatment inconsistent with the Laws of Nations."[35] Lyons's optimism about avoiding more diplomatic conflict and his commentary about an ineffective blockade were premature—he would soon have plenty of work protecting British interests.

In early May 1861 the British Foreign Office decided on a fundamental policy for the American Civil War. Lord Russell advocated neutrality and on May 6 he informed Parliament of the Crown's decision to officially declare it. What did British neutrality mean? The straightforward aspects of this position meant that Great Britain would recognize the Union blockade if it conformed to the Declaration of Paris, and that British subjects were technically forbidden from supplying material support to either side. The neutrality declaration also recognized that a state of war existed between the United States and the "so-called" Confederate States.[36] This meant by implication that the Confederacy possessed belligerent rights—or the right to protect itself with all legal means.

Great Britain's acknowledgment of the Confederacy's belligerent rights infuriated the Lincoln administration. Seward fully understood the legality of Britain's position, but Lyons noted "The sentimental difficulty is the great one." According to Lyons the situation in 1861 confirmed Britain's decision to recognize the Confederacy's belligerent rights. But the ambassador acknowledged, "The present apparent success of the South in founding an independent government is so galling to the North that anything which implies the admission of this self-evident fact irritates them beyond measure." Seward tried to divide the French and British ambassadors on the Confederacy's right to legally defend itself, but to no avail. On June 18, Lyons "prevented an immediate explosion [in Washington] on the subject of the belligerent rights of the South." The secretary of state fumblingly attempted to use the Declaration of Paris to rebuff Britain's position, but Lyons held firm. All parties viewed Confederate belligerent rights in dramatically different terms. Britain deemed them the legitimate offshoot of neutrality. The United States viewed belligerent rights as an overtly hostile act of support for the rebels, and Confederate leaders viewed them as the first step on the path to national recognition.[37]

Seward countered Britain's recognition of Confederate belligerent rights by threatening to close Southern ports. He cited Britain's policy in the *Vixen* affair of 1836 as legal precedent that the US could rightfully pursue this course of action. The difference between a legal blockade and port closure was important. If the US closed Southern ports to neutral ships, ostensibly to make sure that all duties were paid, then the US Navy could legally stop all neutral ships. Port closure was thus outside the norms of blockade law, and the British viewed it as illegal and vehemently protested. Lord Lyons informed his superior on June 24 "[The] critical question is that of closing the southern ports of entry by an Act of Congress without maintaining a blockade regulated by the Laws of Nations."[38]

Apparently, Seward believed he could both observe the international blockade rules and close Southern ports. Lyons disagreed. The British ambassador "urged upon the few men willing to listen" that any US law to close Confederate ports "should at least be so framed as to give the government the option of maintaining a blockade in conformity with the law of nations." Seward reminded Lyons of British policy regarding the 1836 *Vixen* affair in which Lord Palmerston, now Britain's prime minister, had upheld port closures in Circassia despite the fact that Russian forces did not control the territory. Lyons complained to Russell "[American diplomats] rely immensely here upon the case of the 'Vixen' as establishing a precedent for the admission by Great Britain of the principle that a government may close ports without establishing a Blockade restricted by the law of Nations."[39] The dispute over closing Southern ports was an offshoot of other aspects of blockade diplomacy like international legality and Confederate belligerent rights.

President Lincoln called a special session of Congress for July 4 in which closing Confederate ports was on the agenda. Lyons informed Russell on July 2 "If an attempt is made to close the southern ports by Act of Congress . . . instead of by a blockade regulated by the law of nations, I have some hope that the [US] government have been made aware of the extreme danger of attempting to subject British or French vessels to such a system." On July 10 the Republican-controlled Congress introduced House Bill Number 16 "to provide for the collection of duties on imports." The measure contained nine sections that effectually closed Confederate ports. Section 1 initiated arbitrary executive powers so that, "whenever it shall in the judgement of the President, by reason of unlawful combinations of persons in opposition to laws of the United States, [it became] impracticable to execute the revenue laws and collect the duties on imports by the ordinary means," then the president had the authority to create new legal ports of entry with loyal collections agents.[40] If Confederate ports remained rebellious, then Lincoln could close them to outside commerce, redirecting ships to friendly ports for revenue collection. Section 4 forbade "all right of importation" to the closed ports which meant that any vessels attempting to enter could be seized. Opposition from several Democrats was overshadowed by the Republican majority, and the bill passed by a wide margin of 136 to 10.

The Senate referred the port closure bill to the Committee on Commerce. Senators registered some concern that loyal Northern vessel owners, due to partial ownership by rebels, might have their property confiscated. Politicians also debated whether loyal Southerners could have their ships and cargoes confiscated, but the bill passed the Senate 36 to 6 without serious amendment. On July 24 President Lincoln signed the port closure bill into law.[41] He now had the legal authority to prohibit all ships from entering Confederate ports. But did he have the authority according to international law? If Lincoln ignored this aspect of the diplomatic equation, what would be the ramifications with Great Britain?

In late July Seward finally divulged the main reason for the port closure law—to leverage British policy in other diplomatic sectors. Seward "begged" Lyons to explain to his superiors "that it was an enabling not an imperative act; that [it] depended entirely upon the President whether or not it was ever put into execution." The ambassador replied that international law trumped US law on port closure. Seward then snapped that British irritation might still close the seaports. After the verbal scuffle the secretary of state requested Lyons's honest opinion about the port closure law. This was not an official response but Lyons "had no hesitation in saying that Her Majesty's Government did not consider that the United States had any right . . . to close by decree any ports which were not in her own possession."[42] Seward was feeling out his adversary to see whether the legislation in question might extract diplomatic concessions, and when he sensed that it would not, he petulantly threatened enactment. But Lord Lyons did not budge.

Navy Secretary Gideon Welles also endorsed port closure. In an August 5 report to President Lincoln, Welles outlined his arguments for closing Southern ports as opposed to instituting a blockade. The secretary felt uncomfortable and "embarrassed" by the circumstances of a blockade, since under the "rules and principles of international law . . . the Confederate States must be considered and treated as a distinct nationality." He preferred "the closing of the ports, which [was] a legal municipal enactment" that did not confer belligerent status. Welles summed up the dilemma: "If neutral powers have a right to demand that we close the [rebel] ports . . . by such a blockade, then manifestly they have an equal right to claim entrance into those ports under the authority of the Confederate States. To admit this is to admit disunion and revoke our whole policy."[43]

The navy secretary also understood the delicate diplomatic situation with Great Britain. He disagreed with Lord Lyons's opinions about port closure, and he rhetorically asked "Were there no fear of Great Britain, no threat or apprehension from foreign powers, should we hesitate for one moment on this question of closing our own ports?" Welles then made a sobering admission about the prospects of an effective blockade: "To effectually blockade our extensive coast so that there shall be no ingress or egress by the insurgents or by foreigners, is next to an impossibility."[44] Welles advocated port closure, but the blockade decision had been made months before.

Secretary of State Seward continued to threaten port closure throughout September 1861, but he now personally opposed the policy. By mid-September Lyons confidently informed Lord Russell that the issue was dead, and Seward no longer issued relevant warnings in diplomatic discussions.[45] The British ambassador understood from the outset that the law to close Confederate ports was a diplomatic tool in the larger discussion of international maritime law. In retrospect, it appears that the Lincoln administration used the port-closure law as a form of revenge for Great Britain's recognition of the Confederacy's belligerent rights. When British diplomats refused to yield, the American president was left only with a legal blockade conducted according to the Declaration of Paris.

The *Labuan* Affair

Numerous events strained wartime diplomacy between the United States and Great Britain the most famous of which was the *Trent* affair of November 1861. There is little need to reexamine this episode in detail, since other historians have thoroughly analyzed it, but a summary of events will introduce a larger point. In November 1861, Capt. Charles Wilkes of the USS *San Jacinto* stopped the British mail steamer *Trent* off the Bahamas and seized two Confederate diplomats, John Slidell and James Mason. This was a clear violation of the Declaration of Paris and of Britain's neutral shipping rights. Over the next six weeks Lord Palmerston's government and the Lincoln administration faced off over Wilkes's actions.

Lord Cobden of Great Britain noted in a letter to Sen. Charles Sumner on November 29 "The only danger to the peace of the two countries is in the temper which may grow out of this very trivial incident." Cobden provided Sumner with a unique analysis of the British perspective of the *Trent* affair, stating, "Formerly England feared a war with the United States as much from dependence on your cotton as from a dread of your power. . . . Now the popular opinion (however erroneous) is that a war would give us cotton . . . and we, of course, consider your power weakened by your civil war."[46]

Confederate leaders hoped that the *Trent* affair would spark British recognition of their new nation. For his part, Lincoln sought to avoid war with Great Britain while simultaneously upholding Union prerogatives to interdict Confederate resources. Historians have typically analyzed the *Trent* affair as the nadir of wartime relations between the United States and Britain, and as proof of Lincoln's steady leadership by prosecuting "one war at a time."[47] While the *Trent* affair grabbed transatlantic headlines, the event proved to be just one example in which a US warship arbitrarily seized British cargo in international waters under the pretext of the blockade.

In November 1861, around the same time the USS *San Jacinto* initiated the *Trent* affair, the British merchant ship *Labuan* departed Grimsby on Britain's northeast coast. The steamship was owned by the De Jersey Company of Manchester, and it was headed to Havana, Cuba. Subsequently, the *Labuan* headed for Matamoros, Mexico with a cargo of blankets, bagging, and baling materials. The vessel arrived off the Mexican coast on January 1, 1862, and officially registered with the Port of Matamoros.

Several geographical factors complicated the *Labuan*'s situation. The Mexican port of Matamoros does not touch the ocean, but lies about thirty miles inland up the Rio Grande River. In order to access the trade facilities at Matamoros, ships had to unload their cargoes onto smaller vessels, called lighters, to cross the bar at the mouth of the river. Likewise, any return cargo had to be loaded via these smaller boats. This required long periods at anchor off the mouth of the Rio Grande. The area was problematic because the Rio Grande River marked the border between Mexico and the United States, or in 1862 the Confederate state of Texas. According to the Treaty of Guadalupe Hidalgo that ended the war between the US and Mexico in 1848, the waters off the mouth of the Rio Grande were to be commonly used for international trade one league north and south of the river's mouth (a league is 3.0 nautical miles, or about 3.4 miles). The treaty also forbade any blockade of the river's mouth from either the US or Mexico. These neutral waters on the border benefited both the Port of Matamoros and the Texas port of Brownsville on the northern bank of the Rio Grande.[48]

On February 1, 1862, while lying at anchor off the mouth of the Rio Grande, the *Labuan* was seized by the US warship *Portsmouth* commanded by Capt. Samuel Swartwout. The twenty-two gun USS *Portsmouth* allegedly flew a French flag in order to approach the merchant ship after which "a crew . . . boarded the *Labuan*, lowered her [British] colors, which all the time previous had been displayed, removed her from her moorings" and put a prize crew on board. On February 4 the merchant ship, which contained 439 cotton bales when it was commandeered, disappeared from the waters off Matamoros and was underway to an unknown American prize court. Louis Blacker, the British vice consul at Matamoros, considered the *Labuan*'s "seizure . . . to be such a deliberate act of anything short of piracy." The vessel's captain and supercargo—a company representative – both watched helplessly from shore as the American prize crew took their ship away.[49]

Meanwhile the USS *Portsmouth* still lay off the Rio Grande. The day after the *Labuan*'s seizure a small boat carried Vice-Consul Blacker out to the American warship to demand an explanation. The vessel raised a French flag as he approached. Blacker introduced himself to Captain Swartwout as the British vice-consul and asked why the *Labuan* had been taken. The captain "had no explanation to give," noting that the reasons could be ascertained from the American prize court. Blacker pressed the American commander and was told "the *Labuan* had violated the blockade by loading cotton from Texas." Captain Swartwout then declared "that he would not be fooled but seize all cotton and every vessel carrying cotton and violating the blockade, and that he would even seize a vessel in Tampico if cotton were found on board and he knew it to be from Texas." At this point, Blacker officially "protested against the whole act as an outrage to the British flag and . . . British property," but he was interrupted by the American captain, who said "he had nothing more to do with the matter." The British could take their complaints to the prize court.[50] When Blacker asked to which US prize court the *Labuan* would be taken, Captain Swartwout did not know, but he guessed that it would be New York.

The *Labuan* was not the only British vessel in the neutral waters off the Rio Grande. Among the thirteen ships of other nationalities in the vicinity, seven British ships were "loaded and loading" when the *Portsmouth* seized the *Labuan*. Why did Captain Swartwout target this particular merchant vessel? One possible reason was that it was scheduled to bring on board $150,000 in gold and silver. However, the specie and remaining cotton was stuck in the Port of Matamoros after the *Labuan*'s capture.[51] Is it possible that Captain Swartwout was tipped off about the *Labuan*'s outbound cargo of specie? This would explain why the ship was specifically targeted when thirteen vessels lay off the Rio Grande all of which, by Captain Swartwout's definition, were violating the Union blockade. One should always remember that Union blockaders had financial incentives to capture blockade-runners as opposed to sinking them – the lucrative prize money to be divided up among captain and crew.

The Mexican port of Matamoros drastically increased trade during the Civil War due to its proximity to Texas. According to one historian, the Confederate States used a vast network of depots for transporting trans-Mississippi cotton to neutral Matamoros and exported it to Britain. Over three hundred thousand cotton bales were shipped out of the South and numerous cargoes of war materiel were brought into the Confederacy via this route. The location and increased amount of cotton exports out of Matamoros meant this trade was a surreptitious extension of blockade-running through a neutral port.

Union captain Swartwout found additional evidence for extended blockade-running in the fact that the small vessels transshipping cargo from the Port of Matamoros to the oceangoing vessels operated out of

Brownsville, Texas. He promised to capture the lighters if they ventured across the bar into open water. Swarthout's analysis of the situation at the mouth of the Rio Grande was correct. In his view, massive amounts of Texas cotton were being shipped across the border by wagon to be exported out of Matamoros with the assistance of lighters from Brownsville. The annual number of ship departures out of Matamoros increased from one to fifty-two between 1861 and 1864.[52] However, Captain Swarthout still faced the problem of seizing a neutral vessel in international waters, and he had also initiated a de facto blockade of a neutral Mexican port. This latter issue turned out to be part of a larger diplomatic argument between the US and Great Britain.

British officials did not recognize a legal American blockade of neutral Matamoros, but they were alarmed that the *Labuan* was seized without prior blockade notice. Louis Blacker, the British vice-consul at Matamoros, informed his superiors that when the USS *Portsmouth* appeared off the mouth of the Rio Grande on February 1, 1862, "neither the port of [Matamoros] nor Brownsville was blockaded, nor any vessel boarded in that vicinity by a U.S. Man of War." This information was relayed to Lord Lyons in Washington. The British Ambassador was told that the USS *Portsmouth* was "virtually blockading a Mexican port and that the capture of the Labuan" under such a specious and illegal blockade argument was "unwarrantable and arbitrary in every respect."[53] How would the *Labuan*'s capture by a US warship in neutral waters affect blockade diplomacy between Great Britain and America?

Lord Lyons detailed the *Labuan* affair for Lord Russell and the foreign minister believed the case was "one of a very serious aspect." British officials supported the maritime rights of the *Labuan*'s owners and pursued legal procedures to recoup the costs of the seized vessel. However, Russell also recognized that British diplomats needed to address the larger issue of "the principle involved"—US ships seizing cotton in international waters. America had not followed proper procedures and notified the British consulate that a blockade of Matamoros was in effect. Russell ordered Lyons to file an official complaint with supporting legal arguments "that no blockade of that neutral port [Matamoros] did or could exist." Secretary of State Seward responded evasively. When asked whether official US policy included blockading neutral ports and seizing British ships, Seward informed Lyons "No instructions have been given to cruisers of the U.S. to capture neutral vessels [or] bona fide traders to Matamoros."[54]

The ongoing legal debate about blockades between the US and Great Britain now had another facet. Could American ships seize suspected contraband cargo from neutral vessels no matter their location? Sections 2 and 3 of the Declaration of Paris were clear on this issue: "[A] neutral flag, covers [an] enemy's goods, with the exception of contraband of war."[55] The gray area in the *Labuan* affair was that a US captain deemed cotton, presumably grown in Texas, to be contraband, and thus not protected by a neutral flag.

Would Great Britain send warships to Matamoros to protect British merchant vessels? Vice-Consul Blacker informed Sir Alexander Milne, commander of Britain's North American fleet, that he requested "Commodore [Hugh] Dunlop's attention to Matamoros and suggested the expediency of his sending a ship there to protect . . . lawful commerce." Blacker assumed that Dunlop had already dispatched a British warship to the area, but he was wrong. The decision not to escalate the military situation off the coast of Matamoros came from the highest levels of British government. "The Queen's advocate" reported to Lord Russell and the head of the Admiralty ordered Vice Admiral Milne "to provide for the security of British vessels and property at Matamoros."[56]

The Admiralty was well aware of the precarious legal arguments made by both the US captain and the *Labuan*'s owners regarding contraband cargo. The official British position was as follows: "The mere circumstance of the cargo of British vessels, wheresoever found, even on the high seas being (either composed of cotton or any other article) the growth or produce of Texas, will not of itself expose them to capture, assuming that their papers show that such cargo has been purchased and laden on board . . . from a neutral port." Reaffirming the Declaration of Paris, Russell noted "It is not the origin but the property or ownership of the cargo which must determine the question of its liability to capture." After laying out Great Britain's neutral shipping rights, the foreign minister informed Lord Lyons "Unless however in the clearest and most flagrant case of violation of the neutral waters of Mexico by U.S. cruisers acting against British vessels we cannot recommend the resort to force by H[er] M[ajesty's] ships to prevent captures by U.S. ships of war."[57] The murky legal situation of British merchant ships, which were technically in neutral waters but also transporting cotton from rebel states, caused the British Admiralty to balk at offering military protection. Also, the *Labuan*'s seizure by a US warship was only one component of a larger British strategy for Mexico that entailed French intervention.

In the months following the *Labuan*'s seizure, Lord Lyons pressed William Seward to overturn this violation of maritime law. Seward requested more information from Navy Secretary Gideon Welles and confirmed that orders had been given that "no neutral vessel proceeding toward a blockaded port without contraband of war should be seized or detained, unless [it] had received specific notice of the blockade." Instead of intervening in the *Labuan* case, the Lincoln administration thought it best to take no action "until the result of the judicial proceedings at New York should be made known." Seward admitted fault and thought the *Labuan*'s owners and operators were "entitled to damages and costs." He claimed he was unable to influence the court proceedings so the case dragged on through the courts.[58] The secretary of state's reluctance to intervene in the *Labuan* case was a clever snub of British diplomats. Seward knew the incident involved seizure of rebel cotton from a neutral ship—something British officials could not admit to condoning. Lord Lyons could protest all he wanted about violation of international law, but from Seward's perspective the British had known all along that the *Labuan* was carrying contraband cotton from Texas. Neither side could claim to be completely within its legal rights in the *Labuan* affair.

Seward always considered public opinion in his dealings with Great Britain. One should remember that many Northern newspapers applauded the capture of Confederate diplomats on board the *Trent*. Even if the United States had illegally seized the *Labuan* some in the North enjoyed provoking Great Britain. But the impasse over the *Labuan* was not as politically charged as the *Trent* affair; the Northern public was more concerned with other events. In May 1862, the Confederacy appeared on the brink of collapse and there was no need to provoke Great Britain. "[As] we have had complaint enough from England and Englishmen about alleged ill-treatment which their vessels have received at the hands of our navy" declared an article in the *New York Times*, "let us have no complaints of any ill-treatment at the hands of our Courts or their officers."[59] Seward did not experience the same public pressure as he had during the *Trent* affair. He was willing to admit liability in the *Labuan* case, although he refused to personally intervene.

On May 26, 1862, the New York prize court returned the *Labuan* to its owners, but the question of damages remained. The merchants who had chartered the vessel demanded compensation for lost profits. De Jersey Company's owners asked "John Atkinson, managing clerk of the firm" to handle the damage claims. He "estimated that during the three months period of the *Labuan*'s detention in the jurisdiction of the New York prize court, [it] could have carried 6,000 bales of 490 lbs. each from Matamoros." Atkinson calculated the total damages to be £54,780.

In 1863 the British government inquired about the delay in awarding compensation for the *Labuan*'s seizure. Seward informed Lyons that the owners had failed to make a formal claim to the court. For over a year after the ship's release the owner's claims were postponed because "the claimants of the vessel . . . failed to move the proceedings before the court . . . and the delay [was] the consequence of their own blundering." The court asked for a detailed calculation of damages due and arrived at the sum of $190,000. However, this report was not finished until 1868. The US Congress next had to appropriate funds to pay the damages. Heated debate ensued over whether to pay alleged British war profiteers. Finally, the American government compensated the *Labuan*'s owners in 1870. Another claim was settled in 1873 for $38,000 because the merchant ship had been detained for an additional thirty-eight days after the court ordered it released in May 1862. In the end it took eleven years for the scales of justice to produce an outcome.[60]

The *Labuan* affair is a superb example of the back-and-forth diplomacy between the United States and Great Britain as experienced on the margins of international law. Like most rules of war, the Declaration of Paris provided both concrete and nebulous guidelines. For example, the protection of neutral ships and cargo was clear-cut, but the measure of effectiveness as a binding factor was murky and open to interpretation. In the *Labuan* affair America and Britain both claimed to be inside the limits of international law but neither country could completely justify its actions. The Americans presented a strong de facto case that British ships around Matamoros were involved in the illegal trade of contraband cotton, and Great Britain countered with a solid de jure argument that its ships were entitled to trade in neutral ports and take on cargo that was not proven contraband. The Declaration of Paris was not the only rule of war to be stretched to its interpretive limits during wartime and the *Labuan* affair was an excellent example of this reality.

Other Aspects of Blockade Diplomacy: British Crews and Rebel-Centric Captains

The primary issues of American and British blockade diplomacy were laid out in 1861 and 1862. Some matters, like elimination of privateering, were resolved, but others remained contested diplomatic terrain. One disputed aspect of blockade diplomacy concerned captured British nationals taken prisoner aboard blockade-runners. From the US perspective these sailors were serving the Confederacy, but British neutrality technically cloaked them under the legal protections of Her Majesty's government. An ongoing international legal battle ensued between Lord Lyons and William Seward. Lyons tried to leverage neutrality to free British citizens from US prisons. Seward wanted to detain British blockade-running crews for as long as possible without provoking a belligerent response.

Any sailors aboard captured blockade-runners who openly claimed Confederate allegiance could be imprisoned for the remainder of the war. British seamen, however, possessed some immunity from long-term imprisonment due to their country's neutral status, and they could only be detained until their nationality was confirmed. As a result, when a blockade-runner was seized, most crew members claimed British citizenship to evade prison. About 75 percent of the foreign-born crew members captured aboard blockade-runners, resorted to this tactic.[61] Each one of these alleged British citizens became a potential diplomatic incident and both the Lincoln administration and the British Foreign Office sought to protect their legal prerogatives.

It is difficult to determine the number of British nationals captured while blockade-running. At least one thousand and as many as three thousand British sailors were apprehended and temporarily imprisoned by Union authorities during the war. Were these men to be treated as prisoners of war? Britain's Foreign Office had to be careful to distinguish between British subjects with neutral rights and those Englishmen who actively assisted the Confederacy. As historian Amanda Foreman notes, Lord Lyons "as a rule . . . refused to bother Seward with cases involving self-described British Confederate volunteers." But what about captured sailors who professed allegiance to Great Britain and claimed neutrality?[62]

The experiences of captured British blockade-running crews varied depending on time and circumstances. Early in the war, when legal arguments over the blockade were still fresh, it was logical that captured British crews were used as pawns in the back-and-forth between Lyons and Seward. Over the entire course of the war, however, it does not appear that most apprehended British blockade-running sailors were imprisoned for undue lengths of time. Mark Neely points out that the number of blockade-runner prisoners did not keep pace with the number of captured ships from 1861 to 1865. It was unusual, if not illegal, to detain neutral blockade-running sailors for extended periods.[63]

However, as the war dragged on it was evident that previously captured blockade running crews were being recaptured. Navy Secretary Gideon Welles hoped to stop this recidivism. In December 1863 the blockade-runner *Antonica* attempted to slip past the Union squadron off Wilmington, North Carolina. Previously named the *Herald*, the *Antonica* was a serial blockade violator, that had successfully pierced the cordon twelve times. The blockade-runner's captain and crew were captured and sent to New York. At least eighteen of the twenty-six apprehended British crew members claimed they were unaware that their service included blockade-running when they signed on—hardly convincing evidence. Navy Secretary Welles had finally had enough of the repeat offenders. He issued an order in January 1864"British blockade violators will not be released but detained, and any other orders which you may have received inconsistent with this are hereby revoked."[64] Welles's decree made perfect military sense, but it was not enforceable from the diplomatic perspective.

The Lincoln administration had to weigh both military and diplomatic considerations. While Secretary Welles cracked down on British blockade-running crews with indefinite detention, a military commission appointed by Gen. John A. Dix recommended different methods and limited punishment for British citizens. In February 1864, the commission sanctioned full exoneration of imprisoned British blockade-running crews, declaring "No violator of blockade, is by the laws of war, personally liable to punishment for his act." The group further recommended "Forfeiture of ship and cargo and loss of wages are the only penalty imposed by the law of nations for breach of blockade." The legal reasoning for this exculpatory judgement was based on the argument that "blockade-running is an offense against the municipal law of the State or district against which it was committed, and the U.S. courts cannot punish the blockade-runner whose acts have not been done within such limits." In short, US courts lacked the jurisdiction to indict British subjects for alleged offenses on the high seas. The military authorities affirmed "Blockade-runners may be lawfully detained until they are brought ashore, and if needed as witnesses before the prize courts can be held to give evidence." Yet in most other situations, they added, "further detention is an act of power, not of right."[65]

The commission's recommendation countered Secretary Welles's orders to indefinitely detain British sailors. Diplomatic considerations took precedence over military solutions to the problem of British blockade-running crews. As much as many in the Lincoln administration wanted to permanently imprison all such seamen for the remainder of the war, it was not feasible given Great Britain's determination to protect the rights of its citizens. Whatever harm British blockade-runners were doing to the Union war effort by aiding the Confederacy, it paled in comparison with a potential serious rupture of US and British relations.

The status of captured crews from Great Britain was an ongoing diplomatic conflict. In early 1864 Lord Russell told Lord Lyons, "I hope Mr. Seward and Mr. Welles will keep their hands off British subjects as much as possible." British subjects in the North could be imprisoned on suspicion of aiding blockade-runners. This information was usually obtained through captured correspondence, but the foreign minister considered only actual blockade runners, not those communicating about them, legitimate targets for arrest. Lord Russell opined to Lord Lyons "[Blockade runners] can be lawfully condemned . . . [and] Seward ought to content himself with this remedy. . . . Imprisoning seamen who knew nothing of the law of nations and keeping them in duress on account of some villainous letters would be too bad and makes the victims hate the Yankees past all bearing." Russell's conclusive reply was an indirect message to the Lincoln administration "If Seward and his master Lincoln wish to keep on good terms with us, they will do well to refrain from such questionable proceedings."

Lord Lyons informed his superiors that a part of US strategy to deter blockade-running was through "detention of British subjects taken aboard captured vessels." The ambassador remarked "[I have] tried to make Mr. Seward see how dangerous all these illegal proceedings are—but I think he and his colleagues trust to have succeeded in producing a consternation among the blockade runners before they get themselves into any serious difficulty with foreign powers." According to the Lincoln administration, the burden of proof lay with the captured crews. Lyons noted "There is so strong a presumption that the Blockade Runners are owned by the Confederates that [the US government] has a right to call upon the master and crew to disprove this, before they are released, although there may be no proof at all against the individual vessel."[66] From the American perspective all blockade-running crews were assisters of the Confederacy, but Lyons had to protect the rights of British sailors as part of an overall attempt to maintain Great Britain's neutral shipping rights.

The dispute over captured British sailors continued. In May 1864, Lord Lyons informed his superiors that he was "dissatisfied with the government [in America] for maintaining the obnoxious order for imprisoning the Blockade Runners—and for their excessively arbitrary proceedings in some of the cases of the persons under military arrest." To rectify the situation Lyons "pressed Mr. Seward hard." However, presumably because other members of Lincoln's cabinet balked at a solution, Lyons and Seward were unable to make much progress. Britain's ambassador was "far from satisfied" with the Lincoln administration's handling of the issue, and he wished that Seward "had more influence in the government." But Lyons believed he had "reason to complain of Mr. Seward too who, partly . . . [hoped] to conceal his . . . power."[67] In this instance both Lyons and Seward could legally justify their actions, but each hoped to extract positive results from the friction of wartime diplomacy.

In some instances, it appeared that British naval vessels were actively defying the blockade. HMS *Petrel* performed duties in the seas around Charleston, South Carolina.[68] Britain had good reason to maintain a warship in rebel waters; the neutral nation had a right to communicate with its consulate in Charleston. This was an important and delicate diplomatic post for both consul Robert Bunch and *Petrel* captain George W. Watson. Unfortunately for his superiors, the *Petrel*'s commander unwisely showed overt partiality toward the Confederates.

In 1862 HMS *Petrel* had already directly assisted the Confederacy. The legal case of the ship *Oreto* took center stage in the Bahamas. Built in the Liverpool shipyards allegedly for Italian merchants, the *Oreto* was obviously being converted into a Confederate commerce raider that eventually took the name CSS *Florida*. In a summer 1862 court decision the *Oreto* was cleared from any violation of Britain's Foreign Enlistment Act, after which rebel captain John Newland Maffitt took command. Aware of the decision, US vessels waited in Bahamian waters to intercept the newly christened *Florida*. The only comparable American vessel, the USS *Cuyler* closed on the rebel commerce raider, but the American ship was intercepted by the HMS *Petrel*. The British captain forced the US vessel to leave Bahamian territorial waters, and the *Florida* then escaped the harbor—free to terrorize the Union merchant fleet.[69] From the US perspective the HMS *Petrel* had a history of aiding the Confederacy even before the ship's current station at Charleston.

The *Petrel*'s crew was treated with great hospitality while docked at Charleston in 1863. A Royal Navy sailor informed his family "We are amongst the rebels enjoying ourselves very much." He further noted "[The *Petrel*'s] officers are away now for four days in the country hunting."[70] To say that Captain Watson was sympathetic to the rebellion was an understatement. He claimed to have witnessed the raising of the blockade around Charleston, and even provided legal justification for British military assistance to open the port.

On January 30, 1863, Captain Watson allegedly "witnessed the dispersion of the United States blockading squadron off Charleston." He speculated that since the blockade had been forcibly pushed back, "neutral ships now in the port of Charleston would be allowed to proceed to seas unmolested." Watson deferred the legal decision to his superiors, but he embarked on a pro-Confederate justification. The captain asked his superiors to consult Emer de Vattel's *Law of Nations* (1758) regarding the "effect of war on the commerce of neutrals." Watson cited page numbers and argued "The raising of a blockade by a superior force is a total [defiance] of that blockade and its operations." After such an interruption, he contended, "the neutral merchant is not bound to foresee or to conjecture, that the blockade will be resumed: and therefore if it is to be renewed it must proceed *de novo* and without reference to the former state of facts."[71] Watson was claiming that the Union blockade around Charleston, if not the entire US blockade of the Confederacy, was now void until the Lincoln administration issued another official blockade notice.

The episode Watson witnessed was the January 30 attack of the ironclads CSS *Palmetto State* and CSS *Chicora* on the Union blockade squadron. Led by Cmdre. Duncan Ingraham, the assault successfully damaged the USS *Mercedita* and USS *Keystone State* but neither vessel was sunk or captured. After this clear Confederate victory Ingraham ordered the ironclads back across the bar into Charleston Harbor. From the rebel perspective, the blockade had been lifted with military force and could only be resumed with another declaration.[72] To objective observers, however, the Confederates' successful ironclad attack was a temporary blockade reprieve, a naval raid against the Union squadron, not a full-blown military dispersal of the blockade. The *Petrel*'s commander chose to interpret the January 30 attack as proof that the Confederate navy had indeed lifted the blockade.

Watson's argument was flawed in several respects. First, there had been no continual forcible dispersal of the Union blockade squadron around Charleston—only the witnessing of one event by a British officer. Also, Watson's claim was premised on the notion that a temporarily dispersed Union fleet could not reassert the blockade but had to start completely anew, as if the past blockading efforts had never happened. This was absurd. The *Petrel*'s captain wanted a strict burden of proof of legal blockade for the Union, and he also alleged that, until a new blockade could be proclaimed, British merchant ships should be able to freely enter and exit Charleston without US interference.

Watson continued his one-sided legal opinion on blockade discontinuity and necessary legal notice. Once the blockading ships vacated the area if "nothing more came in evidence than the squadron appeared off the port on a certain day, it was held that this would not restore a blockade which had been . . . effectually raised, but that it should be renewed again by notification." On the question of blockade resumption Watson stated "The squadron might return off the port with very different and new intentions . . . as a fleet of observation merely or for the purpose of a qualified blockade only." The captain did not define a qualified blockade. He averred that the squadron "commander might attempt to connect the two blockades together," but he also declared that "this . . . could not be done." Watson evidenced the January 31 proclamation from "the Secretary of the self called Confederate States [who] on the very same grounds addressed a dispatch to the Mr. Consul Mure . . . declaring the port of Charleston SC open." It seemed like Captain Watson was acting more the part of a Confederate diplomat than a British naval officer. HMS *Cadmus* arrived in Charleston on February 2, 1863, with the mission of delivering consular dispatches and resupplying the *Petrel*. The *Cadmus's* captain John Francis Ross noted that two blockade-runners slipped out of Charleston unmolested on February 5, so for outside observers it was plausible that the blockade had indeed been temporarily lifted.[73]

Union blockade commanders were aware of Captain Watson's blatant pro-Confederate actions. Samuel F. DuPont, head of the South Atlantic Blockading Squadron, informed the navy secretary that the "*Petrel* should be ordered out of Charleston by the British admiral or Lord Lyons." DuPont complained of the administration's "liberality" regarding British vessels, and he added "The officer commanding the *Petrel*, from his well-known rebel sympathies, is especially obnoxious."[74] Union leaders were encouraged by the eventual response from the British Foreign Office.

Admiral Milne, commander in chief, North America and West Indies Station, realized this situation required diplomatic attention. He alerted Lord Lyons to the alleged raising of the Union blockade and relieved HMS *Petrel* from duty in Charleston. Milne also informed the British ambassador that his ship commanders were investigating Watson's information about the lifted blockade. "With reference to the alleged raising of the Charleston blockade by the federal squadron being . . . driven off by the Confederate rams," the admiral explained that his commanders were not to make legal or diplomatic decisions without first consulting Lord Lyons. Milne ordered his commanding officers to inform him and Lyons as soon as "the blockade if raised was immediately de facto re-imposed." The admiral wisely confirmed that any legal issue about the blockade was "a question for H[er] M[ajesty's]'s government." "Without [Lord Lyon's] concurrence or instructions from me" Milne said, his commanders were "enjoined to take no direct action in the matter." Admiral Milne doubted that the *Petrel*'s captain had witnessed a raising of the blockade. After deeper investigation Milne realized Watson had been guilty of practicing pro-Confederate diplomacy. The admiral had finally had enough, and Captain Watson was reassigned to a part of the Caribbean not involved in any diplomatic aspect of the Civil War.[75]

The HMS *Petrel* episode highlights the always fragile situation of British blockade diplomacy. The Admiralty, Admiral Milne, Lord Lyons, and even Lord Russell had to maintain a constant vigil over every British official stationed in North America, whether they were consuls or naval officers, to make sure that a single Confederate sympathizer, like Commander Watson, did not disrupt the diplomatic balance between Great Britain and the United States. The *Petrel* incident also shows how one commander, already inclined to Confederate sympathies, could be swayed with local favors, and be persuaded by one-sided rebel proclamations that the blockade had been forcefully removed. All the British high command could do was to make sure such officers were not assigned to Southern ports. The British Foreign Office and the Admiralty performed this difficult task magnificently, taking a measured approach to these situations.

Conclusion

In the nineteenth century British naval supremacy was unquestioned. International maritime policies were largely dictated by Great Britain in the interest of protecting its far-flung global empire. But the Civil War caused a massive expansion of the US Navy that threatened British maritime dominance. The diplomatic arena required careful navigation. The full panoply of British interests conflicted with the main goals of the American combatants. For example, British economic stability, based on cotton imports, collided with Union attempts to deny Southern cotton exports. Likewise, Britain's neutrality and willingness to allow private shipowners to operate blockade-runners clashed with Union blockade policy. The Confederacy benefited from recognition of its belligerent status but it could not seriously interrupt the massive trade between the US and Great Britain, despite the successes of rebel commerce raiders. Nor could the Confederate States convince the British government to directly intervene on its behalf. Neither the US nor the Confederacy got exactly what it wanted from Great Britain, which is a testament to the successful diplomatic efforts of the Foreign Office, and in particular Lord Lyons.

Lyons left Washington, DC in 1864. He departed having achieved most of Britain's diplomatic goals with the United States, and his former adversary Secretary of State Seward now had deep respect for his ability. Despite the periodic destabilizing threats from Seward, Lord Lyons maintained a cool head, calmly implementing the policies laid out by the Foreign Office. Historian Amanda Foreman notes that by 1865, largely due to his wartime service in Washington, the ambassador was "a highly respected representative of Her Majesty's government whose dignified though conciliatory approach in delicate situations made him invaluable."[76]

British interests demanded that the Foreign Office make no egregious diplomatic mistakes concerning the blockade, and in that respect, they succeeded. Despite complaints and one-sided interpretations of maritime law from Union and Confederate officials, the British Foreign Office upheld the legal definition of a blockade. Her Majesty's government expected both combatants to acknowledge Great Britain's neutrality and behave accordingly. Lord Lyons became a lightning rod for Seward's hostile interpretations of blockade legality, but the ambassador ultimately prevailed by preserving British prerogatives and, perhaps more importantly, not being goaded into a conflict with the United States.

Seward used the threat of port closures as a way to satisfy hard-core Republicans in Congress who advocated a hawkish policy with Britain. But Seward also used these closings as diplomatic leverage in an attempt to show just how far the Lincoln administration might go to prevent assistance to the rebellion. The legal argument for shutting down ports was specious in the context of the Declaration of Paris. Seward gladly noted British hypocrisy based on past events, like the *Vixen* episode in the 1830s. Ironically, Lord Palmerston argued for legal port closure in the 1830s and he was prime minister during the Civil War. Despite these inconsistencies Lord Lyons steadfastly refused the Lincoln administration's right to close Southern ports, and he repeatedly channeled legal arguments back to the benefit of British interests under the Declaration of Paris.

Great Britain's insistence on conformity to the Declaration of Paris was imperative to successful blockade diplomacy. So long as British leaders and civilians complied with the letter of the law, neither Union nor Confederate diplomats could claim bias. Some US political leaders, like Charles Sumner, construed Great Britain's neutrality as passive assistance to the Confederacy. Likewise, some Southern diplomats thought that the British were assisting the Union by not applying a more literal interpretation of blockade ineffectiveness. Both of these arguments were tendentious. Lord Russell and Lord Lyons used the Declaration of Paris exactly the way it was intended, granting neutral nations protection from belligerents. Britain's application of the Declaration of Paris was masterful diplomacy that simultaneously safeguarded British interests and maintained a relatively impartial platform for regulation of maritime law. None of the parties to the blockade ever exhibited full compliance with the Declaration. However, of the three nations involved Great Britain most closely followed legal precedent and held others to account for failure to do so. British maritime policy balanced itself on the fulcrum of the Declaration of Paris, and it could lean one way or the other depending on the circumstances, but it was Great Britain that had the greatest long-term interest in international legal compliance.

Britain's granting of belligerent rights to the Confederacy was a sore spot for the United States. Neutrality allowed British citizens to aid the Confederacy with minimal punishment. Great Britain's neutrality had loopholes not only for Southern sympathizers to run the blockade, but also for shipbuilders to construct commerce raiders like the CSS *Alabama*. Despite potential Union retaliation for awarding Confederate belligerent rights, the British Foreign Office's decision was consistent with international law. The Lincoln administration was less concerned with statutory validity than with keeping war materiel from the rebels. Thus, it was unsurprising that the postwar diplomatic tussle between America and Great Britain over the *Alabama* claims exhibited such heated rhetoric from Washington. The Confederates were ecstatic about being granted belligerent status, and they hoped it was the initial move toward British recognition, but this was not to be. However, without the unofficial support of British blockade-runners, it is doubtful whether the Confederacy could have continued the war through 1865.

Britain's blockade diplomacy would have been much easier if it had only consisted of broad policy implementation, but individual cases like the *Labuan* affair and the HMS *Petrel* episode tested the limits of consensus for a legal blockade. In the case of the British merchant ship *Labuan*, all parties were technically within their legal rights. Conversely all parties also interpreted blockade law in an extremely biased way. The case of HMS *Petrel* was clear. British naval officers had a duty to remain impartial regarding the blockade, because one rogue officer could spark war with the United States. The *Petrel*'s commander overtly sided with the Confederacy's interpretation of the blockade, and he had to be removed. The fact that this was done promptly and without incident was important. At any point an individual blockade episode could have escalated into a serious diplomatic crisis, and the fact that this did not occur proves the professionalism and skill of Britain's Foreign Office.

It was a testament to Britain's wartime ability to uphold the definition of a legal blockade that the main postwar diplomatic conflict between the US and Great Britain did not involve lingering questions about the blockade. Instead, the two countries disagreed about responsibility for the British-built Confederate commerce raiders, or the *Alabama* claims. US plaintiffs argued that Britain's "un-neutral neutrality" had caused over $2 billion in damages. This dispute was only resolved by the Treaty of Washington (1871) which sent the two nations to arbitration and was amicably settled in 1872.[77] Owners of blockade-runners had no similar recourse to recover property that Union blockade squadrons captured or destroyed. The few dubious cases of illegal seizure like the *Labuan*'s were eventually resolved in the postwar years as well, but usually in American prize courts. The most impressive feat of blockade diplomacy in the Civil War was Great Britain's preservation of the international rules governing blockades under the Declaration of Paris. This preservation coincided with British interests but it also served as an important foundation for blockade law in the late nineteenth and twentieth centuries.

CHAPTER 2

——————★——————

Blockade Squadrons

THE US NAVY DID NOT HAVE relevant experience to prepare it for the blockade of Confederate ports. The scale and scope of the Civil War blockade dwarfed the naval blockade in the Mexican War of 1846 to 1848 for several reasons. First, the Civil War was a pivotal event from an international economic standpoint. A dominant third party— Great Britain—held vital interests in the outcome. Britain cultivated diplomatic ties with the Union and the Confederacy to achieve its two main goals: avoiding war with the Union and maintaining the flow of cotton from the Confederacy. British blockade-running captains and crews profited from their illicit actions and they claimed the protections of their nation's neutrality when caught. Thus, Great Britain was the greatest source of blockade defiance after the Confederacy itself. Second, the US Navy simply had never attempted any operation of this size, nor did it have the resources to do so in 1861. With determination and ingenuity, Navy Secretary Gideon Welles oversaw the creation and implementation of a vast naval force that interdicted desperately needed Confederate supplies. The Union blockade evolved and improved its tactics over the course of the war, and by 1865 the US Navy had developed the requisite skills to conduct future blockades.

Lincoln Proclaims the Blockade

The timing of President Lincoln's blockade proclamation deserves scrutiny. Many policies in the first weeks of the Lincoln administration arose in reaction to the secession crisis. It is easy for us to forget that the Confederacy possessed great momentum by the time of Lincoln's inauguration on March 4, 1861. Seven Southern states had already seceded, and over the next three months Abraham Lincoln and Jefferson Davis jockeyed to entice undecided states to either stay in the Union or join the Confederacy. This was the greatest strategic battle of early 1861, waged not by armies in the field, but by opposing presidential administrations. Victory likely hinged on the outcome of this struggle for allegiance from the states of Virginia, North Carolina, Tennessee, Arkansas, Kentucky, Missouri, and Maryland. Lincoln's blockade proclamation was inextricably connected with secession crisis strategy and should be analyzed in this context.

The Fort Sumter crisis opened the floodgates of this strategic battle for the undecided states. The rebel attack on the Union flag from April 12 to April 14 initiated a second wave of secession. In response to the Confederate attack on Fort Sumter, President Lincoln called for seventy-five-thousand volunteers to put down the rebellion on April 15. Upper South states reacted to his request with hostility. Virginia seceded on April 17 and North Carolina, Tennessee, and Arkansas eventually left the Union in May and June. But it was Virginia's departure—with its resources, geographic importance, and historical legacy—that delivered the biggest blow to the Lincoln administration thus far, and gave the Confederacy a realistic chance of success. Lincoln needed to respond forcefully—but what to do? He still wanted to prevent the remaining states in the Upper South from seceding. Although he held out hope longer than most, the president recognized that North Carolina, Tennessee, and Arkansas were likely to join the Confederacy. Lincoln's priorities then shifted to keeping Maryland, Kentucky, and Missouri in the Union—and he accomplished this goal masterfully.

Lincoln's blockade proclamation was part of this strategic battle. The events immediately after the firing on Fort Sumter were of vast importance for the trajectory of the war: Lincoln's call for troops on April 15, Virginia's secession on April 17, and finally Lincoln's blockade proclamation on April 19. At this early stage the Lincoln administration's only weapon to stymie further revolt was the promise of future punishment. The Union army and navy were not yet ready to take the war to the rebels, so the president used the only tools available to him—the future ability of US armed forces to bring the rebellion to heel. Both the call for troops on April 15 and the blockade declaration on April 19 were indeed only words, but Lincoln backed them with his resolve. Historian Craig Symonds notes that "the threat of Confederate privateers . . . very likely played a major role in the timing of Lincoln's blockade announcement." Only two days prior Confederate president Jefferson Davis had "announced that he would begin issuing letters of marque to private vessels."[1] This was another major factor in Lincoln's decision to proclaim a blockade on April 19, but most citizens were likely unaware of these maritime legalities. In mid-April 1861 President Lincoln was on the defensive. Lincoln played his available cards—and he played them well—but the blockade declaration was one of the few weapons in his arsenal to stem the tide of secession.

The reasons for the blockade proclamation and the details therein provide insight into Lincoln's strategy (see appendix 2). After listing the initial seven seceded states Lincoln affirmed the legality and necessity of blockading southern ports. He first noted "The laws of the United States for collection of revenue can not be effectually executed." Lincoln stated that the Constitution required "duties to be uniform throughout the United States," harkening back to his first inaugural on March 4, in which he vowed to enforce the laws in the rebellious states. Did Lincoln intend to use a blockade to collect duties? His words implied that he would pursue a port closure policy instead of a legal blockade, and Great Britain strongly opposed port closure. Second, Lincoln mentioned the Confederate "letters of marque" that encouraged privateering against US shipping. Presumably, he intended the blockade to prevent rebel privateers from leaving Southern ports. Third, in case he faced legal arguments against his actions, Lincoln attached the same legality to his blockade proclamation on April 19 as he had to his call for troops on April 15.

These were the first among many of President Lincoln's wartime executive orders, an oft-used method that vastly expanded the president's powers. Lincoln noted that these declarations were intended as immediate actions "until Congress . . . assembled and deliberated on the said lawful proceedings." He wanted to ensure that this blockade declaration conformed to the "laws of the United States and the law of nations." As for the blockade process, Lincoln called for a "competent force" and said that suspect vessels should be notified, warned once. At that point, he stated "If the same vessel shall again attempt to enter or leave the blockaded port [it] will be captured" and sent to a prize court.[2] The policy of seizure after one warning was lenient and rarely used during the war. Lincoln capably laid out the reasons for declaring a blockade, promising a massive naval strategy that played a major role in the Civil War. The president's declaration laid the foundation for what historian Craig Symonds describes as "the greatest naval mobilization in [US] history, one that would not be matched until the months following the Japanese attack on Pearl Harbor eighty years later."[3]

Events in the second wave of secession also influenced Lincoln's blockade policy. Lincoln hoped that Virginia's secession ordinance of April 17 could be reversed once the hysteria subsided, but he could not ignore the capture of Gosport Navy Yard near Norfolk on April 23. In response to the seizure of federal property by secessionists in Virginia and North Carolina, Lincoln expanded the blockade proclamation on April 27 (see appendix 3). He reaffirmed the reasons cited in the original blockade announcement, and he explained the need for extending the blockade to North Carolina and Virginia. The president reminded citizens of what had transpired since he issued the initial blockade decree: "The public property of the United States has been seized, the collection of revenue obstructed, and duly commissioned officers of the United States . . . have been arrested and held in custody as prisoners . . . by persons claiming to act under the authority of the States of Virginia and North Carolina."[4] From Lincoln's perspective, these states had commenced rebellious actions; thus the blockade should be enforced against them as well.

Virginia seceded on April 17, but North Carolina did not officially leave the Union until May 20. This begs the question—did President Lincoln's April 27 blockade expansion unwisely strengthen the secession movement in North Carolina? Due to geography, the hope for keeping the state in the Union drastically decreased with Virginia's departure. However, it appeared that North Carolina was much less eager to secede than South Carolina, and a little less eager than Virginia. In fact, in a February 1861 special referendum North Carolina Unionists won a narrow victory of 47,323 to 46,672. Incoming president Lincoln even considered North Carolina Whig and ardent Unionist John A. Gilmer as his navy secretary as an inclusive olive branch to moderate North Carolinians.[5]

However, events during the secession crisis—in particular Lincoln's call for troops on April 15—pushed North Carolina into the second wave of secession. Gov. John Ellis not only refused the president's request for soldiers, but he also ordered the seizure of federal forts in the state. In response to Lincoln's call for troops, Ellis also ordered the removal of lighthouse lamps, which made the hazardous North Carolina coast even more treacherous. Although North Carolina did not officially secede until May 20, the secessionists had momentum in late April. President Lincoln's extension of the blockade to cover North Carolina merely recognized the de facto state of rebellion. Expanding the blockade did not exacerbate secession in North Carolina since the state government pursued rebellious actions before the May 20 vote made it official.[6]

The Blockade Begins, 1861

The process of building and managing a naval force to blockade the Confederacy was daunting, and it would take time and patience to succeed. Gideon Welles deserves a great deal of credit for overseeing this mammoth task. At the outset of the blockade in 1861 the US Navy possessed only forty-two vessels ready for service—a drastically insufficient pool of resources for the job.[7] Although the blockade was the most significant cause for a naval buildup, the navy secretary also oversaw the creation of river squadrons. Though the Union possessed great shipbuilding capability, construction of quality vessels took time, and the blockade needed to be implemented immediately for both military and diplomatic reasons. The haste to put ships into service meant that converted vessels, sometimes ill-suited for extended duty, were rushed into the blockade squadrons. The Union blockade would have to make do with limited resources until the North's shipbuilding capacity increased squadron strength.

The officers given the initial mission of establishing a blockade faced a Herculean task. The geographic division of the two blockade departments was at Key West, with Flag Officer Silas Stringham responsible for the coastline from Virginia to the southernmost tip of Florida, and Flag Officer William Mervine responsible for the Gulf Coast from Key West to the Mexican border. Expecting this assignment to be accomplished with inadequate resources was unrealistic, but both officers tried their best to provide a stable foundation for the Union blockade.

Flag Officer Silas Stringham was a lifelong naval veteran who in 1861 was in his early sixties, which by the standards of the antebellum US Navy was relatively young. Stringham was given command of the Atlantic Coast blockade, and in the spring of 1861, he pieced it together. On May 1, Welles informed him that President Lincoln had "found it necessary to issue proclamations closing the ports of those States . . . resisting the laws of the Federal Government." This was a minor misstatement since a blockade and port closure—certainly from the British perspective—were two entirely different legal positions. The navy secretary ordered Stringham to "take command of the [blockade] squadron . . . from the capes of the Chesapeake to the southern extremity of Key West." The Union blockading fleet was to meet at Hampton Roads and await Stringham's orders. Welles reminded his flag officer that time was of the essence, and he promised that the necessary supplies and additional ships would be sent as they became available.[8] At this early stage of the war, this was a blockade on the fly, a scraped together naval force that could provide some presence outside Confederate ports until a larger fleet could be deployed.

Over a month after Lincoln's blockade declaration, Stringham was still trying to make sense of his assignment. The navy secretary delivered the available vessels for blockade duty and Stringham assigned them to Southern ports, but more vessels could only be promised. The flag officer realistically informed Welles that blockade squadron tactics were dependent on future resources, stating "Not being acquainted with the force or character of the other vessels . . . I can not now say the exact disposition I shall make of them." Upon arrival Stringham assessed each ship's capabilities for blockade duty. On May 24, he notified Welles "To make the blockade of the Atlantic coast perfect and strict, I require at least from twelve to fifteen more efficient and seagoing vessels. . . . Steamers are preferable." From the start, Stringham recognized that the task overstretched available resources. He reminded Welles "[I will] do with the means I now have all that I possibly can to carry into effect the blockade." Welles then acknowledged the difficult circumstances, but he reinforced the importance of getting the blockade operational. The secretary admitted "The number of vessels sent you is not so large as the Department would wish nor of the description that would be preferred, but we have to conform to existing circumstances."[9] Eventually the blockade was divided into four geographic departments supported by ample naval resources, but in early 1861 Stringham would have to do his best.

Welles reminded Stringham of international blockade law, informing him that, as per the Declaration of Paris, "a competent force must be posted." The flag officer must also "duly notify neutrals of the declaration of blockade," and "allow a reasonable number of days" for them to leave Southern ports unmolested. Welles stressed the legal importance of a continued presence by the blockading squadrons: "A lawful maritime blockade requires the actual presence of an adequate force stationed at the entrance of the port sufficiently near to prevent communication. The only exception to this rule . . . [is] the occasional temporary absence of the blockading squadron, produced by an accident, as in the case of a storm, which does not suspend the legal operation of a blockade."[10] At this stage, neutral ships were given the benefit-of-the-doubt. But blockade-runners blatantly abused the protection of neutrality, and eventually the blockaders became dubious of ships claiming neutral status.

Flag Officer Stringham assessed the situation and implemented the available forces. On May 30, 1861, he estimated the "number and class of vessels" needed to maintain a "strict blockade of the Atlantic coast" as being "five or six for the coast of each State." This turned out to be a severe underestimation. Stringham noted that the blockading ships needed to be "fast and of sufficient capacity to carry coal for some time," and at a minimum, he requested no "less than 20 or 25 vessels" for the entire Atlantic Coast! Even with this small number of ships, the flag officer believed that the blockade squadrons would keep a "strict coast guard in passing and repassing for their coal."[11] It is easy for those with the benefit of hindsight to criticize Stringham's assessment of the necessary resources to prevent blockade-running. But the fact is, he was given an extremely difficult task—the blockade of all Southern ports between Virginia and Key West—and only meager resources to carry it out.

Stringham set about trying to successfully complete his orders, but the assignment overwhelmed him. The spring and summer of 1861 heralded ad hoc blockade implementation in which Stringham put available ships into service as soon as practicable. The correspondence between the flag officer and the navy secretary during this period can be summed up as follows—Stringham requested more resources, and Welles required him to do his best with the available vessels. Neither Stringham nor Welles was satisfied with the result. By September 1861, the spent Stringham felt admonished by Welles and defended his requests for more ships. "That I have not been satisfied with the vessels provided," Stringham noted, "I have been obliged to apprise the Department from time to time, as I considered it my duty to do." But he was unaware that his appeals were construed as inefficiency and weak leadership. Stringham offered to resign. Welles apologized for offending the flag officer's "sensibilities" but explained that he only meant to "press upon [Stringham] the necessity for unceasing activity." In a particular case of bad timing for Stringham, the navy secretary mentioned that the decision was underway to divide the blockade into North and South Atlantic Squadrons, adding that he would accept Stringham's resignation anyway with the thanks of a grateful nation. The flag officer was replaced by a naval veteran and rising star in Washington—Samuel F. DuPont.[12]

The leadership transition coincided with a shift in blockade strategy and tactics. In 1861 coastal patrols were used and it occurred to blockade strategists that focusing on the Confederate ports yielded better results. In May 1861, Stringham had noted that Union vessels had to roam nine hundred to one thousand miles looking for blockade-runners. Shortly thereafter, Navy Secretary Gideon Welles remarked "If you can not line the whole coast with vessels you will use such as you have to the best advantage by closing the most important points." He further declared "[The] primary object [is] to close the principal ports, and with the remaining vessels . . . to perform coast guard service."[13] The overall blockade strategy eventually shifted to port saturation—concentric rings of blockaders outside Confederate ports. However, the North could only implement a port-saturation strategy once its naval resources were fully deployed.

Stringham's counterpart in command of the Gulf Coast blockade was Flag Officer William Mervine, who had passed his seventieth birthday before the blockade's creation. Mervine had a distinguished record, but the task eventually overwhelmed him as well. The US Navy's capabilities in mid-1861 were inadequate to carry out the mission, and Mervine suffered as a result. After the summer of 1861 Mervine understood that officers with more stamina, future longevity, and government confidence were needed to implement the blockade. He resigned gracefully in September 1861, but this was a formality since the Blockade Strategy Board had already recommended a drastic reorganization of the blockade.

Union Blockade Strategy

Union victory in the Civil War required an unprecedented expansion of naval resources in a very short period of time. Nothing on this scale had occurred in the republic's history and by the end of the war, only the British Royal Navy outmatched the numbers and firepower of the US Navy. This massive growth was overseen by Lincoln's secretary of the navy, Gideon Welles, who shepherded the Union's naval resources to victory. Welles was a Democrat from Connecticut, but he was among the most reliable and talented members of Lincoln's cabinet. The secretary possessed an undeviating work ethic that helped him weather the political storms of cabinet intrigue, and it also assisted him in the constant wrangling with Congress and his officers. Although he had detractors, Gideon Welles provided much-needed stability and consistency to naval management. At the outset of this duties in 1861, Welles—like many other high-ranking leaders on both sides—seriously underestimated the depth of his assignment and the resources required for success.

After Lincoln's declaration on April 19, Gideon Welles went to work to blockade the Confederacy's three-thousand-mile coastline. Very few, if any, navies had ever attempted so large a project as blockading a territory of this magnitude while simultaneously supporting armies in amphibious operations. One advantage that Welles had in his long-range planning was that the Union navy did not need to neutralize the enemy's capital ships—the Confederacy had none. In the absence of capital ships, however, Confederate secretary of the navy Stephen Mallory invested his scarce resources in ironclad technology. It was this aspect of the rebel naval program that Welles had to counter with a matching investment, and he did so with mixed results. Union naval strategy centered around two main goals: supporting Northern armies and blockading Southern ports. The navy's support of Union soldiers has been well documented and despite the typical turf wars, by the end of the fighting the US armed forces worked in conjunction rather well. The nagging issue that Welles fretted over from 1861 to 1865 was the intractable problem of stopping blockade-runners. He turned to the opinions of experts to formulate a strategy. In his leadership of the Union blockading squadrons, Welles's personal attributes of patience and perseverance eventually paid off, but not after some trial and error and periodic disappointment.

Neither side possessed a fully developed military strategy at the war's outset. Overall Union strategy was provided by Winfield Scott in what the press dubbed the "Anaconda Plan. The plan had three main components: a blockade of Confederate ports, capture and occupation of the Mississippi River valley, and capture of the rebel capital, Richmond. To a great degree this is eventually how the North won the Civil War, but it would be inaccurate to argue that Union military leaders consistently adhered to the Anaconda Plan as a grand strategy.

Numerous secondary factors, like political considerations, complicated the overall Union strategy. In many cases, Union armies unwittingly deviated from the master plan due to poor leadership and at every turn, the Confederate forces' stubborn defense caused strategic adjustment. The Union navy, however, embarked on the Anaconda Plan in 1861 and consistently achieved its goals. The US Navy played a pivotal role in the conquest of the Mississippi River valley in 1863, and by 1865 the blockade squadrons had developed an ever-strengthening blockade of Southern ports. It would be fair to say that the Union navy excelled with its portion of the Anaconda Plan while the US Army struggled to achieve the basic goals—but this was to be expected since the Confederate navy was not nearly as potent as rebel armies.

Gideon Welles understood that the navy needed a more specific blockade strategy to win the war. Like many other leaders on both sides, Welles found that time and events morphed his understanding and application of blockade strategy. One of the navy secretary's great strengths was his willingness to consult experts for their opinions and assistance. He also possessed forbearance, a quality that served him well when dealing with Assistant Navy Secretary Gustavus V. Fox, a headline-seeking schemer who sought glory for himself and the navy. Welles deserved blame for allowing Fox to operate with a free hand, but in 1861 Welles looked to Fox as a strategic consultant.

The foundation for overall Union blockade strategy was a series of reports submitted by the Commission of Conference—or the Blockade Strategy Board. The group consisted of Gustavus Fox; Alexander Bache— head of the US Coast Survey; Cdr. Charles Davis; Maj. J. G. Barnard— army engineer; and Capt. Samuel F. DuPont—among the most respected career naval officers. Alexander Bache provided the idea for the Blockade Strategy Board, and convinced Fox and DuPont to join in May 1861. By creating the board, Bache cleverly ensured that the Coast Survey would be integrated into Union naval strategy, thus preserving his bureaucratic fiefdom. DuPont chaired the panel, which met from June through September in 1861.[14]

Gideon Welles ordered the board members to focus on two topics. First, they were to recommend the location for capture of "two or more points . . . on the Atlantic Coast [and] similar points in the Gulf of Mexico." This directive was among the Blockade Strategy Board's most important strategic deliberations. The board's final reports led to the joint operations and capture of several strategic coastal outposts that enhanced the blockade's logistical capability. The cooperative amphibious operations and the occupation of Port Royal, South Carolina, and Ship Island in the Gulf of Mexico in November 1861 derived from the members' recommendations. These locations were important logistical bases for maintaining a continual blockade, and they could also be used as staging areas for incursions into the Confederate interior. Welles also requested the feasibility "of closing all the Southern ports by mechanical means."[15] In other words, the navy secretary wanted board members to explore the already popular notion of sinking a stone fleet at the entrance to Southern harbors. This idea was a sham for a couple of reasons. Very strong currents and tides dictated ship channels in ports like Charleston and Wilmington, so the effectiveness of such a plan was limited at best. In most situations, it was downright useless.

In addition, Great Britain considered the closing of ports by such means to be outside the norms of international law, an even more devious method of port closure than the argument based on revenue collection.

The Blockade Board convened on June 27 and over the course of the next twelve weeks issued ten strategy reports. The exact details of the meetings are unavailable, but the covered topics addressed the details of blockade duty. Historian Kevin Weddle notes that almost every conceivable aspect of blockade enforcement was considered "with the notable exception of the legal requirements for an effective blockade." This is probably due to the fact that the board members had scientific backgrounds and wanted to leave legal considerations to the Lincoln administration. DuPont was likely the only member who had considered the legal aspects of the blockade; the other members were recruited for their knowledge of coastal geography and engineering. The other curious omission from the list of meeting topics—in fact it was crossed off the list according to Weddle—was "what force of vessels (number and kind) would be required for the blockade."[16] This stunning failure to assess the required resources for an effective blockade lies squarely with DuPont. He was the career navy officer and the only member with actual blockade experience in the war with Mexico. It is unclear why this omission occurred, but it left a gaping hole in the board's recommendations to the Lincoln administration.

In fulfillment of Welles's request, the Blockade Board recommended seizure of two bases on the Atlantic Seaboard. These two captured ports on the Southern coastline would be used not only "as a depot for coal . . . [but also] as a depot of provisions and common stores, as a harbor of refuge, and as a general rendezvous, or headquarters" for the nearest squadron. Fernandina, Florida—just north of Jacksonville—was highly recommended as a candidate, and eventually Union forces did occupy this location.[17] The board also suggested a trio of sites in South Carolina for a blockade base: Bull's Bay, near Cape Romain just north of Charleston; St. Helena Sound, south of Charleston at the mouth of the Edisto River; and Port Royal, also south of Charleston in the vicinity of Hilton Head Island. Wisely, board members selected the last of these. Port Royal provided a superb deep-water harbor with numerous surrounding islands that could be easily protected from rebel attacks. Also, Port Royal was only a short distance to the mouth of the Savannah River, thus providing easy access to blockade Georgia's largest port city, Savannah. Although Charleston was a bit farther away, Port Royal afforded proximity to South Carolina's most important port as well. On the Blockade Board's recommendation, a joint army and naval force captured Port Royal in November 1861, claiming the first major victory of war for the Union.[18]

The Gulf of Mexico possessed four main blockade targets: Pensacola, Mobile, New Orleans, and Galveston. Blockade Board members provided a detailed geographical description of the entire coast and noted that overall strategy should focus on closing New Orleans. The board also created an extremely detailed narrative, including depths and channel widths, of the three main passes into the Mississippi River. In terms of a general plan, board members opined about a long-standing economic chimera regarding the Mississippi River's importance to the Union's midwestern states, then referred to as the Northwest—Indiana, Illinois, Wisconsin, Iowa, and Minnesota. Confederate leaders hoped that closing the river might jolt these states' economies and cause them to sympathize with the Confederacy, or at least raise a howl with the Lincoln administration. In that the Confederacy sought to wield its economic leverage, these aspirations were similar to Confederate hopes for King Cotton Diplomacy.

However, these desires never came to pass. The Blockade Board recognized as early as August 1861 that the Union's midwestern states were "bound to the East and to the Atlantic Ocean by railroads and by water connections, through canals and the Great Lakes, which render[ed] them . . . independent of the Mississippi." Even if midwestern farmers paid higher transportation costs to move their goods to eastern markets, it was not enough to force them to reconsider their allegiance to the Union. Nevertheless, reopening the Mississippi River to commerce and capturing New Orleans were important goals in Union strategy. But as the board pointed out, rebel possession could not dictate a political uprising in the Midwest. The Blockade Strategy Board crafted a detailed report on how to shut New Orleans off from blockade-running, and Union possession of Ship Island was key to this strategy. Almost equidistant between the Mississippi delta and the second most important Confederate port of Mobile, Alabama, Ship Island was vital to blockade operations in the Gulf of Mexico.[19]

The Blockade Board also recommended the seizure of inland waterways when it enhanced the blockade's effectiveness. Cutting off Confederate ports could diminish imports, but continued interstate and intrastate waterborne transport of goods, particularly on the North Carolina sounds, could dilute the blockade's effectiveness. These inland waters supported low-draft vessels, and they were a supply artery the Union navy needed to close. As a first step, the board recommended the capture of North Carolina's Outer Banks, where the inlets had been a haven for smugglers since the 1600s. The treacherous shallow waters put a premium on local knowledge of the channels. Often, nimble low-draft vessels could not be followed from sea to sound, so the Outer Banks were a perfect natural boundary between blockade squadrons and blockade-runners. Union success here would shut off the numerous inlets and also serve as a springboard for the capture of important cities like New Bern and Plymouth.

Union forces captured Cape Hatteras in August 1861. This operation was the spearhead for other incursions into the North Carolina sounds. As historian James McPherson notes, the seizure of Hatteras Inlet in August 1861 paid instant dividends because US "navy ships seized six blockade-runners approaching the inlet whose captains had not learned that it was in Yankee hands." The North Carolina sounds were also a supply route between Georgia, the Carolinas, and Confederate armies in Virginia, so the Blockade Board prioritized occupation of inlets and ports in the region.[20]

In addition, the Blockade Strategy Board recommended a major geographic overhaul of the blockade. Board members divided duties on the Atlantic Seaboard between the North Atlantic and South Atlantic Blockading Squadrons and those in the Gulf of Mexico between the East and West Gulf Blockading Squadrons. Three of the four newly appointed squadron leaders assumed command in September 1861. The North Atlantic Blockading Squadron operated between Cape Henry and Cape Romain, or from Virginia to mid–South Carolina, and was headed by Louis Goldsborough. Samuel DuPont led the South Atlantic Blockading Squadron, which performed duties from South Carolina to Cape Canaveral, Florida. The East Gulf Blockading Squadron was commanded by William McKean and it covered the coast from Cape Canaveral to Pensacola, Florida. David Farragut assumed command of the West Gulf Blockading Squadron in February 1862, and he was responsible for the Southern coast from Pensacola to the Rio Grande. This difficult assignment contained three important rebel ports—Mobile, New Orleans, and Galveston.[21] The Blockade Strategy Board's division of duties into four squadrons improved chances for success by allowing commanders to focus resources on regional trouble spots, facilitating better command and control of the blockade fleet.

The Blockade Board greatly influenced the long-term effectiveness of the Union blockade. Welles faithfully submitted the group's recommendations to President Lincoln and they were included in the overall naval strategy. Many Civil War historians focus on the blockade only in relation to the Anaconda Plan, and it is true that the blockade was an important component of this basic strategy to strangle the Confederacy. However, Winfield Scott did not go into the particulars of how such an interdiction would function. Navy Secretary Welles was energetic and persistent, but he lacked the background and expertise to craft a detailed plan. However, Welles did have the foresight to convene those who possessed the required skills.

Blockade Strategy Board members made a permanent imprint on US naval strategy, at a time when other elements of overall Union strategy vacillated between egotistical generals and political influence, at least until Grant took command in early 1864. Without question, the board improved the capabilities of blockade squadrons by preparing a road map for success. The immense logistical problem of blockading the Confederacy would be worked out over time, but as scholar Kevin Weddle observes, the "board's most important contribution and its greatest legacy [was] to determine where and how the Union navy would conduct the blockade campaign." More importantly, Weddle notes, board members "defined the Union blockade for the remainder of the war; [and] no other element of Union military strategy was formulated as early and lasted as long as the Blockade Board's proposals."[22] The Blockade Strategy Board set the US Navy on the right path when direction and sound strategy were desperately needed.

The Blockade Matures, 1862–1864

The geographic division of squadrons in late 1861 allowed greater control over local blockade duties. Secretary Welles reminded the squadron commanders: William McKean in the Gulf Coast—Louis Goldsborough in the North Atlantic—and Samuel DuPont in the South Atlantic—of "the importance of a rigorous blockade." Welles wanted an effective blockade of all rebel ports, ordering that "there should not be a concentration of vessels at any given point, but that they should be spread so as to make the blockade effective throughout the whole extent of coast." He reinforced the blockade's international legal ramifications and encouraged the squadron leaders to be resolute. He promised to supply the flag officers with ample ships and resources, but he urged them in the meantime to persevere. In 1862, Welles delivered on his promise of more resources and had overseen the purchase and construction of about 250 additional ships, many of which were distributed to the blockade squadrons.[23] One of the navy secretary's greatest achievements was remaining steadfast that an effective blockade could be achieved, and he transmitted that confidence to the unit leaders.

The new squadron commanders reaffirmed the legal principles of the blockade. Although the units had been geographically divided, making command and control much easier, new ships, captains, and crews were joining their ever-growing ranks. Flag Officer Louis Goldsborough, commander of the North Atlantic Squadron, reminded his captains on September 28, 1861, of the blockade's legal details. He reinforced the usual reminders to "notify neutrals" and keep "an adequate force" to prevent passage, but he also explained that port closure was still a possibility. Goldsborough told his captains "Until the ports are closed by proclamation (. . . declared to be no longer ports of entry)" neutrals were to be seized only after prior notification.[24] The task of disseminating and maintaining blockade legalities was an unappreciated aspect of the squadron commander's role, but one that Welles and the Lincoln administration understood was crucial to diplomacy.

As Union victories in early 1862 mounted along the Atlantic Coast, Lincoln officially lifted the blockade of some Southern ports. Union forces captured Port Royal, South Carolina, in November 1861 and won important victories in early 1862 in North Carolina at Roanoke Island, New Bern, and Fort Macon, which protected Beaufort. However, the most impressive Union naval triumph was the fall of New Orleans in April 1862. Lincoln wanted normal trade resumed from these ports as soon as possible. In addition, Northern textile factory owners coveted the cotton crops of the South Carolina Sea Islands and cotton exports from the Crescent City. On May 12, 1862, President Lincoln ordered that the blockade of these "ports . . . be safely relaxed with advantage to the interests of commerce."[25] The power to collect duties on imports and exports was thereby reinstated. This must have been supremely satisfying to Lincoln, since it was under this legal authority in 1861 that he had asserted his power of military intervention at Fort Sumter and Fort Pickens.

Some elements of blockade strategy could only be improved by the learning curve of war. For example, the potential of steam-powered blockade-runners was self-evident and denying the vessels access to fuel was a goal. Coal supplies in the Confederacy were unreliable, so most blockade-runners looked elsewhere for fuel, particularly Great Britain and its colonies. Well-financed shipowners sought anthracite coal because it was purer than regular coal and did not emit a telltale black cloud when burned. Although more expensive, anthracite coal also made blockade-runners virtually invisible at sea. Great Britain and the United States were the main sources of this fuel and there was little the Lincoln administration could do to prevent blockade-runners from obtaining it in Great Britain, but the US could curb the supply from eastern Pennsylvania. On April 12, 1862, Welles urged President Lincoln "It is of the greatest importance that the exportation of anthracite coal . . . should be absolutely prohibited." Welles noted that US exports were fueling Confederate blockade-runners since anthracite was being accessed in both Nassau and Havana.[26] It should not have taken a full year before the Union naval high command figured this out, but in the end, anthracite coal became more difficult to obtain.

Overcoming Geography and the Technology Gap

The logistical problems of the blockade were daunting enough but grappling with the actual conditions of blockading rebel ports further complicated matters. Each Southern port possessed its own unique natural characteristics. For example, Charleston had four channels through which deep-draft boats could access the harbor: Maffitt's, North, South, and Main Channels all fed into Charleston Harbor from different directions. The channels were not far apart in distance, but each one needed to be closely guarded and the intervening shoals could prevent mutual support by deep-draft blockaders. Eventually, Union occupation of Morris Island in 1863 assisted in curtailing some blockade-running through the main ship channel, but Charleston proved a difficult assignment for the blockade squadron.[27]

Another important port on the Eastern Seaboard was Savannah, Georgia. Unlike Charleston, whose deep-water harbor was adjacent to the sea, Savannah lay thirty miles upriver from the Atlantic Ocean on the Savannah River. The city's main export was the cotton produced in central and southern Georgia—and to some extent in western South Carolina—which could be floated down the river and loaded for transshipment to New York and then to overseas markets. Union blockade forces attempting to stop commerce to Savannah did not need to capture the city, but merely bottle up the river's mouth, which Fort Pulaski protected.

Flag Officer Goldsborough noted the difficulty of blockading Savannah in October 1861. He requested no fewer "than four active steamers . . . [to] effectually blockade" the port, but he also confessed the task would be nearly impossible "without withdrawing vessels from other points" since he had "none" on hand for the task.[28] As more blockade ships became available in 1862, the Union squadron adequately covered the shallow backdoor approaches to Savannah. These vessels, combined with a potent fleet off the Savannah River's mouth, made Georgia's most important port a difficult blockade-running destination.

One of the most challenging naval assignments was Wilmington, North Carolina, which by 1864 had become the Confederacy's most important blockade-running entrepôt. The port's natural geography worked against the blockade squadrons. Cape Fear, the point that jutted out into the Atlantic Ocean at Smith Island (today called Bald Head Island), was a formidable maritime obstacle that both protected Wilmington and gave an advantage to blockade-runners. Extending for thirty miles off the tip of Smith Island, Frying Pan Shoals was one of the most treacherous stretches of shallow water on the Eastern Seaboard. For centuries, ships and crews had met their demise on this shoal, contributing to the North Carolina coast's reputation as the "Graveyard of the Atlantic." Frying Pan Shoals proved to be an immense obstacle for Union blockade squadrons as they patrolled both inlets into the Cape Fear River and Wilmington.

The city of Wilmington lay thirty miles up the Cape Fear River which emptied into the ocean between Oak Island and Smith Island. This entrance was called Old Inlet since it was the natural terminus of the Cape Fear River. The other access point was New Inlet created in 1761 by a hurricane that breached the barrier island (New Inlet was later closed by the Army Corps of Engineers in 1881). Thus, the Cape Fear River and Wilmington could be accessed by two inlets—which is not that impressive except in one regard. The distance between Old and New Inlet on the Cape Fear River side—the distance for blockade-runners looking to run out of Wilmington—was only about five miles. In contrast, the travelling distance for Union blockade squadrons to support each other at the other inlet—after being forced to go around Frying Pan Shoals—was about forty miles. This was one of the most important, and overlooked, examples of the Confederate advantage of interior lines. Blockade-runners loaded their outbound cargoes at the Wilmington docks, then floated downriver, in between Old and New Inlets, and surmised which exit was most favorable. When the decision was finally made to dash out of the inlet, the Union squadrons were too far apart to combine for the chase. In effect, the Union navy was required to keep two blockade squadrons off of Wilmington, one at New Inlet and one at Old Inlet, to maintain an effective blockade.

Union commanders admitted the Cape Fear area posed enormous difficulties. Cdr. J. W. Livingston of the USS *Penguin* notified blockade commander Silas Stringham in August 1861 that this lone ship was definitely not sufficient to cut off Wilmington. Livingston, in a severe case of underestimation, stated, "It requires two vessels to effectually blockade Cape Fear [because] it has two mouths." Commander Livingston summarized the nature of the problem for blockade squadrons for the remainder of the war: "To reach one [inlet] from the other a cruise of 40 miles is necessary, and the enemy always hoisted a flag on the light-house to indicate which side the blockading vessel may be, and making signal lights at night." The notion that one vessel could be effective with this disadvantage of maritime geography was ludicrous. Livingston ended his August 15 message by saying he was running low on coal and with the weather turning foul, he decided to return to Hampton Roads—leaving Wilmington with no Union blockade presence at all![29]

The natural obstacles in the Cape Fear area were a constant nuisance for the blockade squadron. In April 1861 a Union captain informed North Atlantic Squadron leader Louis Goldsborough that, due to resupply, his blockade force would be "only two vessels off Wilmington, one off each entrance." Neither of the two remaining ships could come to the other's support in a timely manner. The captain concluded that his "force [was] totally inadequate to maintain an efficient blockade." Union naval production would eventually overcome this paucity of squadron strength, and a full-size complement of blockaders would be available for both inlets.

As late as August 1862, the Union blockade force off the Cape Fear River was not fully operational. Cdr. J. F. Armstrong informed his superior "Our present force here is small [because] one vessel is of necessity constantly away for coal." Because the ships varied in capacity, he added "It is almost impossible to have only one absent at a time." Coal resupply was a constant problem for maintaining an active blockade, and the Cape Fear's natural obstacles exacerbated the issued. It was difficult for the squadrons to reinforce one another between Old and New Inlets when ships were away for resupply. Armstrong recommended "There should be a force sufficient to allow one vessel to be absent from each side [of Frying Pan Shoals] without reference to vessels on the other." The commander asked for at least ten vessels—five for each inlet—but even that number was too few. In reality, he admitted that each inlet could be "guarded at most by three, and of necessity often by only two vessels." Armstrong knew the blockade-runner

Kate was preparing for an outbound trip and could pick an inlet based on the comparative weakness of the squadrons. Indeed, the *Kate* took full advantage of the natural geography and made a successful run out of Wilmington on August 26.[30] From review of the available evidence, it appears that the Union blockade squadron off Wilmington did not achieve a sufficient number of vessels until 1864.

As late as August 1864 Gideon Welles despaired over the Union's inability to cut-off incoming rebel supplies. After Adm. David Farragut's capture of Mobile Bay earlier in August, Welles was relieved that this important Gulf port was now closed to blockade-runners. However, the navy secretary continued to worry about the effectiveness of his blockade squadrons, and in particular about closing the Confederate port of Wilmington. He wanted to "arrange for changes in command of our Squadrons" and despite rumors of complicity between the squadrons and blockade-runners, he gave "no credit to the newspaper gossip of connivance on the part of [Union] naval officers which many good men believe." Welles noted, however, the "want of effective action" among his squadrons, saying, "[It] makes Wilmington seem an almost open port."[31]

The next major goal of Union strategy, according to Welles, should be Wilmington's capture. Declaring "something must be done to close the port of Wilmington" he further stated, "[If Union forces] could seize the forts and close the illicit traffic, it would be as important as the capture of Richmond."[32] Even as other Confederate ports were captured through 1864, which freed-up more blockaders to focus on Wilmington, Welles still worried that the blockade-runners held the upper hand in the contest. Until the port could finally be closed, the rebel lifeline of supplies would continue to flow.

The Confederates in Wilmington, however, were beginning to notice the presence of increased blockade squadron strength. Maj. Gen. W. H. C. "Chase" Whiting, rebel commander of the defenses around Wilmington, remarked in September 1864, "The difficulty of running the blockade has been lately very great." Whiting also noted "Far more than the average of [blockade-running] ships have been lost."[33] By this late stage of the war Wilmington was the most important blockade-running port for the Confederacy, and now the Union high command realized that fact. But blockade-running into Wilmington continued until the Union capture of Fort Fisher in January 1865.

Advances in steamboat technology in the 1860s were a crucial aspect of the contest between blockade squadrons and blockade-runners. The Civil War occurred at the crossroads of the transition from sail to steam power. One should not forget that the heyday of sail power was in the 1850s with the impressive clipper ships and their speed records from New York to San Francisco and around the globe. Sail power remained an important part of most shipping in the 1860s, but for the most technologically advanced blockade-runners, it was simply an additional source of speed used only in desperate circumstances.

The most successful ships tended to be fast, well-designed, steam-powered vessels, specifically constructed to run the blockade. Their main aspects were low profiles, shallow drafts, camouflaged exteriors, and, most importantly, superior speed. In addition to these design advantages, some engines powered a system of twin-screw propellers, which meant a runner could change course almost instantly without a wide turn. Some Union blockade squadron vessels also had twin-screw propellers. But if a blockade-runner had this technology and the Union blockader did not, it would be extremely difficult for the runner to be captured. With immense profits to be made, and with well-financed firms paying for construction of new blockade-runners, it became obvious by 1863 that, the new fleet of blockade-runners technologically outmatched their pursuers in most cases.

Union blockade captains and squadron commanders acknowledged the technology gap. In March 1863, Cdr. A. Ludlow Case, aboard the USS *Iroquois* stationed off Cape Fear, opined to his superior "The class of vessels now violating the blockade is far different from those attempting it a year ago." Samuel DuPont noted the improved technological design of blockade-runners in May 1863. DuPont requested more ships from the navy secretary to counter the "increase in the number of steamers . . . of greater speed and less draft." He stated that it would be "simply impossible to maintain a stricter blockade" of Charleston with the quality of vessels now on hand, which exhibited "great inferiority of speed" compared to the runners.

As late as December 1864, Rear Adm. David Dixon Porter, recently appointed commander of the North Atlantic Blockade Squadron, commented to Secretary Welles about the technological superiority of the blockade-runners. Dixon blamed profitability, and he informed the secretary, "Blockade running seems almost as brisk as ever, and I suppose will continue so as long it remains remunerative." According to Dixon, the reason for continued running attempts despite strengthened Union blockade squadrons was a "new class of blockade runners . . . entirely built for speed." Dixon's block-aders were capturing or sinking more vessels, but the fact that ships contin-ued to test the blockade proved "the immense gains the runners make."[34]

The technology gap between squadrons and runners was overcome through sheer numbers. In a one-on-one chase, few Union vessels could catch a top-notch steam-powered blockade-runner. Rear Adm. David Dixon Porter later admitted that the Union blockade squadrons "never had a vessel that could run down a blockade-runner during the whole war, ex-cept the *Vanderbilt* and two others."[35] However, the Union forces had two advantages—they had increasing numbers of ships to concentrate against the runners, and they knew where the runners were headed. At some point, the ships running the blockade had to dash into port, and it was there that the squadrons pounced.

The Prize Factor

Blockade duty was an often tedious, even boring, service occasionally bro-ken by moments of excitement. For ambitious naval personnel looking for military glory, blockade duty was not as high profile as other assignments. In terms of professional reputation, blockade commanders had little to gain and much to lose. So aside from patriotism, why did sailors and officers so willingly serve in a less respected branch of the service? The answer is prize money. The system of prize courts and money awarded to crews is one of the least-known aspects of Civil War blockade history—at least for those who are not maritime historians. According to one historian of the US Navy prize system in the nineteenth century, "Prize money may have been the persuasive force which brought some officers into the Navy" in the first place. During the Civil War, when inflated currency devalued their base salary, "only prize money proved the salvation of many officers."[36]

US law allowed enemy ships and those carrying contraband for the enemy to be seized and sold at auction. The foundations of American prize law dated back to 1799, when an incentive was added to spur outmatched Amer-ican ships to grapple with both British and French vessels. This was the era of the Quasi-War with France and the British Orders in Council, which established impressment of US sailors. The 1799 prize law declared, "Ships and vessels, being of superior force to the vessel making the capture, in men or guns, shall be the sole property of the captors, and all ships or ves-sels of inferior force shall be divided equally between" the government and the crew. Prize money was to be divided by percentages according to rank. The captain claimed three-twentieths of the total prize, and if a fleet commander presided—during the Civil War this was the blockade squadron commander—then that officer could claim one-twentieth to be taken out of the captain's share. According to the 1799 ordinance, any ship "in sight" when the capture was made could claim a portion of the prize. This aspect of the law was modified during the Civil War on a case-by-case basis with the requirement that prize claimants had to prove they assisted in some way with the capture.[37]

The prospect of prize money sometimes caused conflict among squadrons over who should share in a capture. In May 1862, the USS *James Adger* and USS *Keystone State* captured the *Elizabeth* trying to run the blockade. Not surprisingly, sixteen other Union blockade vessels claimed a share of the prize money. The claimants argued that although they "were not present at the time of the capture," they were "entitled to a share of the prize money . . . upon the grounds that . . . many of them were within view at the time . . . [and] that the capture was made within the limits of the blockade of this place."[38] This was eventually sorted out at the prize court, and in the future the "in-sight" aspect of prize sharing was dropped.

Blockade squadron commanders held lucrative posts and accumulated impressive sums of prize money. At a time when rear admirals were paid an annual salary of $5,000, North Atlantic Blockading Squadron leader Stephen P. Lee claimed $109,689.69 in prize money, and his successor, David Dixon Porter earned $91,528.98. South Atlantic Blockading Squadron head Samuel F. DuPont claimed $57,093.25 in prize money and West Gulf Blockading Squadron commander David G. Farragut earned $56,270.67. Porter's prize money is of special interest since he was only a squadron commander from September 1864 until the end of the war. However, Porter had already amassed some prize money from confiscated cotton during his command of naval forces on the Mississippi River earlier in the war.[39] Promotion to blockade squadron commander proved to be a lucrative assignment.

During the Civil War prize courts existed in Boston, New York, Providence, Philadelphia, Baltimore, Beaufort (North Carolina), Key West, and New Orleans. The major functions of prize courts were investigating the legality of seizure and then either returning or distributing the property accordingly. Owners of captured vessels were given an opportunity to argue that their property had been illegally taken and should be returned (see discussion of the *Labuan* affair in chapter 1). However, the legal advantage lay with those who brought the prize to court. In addition to the fact that the seized vessels were already suspected of aiding the rebellion, the government had a financial interest in awarding the prize to the captors.[40] Once the government decided against the shipowners, the sale proceeds were then divided among the courts, the government, and the officers and crew of the vessel responsible for capture.

According to British documents, ships taken to US prize courts sometimes had their cargoes stolen or sold before a court decision. This made sense for perishable cargo since the shipowners could recoup losses in cash value, but cotton was another story. In May 1863, the British-flagged ship *Tampico* was seized by the USS *Cayuga* in the Gulf of Mexico. The *Tampico* carried 112 bales of cotton, which was off-loaded in New Orleans and sold at auction before the prize court's verdict. Union officials could have argued that the *Tampico*'s owners would be reimbursed by the sale price of the confiscated cotton, but cotton was not a perishable commodity, and Union officials could have waited for the court's decision. In other cases, British records indicate that other cargoes were looted or destroyed before the prize court's conclusion.[41]

If a prize could not be captured, one assumes that squadrons would attempt to sink runners. However, as late as January 1863, one blockade captain inquired "whether, after he [had] used every means in his power to prevent vessels from running the blockade" he was "justified in firing" at violators. Welles replied that the captain was indeed "justified in firing into such vessels," surprisingly adding, "[To] resort to this expedient would be painful, but the blockade must be enforced."[42] The fact that the navy secretary, a squadron commander, and a blockade captain debated whether to fire on a blockade-runner in 1863 is astonishing! One might assume that this question had already been decided—if it needed to be decided at all—at the blockade's outset in 1861.

In July 1864 the State Department received a concerning communiqué from the US consul in Liverpool regarding the blockade squadrons. The consul informed his superiors "Many vessels succeed in violating the blockade because the blockaders do not fire on them, being anxious to secure prizes," and he observed that the blockaders were "unwilling to run the risk of sinking or injuring vessels." This troubling assertion was sent through Navy Department channels down to the squadron commanders. Rear-Admiral Lee reminded his commanders "The first object of the blockade is to weaken the enemy by preventing his cruisers from going in or out." It is a testament to the motivation of prize money that Lee had to reaffirm this basic goal for his captains in 1864. But the captains, with Lee's support, refuted the consul's claim. Captain Glisson of the USS *Malvern* replied to Lee's report by saying there was "no foundation . . . for these assertions." Glisson remarked that a handful of specialized vessels might get through the blockade, but it was not for want of effort. He recommended that any forthcoming charges "should be denied officially."[43] The US consul in Liverpool was apparently repeating rumors circulating among British blockade-running captains and crews. However, it is possible that ship captains' unofficial policy to secure a prize was hampering official Union blockade policy.

Despite official claims to the contrary, incentives existed to capture blockade-runners instead of destroying them. It can be argued that blockade squadrons had a pecuniary inducement—if they realized capture was unrealistic during any particular chase—to allow the runners to escape, so that the same ones might be captured the next time. This view of blockade duty is counterintuitive to the fundamental strategic understanding of the Union blockade, but it was a realistic aspect of the day-to-day culture of blockade squadrons. The potential for prize money was a major component of blockade squadron service, and it should not be overlooked as a factor in analyzing the blockade's effectiveness.

Port Saturation: Outside and Inside Blockades

The strategy of port saturation, by which the squadrons focused resources on key rebel ports, was not implemented in the early months of the blockade. Surprisingly enough, this tactic gradually evolved as a fundamental aspect of blockade strategy. In January 1862, Gideon Welles reminded South Atlantic Blockading Squadron commander Samuel F. DuPont, of "The importance of a rigorous blockade at every point under your command can not be too strongly impressed."[44] Welles recognized that this order would stretch DuPont's resources, and in effect it weakened the blockade of Charleston. But the navy secretary was willing to temporarily loosen the grip on Charleston in order to cover the numerous bays and inlets in the commander's sector. This complete-coverage strategy likely stemmed from a desire to have the appearance of a ubiquitous blockade to allay British legal arguments. In 1861 British and American diplomats were in the midst of an ongoing debate about the parameters of a legitimate blockade as per the Declaration of Paris, and British officials insisted that Union vessels be visible to maintain legality. But as more Union maritime resources became available in 1862, the strategy of port saturation was finally implemented. As the war dragged on and blockade strategy evolved, port saturation was the fundamental tactic, and the deployment of vessels constituted an inside and outside blockade of rebel ports.

The outside blockade was the typical assignment for the most seaworthy Union vessels. Outside blockaders needed to keep pace with the ships trying to break through the cordon, and thus they frequently cruised several miles off the coast of Confederate harbors. Ships on the outside blockade also needed to be available for pursuit at a moment's notice. They needed to be swift, but they also needed to carry enough armament to cripple runners and protect the fleet from rebel naval attacks. One of the most efficient vessels in the Charleston sector was the USS *Keystone State*, which was the reason South Atlantic Blockading Squadron leader Samuel F. DuPont ordered her captain to "cruise along the coast" from around the Georgia border up to Charleston, "maintaining an outer blockade." The obvious difficulty for outside blockaders was the vast area to be patrolled. After criticism from the press and politicians, DuPont remarked that the blockade of Charleston required "an arc of 13 miles . . . and although it might be supposed that eight steamers and four sailing vessels would cover this," reality dictated that more steam-powered ships were needed "to render the running [of] this blockade impossible."[45]

As a result of their duties, outside blockade vessels were required to be in good operating condition. These ships were the chasers, which meant their engines needed to be maintained to optimal standards. It was necessary for the outside blockaders to be "under steam" within moments, so inefficient ships could be a serious weakness. Rear Adm. John Dahlgren noted that constant need for repairs had caused "the outer blockade [to be] rather low sometimes."[46] However, it was essential to effectiveness to keep the outside blockade vessels in prime condition.

What was the limit of blockade squadron pursuit, if any? Rear Adm. S. P. Lee asked Secretary Welles whether a range limit existed for the outside ships in the cordon. Welles vaguely responded that a second line could be established "just outside of the line occupied by the vessels in blockading," and that pursuit beyond that point was acceptable. Welles allowed squadron leaders great leeway on resource allocation in their respective zones, since certain vessels were more adapted for coastal service and others for

high-seas pursuit. The navy secretary did not "propose to suggest any particular positions for . . . vessels," and he thought each squadron commander
should use his best judgement.[47] In this bottom-up way, the strategy of
complementary inside and outside blockades was developed in each of the
squadrons.

The outside blockade required the fastest ships capable of keeping pace
with the blockade-runners on the high seas. Captain O.S. Glisson of the
USS *Santiago de Cuba* commanded one of the best ships in the Wilmington squadron. He informed his superior that his vessel was "the fastest on
the blockade," but he also admitted, "There are but few blockade runners
that go less than 14 miles per hour." If an effective outside blockade was to
be upheld, Glisson recommended "one or two vessels that . . . run 15 or 16
miles per hour" to chase runners, stating "[The] offshore blockade . . . is
the only one that the blockade runners dread." Rear Admiral Lee decided
to give Captain Glisson jurisdictional control over the blockade of New
Inlet at Wilmington, and the leeway to assign vessels to the inside and outside blockades accordingly. Lee allowed Glisson to "station not exceeding
two-fifths" the total squadron strength "to cruise offshore on [an] outer line
of blockade." Lee warned, however, that an effective inside blockade was
never to be weakened "in preference to outside cruising."[48] Just as Welles
had granted squadron commanders the ability to distribute resources, so
too did Lee allow his captain to allocate his vessels between the inside and
outside blockade.

One reason to station Union ships on the outside blockade was to protect
them from Confederate naval attacks. On several occasions Confederate
ironclads made forays against Union blockade squadrons—the CSS *Virginia* (1862), the CSS *Palmetto State* (1863), and the CSS *Atlanta* (1863) all
did so. In June 1863, runaway slaves informed squadron leader DuPont that
the rebel ironclad CSS *Atlanta* was preparing to leave Savannah for an assault. DuPont then ordered the USS *Cimarron* to move from inside the bar
to the outside blockade since the "vessel could not for a moment contend
against an ironclad."

Another famous rebel strike on Union blockade ships was the February 17, 1864, attack by the rebel submarine *Hunley* against the USS *Housatonic*. The *Hunley* bypassed the inside squadron of Union monitors and
instead targeted the outside blockade vessels. In the wake of the first successful submarine attack in history, Rear Admiral Dahlgren ordered all
ships in either blockade to take countermeasures. Dahlgren warned that

anchored blockaders were not safe, and that "vessels on inside blockade had better take post outside at night" and "keep underway when the sea is smooth" until their safety could be ensured.[49] As it turned out, the Confederates did not embark on a widespread submarine campaign, but the *Hunley*'s success forced the Union's inside blockade vessels to be more cautious.

The most distant posting for the outside blockade was around transshipment points like Nassau in the Bahamas. Between five hundred and six hundred miles lay between Nassau and major Confederate ports, and Union blockaders forayed into Bahamian waters to catch blockade-runners as they left Nassau. This posed serious diplomatic problems. The British claimed US violation of their territorial waters despite the legal limit for international waters being only three miles out to sea. The Bahamas' geography, including many small islands covering a wide swath of the Atlantic, meant blockade-runners could technically stay in British waters for about a third of the voyage to rebel ports—but doing so was hazardous. Nassau was a neutral port that Union ships could not officially blockade. British authorities, upset by the US naval presence, threatened to fire on American ships, but that never occurred.[50] After 1862, the Union was dissuaded from this tactic for several reasons—first, the potential for unnecessary diplomatic conflict with Great Britain; second, the immense amounts of coal required for such cruising; and third, the focus of blockade-running shifting heavily to Bermuda in 1863.

Joseph Crawford, British consul in Havana, was offended by the US Navy's presence near that transshipment point. In May 1862, Crawford complained to superiors that US blockade squadrons had no right of seizure on the high seas "at a distance from their coast." Although Havana was not nearly as distant from American territorial waters as Nassau, the consul felt a defense of British commerce was necessary. He noted that blockade-running would continue so long as profits remained high and adventurous types endeavored to try their luck, and there was little he could do to prevent it. However, it was US naval interdiction of legal trade that Crawford found "quite objectionable." He opined to his superior that some blockade-running out of Havana was "no excuse for attempt[s] to enforce the blockade by proceedings not sanctioned by international law."[51] Crawford's frank assessment was a microcosm of Britain's overall policy—permissiveness toward blockade-running coupled with protection of British commercial rights.

Despite these duplicitous British protests, American vessels continued to seize suspicious ships far away from rebel ports. When a very "valuable" British-flagged cargo was seized, British officials objected to US secretary of state William Seward. The capture of a small sloop typically prompted a perfunctory memo to Seward, whereas seizure of large cargoes sometimes sparked a multipage legal defense for the ship's return. The British steamship *Circassian* is an excellent example of how both the United States and Great Britain handled disputed captures. Throughout the drawn-out diplomatic spat over the *Circassian*, the secretary of state transitioned from initial obstinance to an apology. Seward assured Great Britain that, going forward, US blockade captains would be less aggressive toward British-flagged vessels. But, Seward noted, this apology did not detract from the fact that some British vessels carried contraband and searches needed to continue. Both sides regarded this temporary resolution as agreeable. The *Circassian* episode showed that both sides understood their legal ground in international law, and seizures on the high seas were not as clear-cut as those seizures by blockade squadrons around Confederate ports.[52]

The inside, or close, blockade was designed to thwart runners that hugged the coastline. Captains seeking to break the blockade used their lighter draft as a defensive tactic, running dangerously close to shore to keep the deeper-draft blockaders at bay. Blockade-runner captains also understood that the shoreline provided camouflage and occasional rebel artillery support. For these reasons, a favorite tactic of blockade-runners was to dash through the outer ring of blockaders into shallow waters, and then steam to port skirting the surf's edge. Partially to counter this tactic, squadrons developed a cordon termed the inner/inside blockade, or close blockade. The mission of the inside blockade was multifaceted. One goal was to occupy inlets and harbors with lighter-draft vessels and capture blockade-runners trying to use shoreline tactics. Another mission of the inside blockade was to complement the outside blockade and act as the catcher of last resort for inbound blockade-runners, or as a first warning system for outbound ones. In some cases, close-blockade vessels were stationed inside the bar of rebel harbors, making them a tempting target for Confederate attacks. The inner blockade performed a variety of functions, but it was typically less involved in long-distance pursuit.

The inside blockade evolved as necessity and resources allowed. Another mission for the inside blockade was to interdict intercoastal water traffic. For example, shortly after Union forces captured Port Royal Sound in South Carolina in November 1861, they established an inside blockade.

Cdr. J. S. Missroon of the USS *Savannah* ordered two smaller draft vessels to "keep inshore" of his larger vessel at night, and also to remain "within signal distance, with a sharp lookout . . . ready to move at the instant." The Union expanded this tactic to interdict intercoastal waterways between Charleston and Savannah in December 1861. There was no distinction between inside blockaders and the other blockade vessels—they were part of the same squadron and meant to complement one another. In December 1861, blockade squadron leader Samuel F. DuPont ordered the USS *St. Lawrence* to "cruise" the South Carolina coast below Charleston while "approaching as near as possible the various harbors, inlets, and ports." DuPont reminded the captain that he "should keep up an outer line of cruising and blockading," but he contradictorily ordered him to "Perform the duty as close to the coast as you can."[53] In the early stages of the blockade, it appeared that ships might easily switch between inside and outside blockade duties.

A major factor for an effective inside blockade was obtaining enough steam-powered light-draft ships. In March 1862, squadron leader DuPont was "pressed for want of the light-draft vessels." That August, a blockade commander off Wilmington opined that "small steamers to be stationed as lookouts would be of great service," and that the "larger ships" could be "ready to run to their assistance." As late as November 1864, Union blockade captains requested additional support for the inside blockade. One ship commander off Wilmington suggested, "There should be at least one small, swift vessel patrolling the coast, close in on nights." This tactic was meant to counter "runners . . . coming down the shore and getting in the 'pocket' under the fort."[54] Blockade-runner captains frequently used this method of getting into the "pocket" under the protection of Fort Fisher, and additional inside blockade vessels were intended to thwart them.

Cooperation between the outside and inside blockades was pivotal for success. A system of signals using color-coded rockets informed distant blockade ships of an outbound or inbound runner. On a successful inbound capture, the chasers on the outside blockade pursued their quarry into the waiting trap of the inside blockade vessels. In July 1863, this tactic worked to perfection. A blockade-runner was spotted "trying to run into Charleston" when the USS *Canandaigua* and "other outside blockaders" gave chase. The USS *Catskill* lay in wait, "anchored . . . on picket duty," and the combined pursuit forced the runner aground, after which it was "fired by [the] crew . . . and [was] now a total wreck."[55]

Resource allocation between the two lines could mean the difference between success or failure. Capt. C. F. Green noted that enough vessels were needed on the outside blockade to initially spot runners. He suggested that all ships "that could be spared from inside the bar should be sent out nightly" since only three ships were on the outside blockade at that time. In this instance, squadron commander John Dahlgren worried that the outside ships might be vulnerable to attack from rebel ships being constructed in Great Britain—so there was no safe blockade posting. Dahlgren informed his superiors of the great "distances to be gone over" between the two blockade lines. "The outside blockade extends over several miles," he stated, "and is of itself 4 or 5 miles from the inside [blockade]." At the same time, the inner line was "spread 3 or 4 miles."[56] These distances, in addition to other natural obstacles like weather and tide, meant that close cooperation between the outside and inside blockade lines was paramount to ultimate success.

Cooperation meant that one line—either the inside or outside blockade—might temporarily be weaker than the other. For example, in late 1863 and early 1864 off Charleston, squadron leader John Dahlgren noted, "[The inner blockade] of the harbor is maintained by four monitors," and the "outer blockade . . . consists of a few vessels only."[57] In this case the monitors proved a serious obstacle to runners as they entered Charleston Harbor, so a weaker outside blockade was not necessarily an issue. However, the reliance on monitors to bottle up rebel ports was problematic since they were notoriously unseaworthy, as witnessed by the sudden sinking of the USS *Weehawken* on December 6, 1863, near Charleston. The *Weehawken*'s demise stemmed from its inability to weather stormy seas.[58] Thus the inside blockade could not rely solely on floating gunships to contribute to an effective blockade.

The inside-outside blockade always contained at least two lines, but it was possible to create a more in-depth blockade. In 1864, Rear Adm. Stephen Phillips Lee implemented on the approaches to Wilmington what blockade historian Robert Browning Jr. describes as "the most complicated system of blockade used by any squadron during the war." Lee created a system of "four seaward lines of cruisers" with the usual complement of insider blockaders—or "bar tenders" since they were posted inside or in close proximity to the bar—and outside chasers who could bring the blockade-runners to heel.[59]

Availability of ships was the main factor in augmenting the inside-outside blockade, and the capture of rebel ports freed up additional resources to reinforce squadrons. As a result, the tactic of port saturation grew more potent as the war dragged on and the inside-outside blockades became stronger. Historian Bern Anderson notes that in 1863, "when Admiral Dahlgren moved his ironclads inside the bar off Charleston . . . blockade running practically ceased." This assertion is accurate to a degree since the ironclads were also part of the larger 1863 military campaign around Charleston, and having a force inside the bar was a definite improvement of the blockade's defense in-depth. The military focus on Charleston in 1863 diverted blockade-runners to less dangerous ports like Wilmington, and in response an inside-outside blockade was developed there in 1864 with about thirty-two blockade vessels.[60]

Port saturation strategy and the evolution of the inside and outside blockade laid the foundation for blockade success. Squadron deployment was key to improving the capture rate, and Union vessels constantly adapted to blockade runners' changing tactics. The presence of at least two lines of blockade, and sometimes even more depth of patrols, meant that blockade-runners had to navigate a system of entrapment as they approached or left Confederate ports instead of merely outrunning their pursuers. The possibility of capture increased as the war continued, partially due to the new inside-outside blockade system, and also due to the additional number of available Union vessels. By 1864, Union blockade squadrons had a sound strategy and improved tactics to ensnare blockade-runners, and as a result, blockade-running became far more hazardous.

Growing Pains: The Blockade's Path to Success, 1862–65

Concerns about the blockade's effectiveness in 1861 were commonplace and very understandable. The Union's shipbuilding capacity had not yet come into fruition, and squadron commanders were frustrated until a full complement of blockaders could be put to sea. Flag Officer Goldsborough stated in November 1861 that he was desperate "for efficient steamers to maintain the blockade," and he noted the extensive repairs needed for his existing fleet. Welles encouraged Goldsborough to do the best with the ships at hand, reminding him "A large number of most efficient steamers are being pressed to completion." Welles haughtily pointed out, "The [Navy] Department desires to assign these . . . to those officers who have performed at sea most faithfully the duties of the blockade."[61] The message was clear—squadron commanders who captured blockade-runners with little complaint about resources would be rewarded with more vessels. However, the complaint about insufficient vessels was a recurring theme from most squadron commanders up to 1865.

State Department consuls in England kept Gideon Welles informed of potential blockade-runners. In the wake of the *Trent* affair in late 1861, the Lincoln administration was eager to know the diplomatic mood in England, and the way in which the blockade fit into Confederate diplomatic strategy. In early 1862, Secretary Welles forwarded the following statements to squadron leader Samuel DuPont: "The Confederates have labored very hard to create the belief [in Great Britain] that the blockade offers but little obstruction," and "[The rebels have claimed] at Lloyd's [Insurance Company] to have a list of 1,000 vessels which have passed the blockaded ports."[62] This rebel claim was a gross exaggeration, but the fact remained that Union squadrons needed to successfully capture some high-profile blockade-runners in 1862 to confirm the blockade's legal standing.

By June 1862, Welles proudly declared his approval of the blockade, telling DuPont, "The recent capture of so many vessels attempting to run the blockade is giving great satisfaction to the country . . . [and] John Bull [Great Britain] is realizing the efficiency of the blockade."[63] After one full year of implementation, it appeared that the US Navy had constructed a sufficiently effective blockade of Confederate ports. In 1862, any objective argument about the blockade's legality could be put to rest—this was clearly no paper blockade. However, despite this encouraging start, high and low points, captures and escapes, caused the blockade's effectiveness to fluctuate until 1865.

In March 1862, Assistant Navy Secretary Gustavus Fox chastised squadron commander Goldsborough over a much-publicized blockade breach. On February 28, the Confederate government-owned blockade-runner *Nashville* brazenly cruised into Beaufort, North Carolina. The ship then left Beaufort and slipped into Georgetown, South Carolina, thus piercing the blockade three times in a matter of days. Fox considered this single blockade violation "a terrible blow to . . . naval prestige" that diminished the effect of recent captures. The feeling in the Navy Department, according to Fox, was severe depression. Declaring, "This is not a blockade," the secretary instead compared the situation to the Union army's first major defeat "It is a Bull Run to the Navy." Fox's hyperbole aside, the Union navy expressed serious concern about complacency among the blockade squadrons. On March 28, Secretary Welles warned squadron command-ers about negligence and the necessary remedy. Welles ordered that each blockade violation be investigated by "a court of enquiry." If negligence was uncovered, then military courts would judge offenders.[64]

In the spring of 1862, concern about the blockade's effectiveness was also evident in some political circles. Rumors of effortless blockade-running at Charleston from British consul Robert Bunch sparked an outcry in North-ern newspapers and among some politicians. Sen. John P. Hale, Republi-can from New Hampshire, chaired the Committee on Naval Affairs and questioned the blockade's efficacy. Gideon Welles asked South Atlantic Blockading Squadron commander Samuel F. DuPont about the allegations, and DuPont adamantly refuted the Senate committee's assertions. DuPont argued to his superiors in the Navy Department, "Much has been said in the papers . . . of the utter insufficiency of the blockade, and a too ready credence given by our public functionaries . . . to the representations of parties interested in making out a case against the [blockade]." He pointed out that he was among the few naval officers who had blockade experience in the Mexican War, and with this empirical knowledge, he stated, "No blockade in the history of the world has ever been more effective."[65] Aside from this unproveable boast, DuPont correctly asserted that the Union blockade was succeeding despite the difficulties that previous blockades did not encounter, like the extent of Southern coastline and the advent of steam technology.

DuPont's superiors in the Navy Department supported his claims and came to his defense. Secretary Welles composed the official reply to the committee, and he admitted, "There have been instances when the block-ade has been evaded." However, considering the resources available and the obstacles to overcome, he was surprised "the violations [had] not been vastly more numerous." Welles pinned some of the blame on the necessity of joint operations with armies, but he believed that these missions did not "render the blockade inefficient." The navy secretary gave an unqualified endorsement to DuPont, and he pointed to inflation in Confederate ports as evidence that the blockade was working.[66]

Gideon Welles was challenged with operating an effective blockade, but Union armies also periodically asked for assistance. Waterborne supply and support of Union armies was vital to strategic success, and the US Navy played an important role in many Union army campaigns. The argument to divert blockade resources to assist in land campaigns was a constant factor in Welles's handling of the Navy Department, but the temptation to weaken the blockade was occasionally rebuffed. In March 1862, Welles agreed to lend available naval resources to McClellan's Peninsula Campaign, particularly for the purpose of capturing Norfolk, home port for the still-potent CSS *Virginia*. But this case was among the few exceptions, as Welles was "extremely reluctant to take any measure that would even temporarily weaken the efficiency of the blockade."[67] As the war dragged on into 1862, the navy secretary became more attuned to cabinet squabbles over military resources, and he learned to protect squadron supplies with a jealous regard for blockade prerogatives.

In October 1862 a dispute erupted between the army and navy commanders around Norfolk, Virginia. The blockade squadron under Rear Adm. S. P. Lee disputed the authority of Maj. Gen. John A. Dix to receive supply vessels at his discretion. Dix informed Lee that the clearance was given by "the Secretary of the Treasury, under special permit." Lee countered by saying that he would honor permits from the treasury secretary, "but not [those] given by any other officers"—in other words, not those from an army general like Dix. The rear admiral declared, "No vessel will be allowed to pass . . . until her permit and manifest have been examined by me." Dix argued that since Norfolk was under Union occupation, then the blockade of that port was over. Supply vessels from the North should be allowed to freely come and go without interference from the Union navy. The supply vessels at the center of the dispute were the *Marblehead* and the *Conrad Fox*. Welles finally intervened on behalf of his squadron commander, opining, "The rule which General Dix applies to Norfolk, denying that it is a blockaded port, would exempt any port on the whole coast, with the exception of Wilmington and Charleston, from blockade, for all are held by military occupation."[68] This clash over who determined legitimate cargo was a three-way competition for control between the War Department, the Navy Department, and the Treasury Department.

Welles took his complaint to Treasury Secretary Salmon P. Chase and noted that General Dix was arbitrarily selecting which vessels could enter Norfolk. Welles argued this system would "lead to favoritism and demoralization," adding "The blockade ought not thus be abused and prostituted." He further pointed out that Lincoln would need to officially end the blockade of Norfolk in order for normal trade to resume. Until that time, the interdiction would apply to all ships entering Norfolk, and General Dix did not have the authority to exempt vessels. If the current situation persisted, Welles argued, then the naval presence was "not [a] blockade, but a perversion of it." The navy secretary declared that army officers could not bestow special privileges on ships, and that either the blockade be fully implemented or "the port should be open to all." Any deviation from this rule, Welles believed, would "bring the whole blockade into disrepute."[69]

This local disagreement about blockade rules had escalated to a cabinet-level tussle. Welles understood that if he backed down on this issue, then local Union officers at other Southern ports might decide whether vessels were carrying legal or contraband cargoes—a task blockade squadrons were more qualified to carry out. Welles temporarily fended off additional claims from General Dix, who had solicited support from Secretary of War Edwin Stanton. The navy secretary informed Stanton that the blockade remained in force at Norfolk, but the president eventually resolved the conflict within his cabinet. Lincoln sided with the Army and Treasury Departments and ordered that ships "be allowed to pass from [Norfolk] . . . to [their] destination to any port not blockaded by the United States."[70] This meant that Union army officers would be responsible for any contraband that flowed in or out of occupied Southern ports.

Welles and the blockade squadrons lost this round of the internecine cabinet power play, but this was the correct decision. The main focus of blockade resources needed to be on rebel-held ports, not Union-occupied ports. Army control over ship cargoes in these occupied zones opened opportunities for contraband smuggling from the Northern states to the South, but the US Navy's main goal was preventing rebel resupply from abroad, not focusing on goods sent from unscrupulous Yankee merchants. In fact, this is one of the relatively unknown dirty secrets of the Civil War—that both sides kept illegitimate trade channels open for their mutual benefit. The typical trade-off was that the Confederates got medical supplies and the Union got cotton, but it is evident that both President Lincoln and Jefferson Davis looked the other way at this illicit trade.

Joint army-navy operations also caused conflicts about confiscated materials. For the navy, prize law for high seas vessels was clear-cut, but what about contraband seized in cooperation with the army? In June 1863, Rear Admiral Lee asked for guidance from Welles about a joint-operations mission in which the navy assisted in "the capture of mules and corn for the army." Lee inquired "whether it [was] proper for the Navy to make such captures." The navy secretary cited a recent law and replied that naval officers were not required to remit "such articles to the special agent of the Treasury Department." Rather, it was "proper for the Navy to make such captures and to use them if necessary."[71] The conflicts caused by joint-operations

with the army troubled Welles, but he typically did an excellent job of en-
suring they did not detract from the blockade.

In 1863 Welles was particularly concerned about the Cape Fear region
and the difficult blockade of Wilmington. Blockade commanders stationed
there consistently clamored for more and better vessels. In May 1863, Capt.
Charles Boggs, aboard the USS *Sacramento*, warned Rear Admiral Lee
that the weak blockade force invited rebel attack and supported Confederate claims of a "paper blockade." He notified his superior, "The force now
on either side of the [Frying Pan] shoal is far too small to make an effective
blockade, as evident by the number of vessels that get in and out during
the night." Boggs felt it to be his "duty to lay the case plainly" before his
superiors, and he declared, "Every officer displays the utmost activity and
zeal in performance of his duty, but we must not be expected to perform
impossibilities." Rear Admiral Lee endorsed Boggs's complaint, and he
transmitted the harsh reality to Welles with this opinion: "The blockade
requires more and better vessels and must eventually fail without them."[72]

Welles was inured to the continual complaint about inadequate resources.
He could see the blockade big picture—the capture rate was improving
in 1863—whereas regional squadron commanders only understood their
own troubles. In fact, Wilmington attracted more blockade-running attempts due to the Union military campaign against Charleston that started
in April 1863. Rear Admiral Lee reiterated his request for more vessels in
August and stated, "It is generally felt by the officers here that the blockade
of [Wilmington], the most difficult port to close . . . is exposed and inefficient from the want of many more and suitable vessels." Welles maintained
his patience with Rear Admiral Lee despite at least two more requests for
more resources in late August and early October 1863. The navy secretary's
perseverance and leadership eventually paid dividends.[73]

Welles's confidence in ultimate success was eventually infused into Rear
Admiral Lee. In February 1864, Lee noted that additional vessels and improved tactics on the Cape Fear station had "greatly increase[d] the hazards
of blockade running and consequently the efficiency of the blockade." Lee
crowed to Assistant Navy Secretary Gustavus Fox that his blockaders off
Wilmington had captured or destroyed twenty-six blockade-runners since
last July. "Can the history of the blockade beat this?" he asked rhetorically.[74]
As it turned out, 1863 proved to be a banner year for the blockade squadrons (see chapter 5 for statistical evidence), and Lee deserved some credit.

In 1864, the conflict over whether to denude blockade resources for cooperation with army campaigns continued. In April of that year, Welles ordered Rear-Admiral Lee not to weaken his grip on Wilmington to assist with any army campaign "except by special direction" of the Navy Department.[75] U. S. Grant was calling for all available support for his upcoming spring campaign in Virginia. In this case, the Wilmington blockaders likely would have been used to support Maj. Gen. Ben Butler's campaign at Bermuda Hundred southeast of Richmond. While Welles wanted to maintain an effective blockade of Wilmington, April 1864 heralded serious concern about the readiness of Confederate ironclads on the North Carolina Sounds—the CSS *Albemarle* and the CSS *Neuse*. As it turned out, the CSS *Albemarle* provided crucial assistance in the rebel capture of Plymouth, North Carolina, but the CSS *Neuse* did not make it into action. Despite the threat from two rebel ironclads and Grant's request for all available resources to support the spring campaign, Welles continued the Union blockade's grip on Wilmington—the Confederacy's most important blockade-running port by 1864.

The decision to assault Wilmington finally came in the fall of 1864. The original plan approved by U. S. Grant was to begin in October, but the operation was postponed. Navy Secretary Welles worried about the continued delay of joint operations against the port. He aired his concerns to President Lincoln about the diminishment of the blockade fleet as vessels awaited the assault. Welles noted that there were 150 ships in the North Atlantic Blockading Squadron, and that "every other squadron ha[d] been depleted . . . to strengthen this expedition." The ships were "an immense force lying idle, awaiting the movements of the army." Welles opined that "the retention of so many vessels from blockade and cruising duty [was] a most serious injury to the public service," and if further army delay ensued, then he desired that the "ships may be relieved and dispersed for other service."[76] The secretary remained steadfast in maintaining an effective blockade.

Conclusion

The only surefire method of stopping blockade-runners was to capture Confederate ports, which Gideon Welles understood was the ultimate multiplier of the blockade's effectiveness. He told Samuel DuPont in early 1863, "The withdrawal of blockade vessels" for other duties "renders the capture of Charleston and Mobile imperative." However, capturing Confederate ports required army assistance, and this was sometimes not a strategic priority. The unsuccessful assault on Charleston from April through October 1863 ended without Union capture of the city, although it did divert some blockade-running traffic to Wilmington. Thus in 1864, Wilmington became the most important blockade-running port. The Union high command did not focus on Wilmington's capture until that fall, and Union forces did not effectively seize the port until January 1865, when Rear Adm. David D. Porter could finally report that it was "hermetically sealed against blockade runners."[77] However, this declaration could only be made thanks to the army's capture of Fort Fisher. This is an important point—no matter the size of blockade squadrons, the best way to stop blockade-running was for Union land forces to seize Confederate ports.

In some cases, it was unnecessary to capture the city itself, but only the territory surrounding maritime entrances. For example, Union armies did not need to seize Wilmington or Mobile; they could simply occupy the maritime approaches to prevent blockade-running. As the war dragged on, the list of Union-occupied Southern ports grew to include New Orleans (April 1862) and Mobile (August 1864). Outright capture served two strategic purposes for the blockade squadrons. First, once a major Southern port was captured, blockade-runners were forced to try their luck at another port, thus limiting their options. Second, naval resources previously earmarked for duty at a captured rebel port could be utilized by other blockade squadrons, thus strengthening those units' numbers. Both Union and Confederate leaders understood this strategy and confronted it with the resources available.

On June 23, 1865, Pres. Andrew Johnson officially ended the Union blockade of the South. Looking back over the previous four years, Gideon Welles could take pride in overseeing one the largest maritime mobilizations in American history. Welles noted that during the war the US Navy purchased 418 extant ships and contracted for another 208—which put the total naval strength in 1865 at about 626 vessels.[78] The US Navy had evolved from a small but respectable force to a serious future contender for maritime dominance—but that lay in the future.

The US Navy's experience with the Civil War blockade was impressive because no mission approaching this magnitude or duration had ever been attempted. In that light the Union blockade of the Confederacy should be regarded as an example of the United States fulfilling its maritime potential during a national emergency. To be sure, unreliable vessels were hustled into service with little thought of their capability, like the USS *Stars and Stripes*, which took part in the 1862 Roanoke Island campaign, but in 1878 the vessel, renamed the *Metropolis*, sank off the North Carolina coast with the loss of eighty-five lives. Other Union ships, however, were first-class warships—like the USS *Niphon*, USS *Santiago de Cuba*, and USS *Keystone State*—and these vessels represented the modern fleet into which the US Navy was evolving.

Another important factor was that the Union blockade got the chance to grow and operate largely without the interference of enemy capital ships. The blockade was a huge task that had never been attempted on this scale, and the lack of a major enemy maritime threat allowed the US Navy to practice the skills of a modern blockade without existential interference. Gideon Welles and the Union blockade squadrons could proudly reflect on their service and rightly boast that they had played an important role in Union victory.

CHAPTER 3

———★———

Blockade-Running

THE BUSINESS OF blockade-running was not the only boom economy of the Civil War, but it was the most adventurous. The immense profit to be made on a single trip through the Union cordon attracted a variety of business interests to the trade, from the well-organized merchant houses to hastily convened groups of schemers. Although less motivated by profit, the Confederate government and Southern state governments became involved in, and dependent on, blockade-running as a fundamental means of supply. Blockade-running was the Confederacy's system of international trade, so if the would-be nation was to establish credibility abroad, maintaining commerce despite the blockade was vital for national legitimacy. Blockade-running narratives comprise some of the most fascinating tales of the Civil War. This chapter will focus less on these exciting stories, and more on some overlooked aspects of blockade-running.

Sail-Powered Blockade-Running

Although most successful blockade-runners were steam powered, a few sail-powered vessels tested the Union blockade. Sail-powered blockade-runners tended to be smaller vessels that plied the coastal waters with smaller cargoes. These boats depended on a shallow draft and the ability to hide in plain sight. Larger sail-powered blockade-runners, as historian Stephen Wise notes, operated "only during the first months of the war . . . and this was only for outward runs as their owners refused to risk their vessels a second time against steam warships" of the Union blockade squadrons.[1] However, some small, sail-powered runners continued to test the Union blockade.

The early days of blockade-running allowed sailing vessels an opportunity to sneak into rebel ports before the Union blockade was fully implemented. One such episode was the remarkable story of the sailing ship *Standard* and her two crew members James Dickson and Thomas Hernandez. In late 1861, Hernandez visited Dickson in Newark, New Jersey, and they hatched a plan to smuggle goods through the blockade. Their chosen destination was Savannah, Georgia, to which each man had strong ties. Dickson was a former merchant, and Hernandez, more importantly, was a Savannah River pilot. This combination of merchant capital and local maritime acumen made for the perfect blockade-running relationship— at least on paper.[2]

After concocting their scheme in Newark, Dickson and Hernandez stowed away on board the *Lilly Dale* out of New York City bound for Halifax, Nova Scotia. After a harrowing journey, during which they encountered severe storms in December 1861 and even ran aground, the would-be smugglers arrived in Halifax in early January 1862. For the next six weeks they enjoyed themselves in the port city, "dancing and fiddling and singing, and feasting," and on February 21, 1862, they departed on board the *Standard*.[3] The merriment of six weeks in Halifax was about to be contrasted with a terrifying ordeal at sea.

A man called Captain Blanch commanded the *Standard*, and Dickson and Hernandez, and seven others served as crew members. The *Standard* had a nine-foot draft and was 110 tons. Its freight included a shipment of medicine, lead, guns, caps, and dry goods technically bound for Matamoros, Mexico, but everyone on board knew the ship's true destination was Savannah, Georgia. The adventurous smugglers were finally underway.

The *Standard*'s story highlights the realities of sail-powered blockade-running. The vessel's crew were blockade-running amateurs who decided on the spur of the moment to give it a try. For them, breaking the Union blockade was a get-rich-quick scheme. It seems that Dickson and Hernandez considered their scheme a lark, an endeavor to line their pockets and provide a great story to tell in their golden years. This was—and still is—a major misconception about blockade-running in the Civil War. The most successful blockade-runners were serious businesspeople who invested generously in the best equipment and captains. Ill-planned attempts at slipping past the Union cordon with inferior vessels and less knowledgeable crews often resulted in ships' and seamen's capture.

The *Standard*'s journey turned dangerous as soon as it left Halifax. From February 24 to March 7, the ship was hit by continuous storms in the North Atlantic. Captain Blanch and the crew were forced to ride out the treacherous seas for almost two weeks, during which time they were blown far off course to a longitude east of Bermuda. On the helplessness of the *Standard* in this lengthy storm, Dickson remarked, "The sea was now washing our decks . . . [and] dark masses of water would come thundering down on us." Another storm hit the *Standard* from March 16 through March 20, but this gale at least blew the crew in the right direction. Dickson mused about the terror of surviving these storms, and he questioned "what more appalling sight in the entire universe [there was] than an angry raging sea." The *Standard* survived again, and now the thrill of running the blockade became possible. If conditions remained favorable, Dickson noted, "We will be in the Gulf [Stream] after which a few hours will decide whether we shall arrive on the coast of the Confederate States or be taken by a Yankee as a prize."[4] After enduring a dangerous trip on the Atlantic, the sailing ship *Standard* was finally in position to run the blockade and complete the adventure.

As the *Standard* prepared for the final dash into the Georgia coast, Dickson and the crew were "getting everything in readiness for running in or running away from the Blockaders." He noted the final tactic was to wait until nightfall, get closer to the shore, and then catch the next tide. If the breeze permitted, the *Standard* could then race into the coast with little chance of detection. The crew spotted a Union blockade steamer, but it did not see them. On March 30 the *Standard* made its final run into the Georgia coast near the town of Darien. At this pivotal moment, Dickson acknowledged the disadvantages of sail-powered ships. He admitted "the absolute necessity of steamers alone attempting to run the blockade," since sailing vessels were helpless without the wind and could make "easy prey to the enemy."[5] The *Standard* was not yet in the safety of rebel waters.

The would-be blockade-runners did not come to port in Savannah or Brunswick, Georgia, but instead came into Sapelo Sound, a back channel of St. Catherine's Island. From March 30 to April 1 the *Standard* ran aground, increasing the danger of capture. The captain and crew realized they needed to find a safe harbor. It was only a matter of time before a Union blockade ship learned of the *Standard*'s position, and this occurred thanks to the information of runaway slaves. Captain Blanch took the *Standard* up the nearest inland waterway—the North Newport River—and docked at Melon Bluff on April 3. The next day, the captain traveled to Savannah to arrange for sale of the smuggled goods. On April 15 the mercantile house of LaRoche and Bell auctioned off the *Standard*'s cargo.[6] The *Standard* had accomplished a successful blockade run, but its success also sealed its fate.

Union commanders were aware of the blockade breach and sent two gunboats in pursuit. The USS *Potomska*, captained by Lieut. Cdr. Pendleton Watmough, and the USS *Wamsutta*, captained by Lieut. Cdr. Alexander Semmes, were dispatched to investigate the situation and capture the runner. As the Union gunboats ascended the North Newport River, local rebel militia forces mobilized and awaited their arrival. To prevent these ships from ascending farther, rebels decided on April 25 to scuttle the *Standard* in the channel. Shortly thereafter the only visible remnant of the blockade-runner—the superstructure—was torched as evidence that Yankee gunboats no longer had a prize to take.[7] The Union foray in pursuit of the *Standard* resulted in some light skirmishing between the gunboats and local defense forces, but the US flotilla was content to resume blockade duties out of harm's way.

The saga of the sail-ship *Standard* is an informative narrative about a little-covered aspect of blockade-running. From the start, the amateur status of the entire affair was evident. It was a risky venture since the *Standard* was solely dependent on sail power, and although Dickson and Hernandez were familiar with the mouth of the Savannah River, little else predicted success. The episode's protagonists—James Dickson and Tom Hernandez—were adventure seekers looking to make a quick profit, and each man responded differently to his experience on board the *Standard*.

Tom Hernandez was captured in July 1862 on board another blockade-runner. He subsequently returned to Savannah, then served as pilot for the rebel ironclad CSS *Atlanta*. Hernandez was then wounded in the June 1863 battle with the USS *Nahant* and USS *Weehawken* and captured. After a stint in a Union prison, he returned to service in the Confederate navy until the war's end. The experience on board the *Standard* apparently did not deter Hernandez from using his talents as a river pilot for more blockade-running and for the Confederate navy. Based on his activity after the trek on board the *Standard*, it appears that Hernandez was motivated by Confederate nationalism, not just profit.

James Dickson was apparently less enthusiastic about continued adventure, but he did manage to travel to Nova Scotia and get married in 1864. Dickson raised a family, but little is known about his life from 1862 until his death in 1878.[8] It is doubtless that numerous others attempted to run sailboats through the blockade like Dickson and Hernandez. Yet few left written accounts of their activities, so it is difficult to gauge whether the *Standard*'s experience was normal or atypical.

Sail-powered blockade-running significantly diminished in 1862. Historian Marcus Price notes, "During the second year of the war there began a shift from sail to steam that was to continue at a steadily increasing rate until blockade running ceased." A perfect example of this transition was the capture of the sail-powered blockade-runner *Stephen Hart* off the Florida coast in January 1862. The runner contained large quantities of rifles, ammunition, and accoutrements purchased by Confederate overseas contractor Caleb Huse. The costly capture of the *Stephen Hart* "was a valuable lesson . . . [and] no major shipment of . . . stores would ever be made again via sailing vessel."[9] Only a foolhardy entrepreneur would continue to risk capture of a sail-powered blockade-runner after 1862.

William Watson was among the brazen seamen who continued to attempt blockade running after 1862 using only wind power. He recounted running out of Galveston, Texas, in 1864 under sail aboard the *Rob Roy*, and he described his tactics, after clearing the shallows at night: "The object now was to get as far out to sea as possible before daylight, and this was the all-important object of a sailing vessel running the blockade on an outward trip." Watson noted the difference in timing for inbound and outbound runs of sail-ships. Early evening was the best departure time for sailing vessels so as to put maximum distance between the blockaders and the runners under darkness, while the late evening or early morning hours were best for inbound runs because the blockade sailors were less attentive.[10]

The obvious limitation to successful sail-powered blockade-running was the unpredictable nature of the winds, tides, currents, and visibility at sea. Winds were especially important, since the ships' main power source could falter at any time. Capt. William Watson recalled one such incident and the only available means to evade capture: "About one p.m. it was dead calm, and we lay helpless. We lowered every sail and lay under bare poles, so that we would not be so easily seen from a distance. This I afterward found to be an excellent plan, as we would be less apt to be observed at a distance of seven miles than at a distance of twelve miles with sails up."[11] This method of hiding in plain sight worked for Watson on this occasion, but any blockader that spotted a sail-powered runner in calm winds could make an easy capture. Sometimes, however, shallow-draft vessels could evade a large blockader by heading into shallow waters.

Capt. William Watson actually touted the few benefits of sailing schooners as compared to steamers. He explained, "Most of the steamers were swift paddle boats of light draught of water, mostly built on the Clyde, and purchased for this trade on account of their high speed; but there was now some difference of opinion as to whether they were more safe and profitable than [sailing] schooners." Watson pointed out that the ships' "original cost was high so that there was always a large amount of capital at risk." In addition, "they consumed a large amount of coal, and . . . this article was not to be had in the Confederate States." In the captain's opinion, the fuel-to-cargo ratio offset the steamers' advantage. He noted, "Their carrying capacity was small, and this was still more hampered by the large amount of coal they had to carry, and when loaded down with coal and cargo their speed was greatly impaired."[12]

Despite Watson's critique, most blockade-running captains still preferred the faster coal-fired, steam-powered blockade-runners over sailing schooners. Watson was also being hypocritical. While it is true that necessity forced the fastest steamers to limit their cargo space in exchange for speed, the captain's sailing schooner, the *Rob Roy*, was constrained by the same limitations—but without the advantage of steam-powered propulsion. Watson's opinion was in the minority, since a vast majority of blockade-running captains preferred reliable steam power to sails.

Sail-powered blockade-running continued throughout the war in specialized circumstances. As witnessed by Watson's experiences aboard the *Rob Roy*, the western Gulf of Mexico was geographically suited for sail-ships traveling between Galveston, Matamoros, Tampico, and even Havana. Historian Andrew Hall asserts that sail-powered blockade-runners "in Texas, and the Gulf of Mexico . . . contributed a great deal to the aggregate total of cotton supplies and people trading between the Confederacy and neutral ports in Cuba, Honduras, Jamaica, and Mexico." Hall notes that although the relative cargo capacities were small, sail-powered vessels "attempted more than 2,200 one-way trips" in the region, "getting through the Union cordon more than 80 percent of the time."[13] The coastal geography and proximity of foreign ports made sail-powered blockade-running in the western Gulf of Mexico a viable business.

Sail-powered blockade-runners continued attempts along the Southern coast throughout the war, but they did so with limited success. In March 1864 the captain of a Union blockader along Georgia's shoreline remarked, "Three-fourths of steamer blockade-runners get through, and about one-fourth of sailing vessels." This lack of success by 1864 meant that fewer sail-powered attempts were made. Historian Robert Browning Jr. shows that in the case of the North Atlantic Blockading Squadron, sail-ships apparently made fewer attempts to break the Union cordon. In statistical tables for blockade-runners using both steam and sail power from 1861 to 1864, Browning notes the increase in captured or destroyed steam-powered blockade-runners from zero in 1861 to forty-five in 1864. But the decrease in captured or destroyed sail-powered blockade-runners from twenty-eight in 1861 to two in 1864 shows that the overall number of attempts dropped due to the high probability of getting caught.[14] Of course, these statistics apply only to the North Atlantic Blockading Squadron, but one can assume that fewer sailboats tried to run the blockade in 1864 than in 1861 all along the Southern coast due to their relatively lower chance of success.

Pilots, Tactics, and Intangible Cargo

One of the most important blockade-runner crew members was the pilot. The typical blockade-running ship was crewed by a captain, seamen, a supercargo, and a pilot who intimately knew the entrances to a Confederate port. Regrettably, very little scholarship has been produced about Civil War pilots. In peacetime, these local seafarers guided ships safely into port, and they proved an integral part of maritime commerce. During the Civil War, their specialized knowledge of channels, depths, currents, and shoals became priceless information for blockade-runners. Local historians have contributed to the pilots' role in blockade-running, but the only comprehensive work on these seamen (that we are aware of) is *Masters of the Shoals: Tales of the Cape Fear Pilots Who Ran the Union Blockade* by Jim McNeil (2003). McNeil's magnificent book preserves the stories of Wilmington's blockade-running pilots for other historians. Alas, if other local historians of Southern ports compiled similar studies, a more complete picture of pilots' important role in blockade-running might be possible.

Twenty-first-century ship captains are fortunate to have easy access to navigational charts. Instant data on depths and channels and up-to-date charts from GPS (Global Positioning System) make modern navigation safer and far more reliable than its nineteenth century counterpart. Even when technology fails, today most channels to ports are well marked with green and red way points that can even be seen at night due to their blinking lights. However, shoals still alter charts, and local pilots are still needed to guide large cargo ships across the bar and safely into harbor. In the mid-nineteenth century, pilots personified a vast store of maritime knowledge about the waters around their home ports. In a sense, pilots were walking,

talking GPS charts, but they were also much more. These seafarers knew
the types of sand to be expected on approaching a port, and could estimate latitude and longitude from a sounding, or depth reading. Temporary
shoals, tidal effects, depth variations, and all manner of localized maritime information were contained in a pilot's mental library. Even though
blockade-runners only needed them for a few hours at the beginning or end
of a trip, pilots' familiarity and expertise with local navigation could mean
the difference between a successful blockade run or a total loss.

As a result of their unique skill set, pilots were accorded special status
in Confederate ports. They required certification by a state agency, and
they were well compensated for their skills. During the war, historian Jim
McNeil observes, "the Cape Fear pilots [were] still governed by the state
Board of Commissioners of Navigation and Pilotage . . . [and] bonds were
required as established" in a 1784 North Carolina law that regulated the
trade. In addition, "Pilots received separate licenses for [guiding on] the
river and the bar," depending on their specialized knowledge. The pay for
experienced pilots was very good by standards of the day. According to
McNeil, in the 1860s, "a pilot's fee for taking a vessel from Wilmington to
past the bar, or from the bar up the river to the port, was set at $200 each
way." Wartime demand vastly increased that already impressive rate, since
"pilots of privately owned blockade runners could earn as much as $5,000
in gold per trip." During the war, at least seventy-seven maritime pilots
operated out of the Cape Fear - Wilmington area, so one can surmise that
several hundred of them were available for blockade-runners throughout
Confederate ports like Charleston, Savannah, Mobile, and Galveston.[15] No
intelligent, well-financed blockade-running entrepreneur would dare to
test the shoals of Confederate ports without a pilot.

Pilots were so pivotal to the Confederate war effort that they were not
subject to conscription. The Confederate Congress passed the first draft
law in April 1862, and river and coastal pilots were among the exempted occupations. On April 21, Congress exempted "all pilots and persons engaged
in marine service" from the armed forces. As the heavy toll of the war in
1862 depleted Confederate manpower, Confederate congressmen decided
to close some of the exemptions in October, but pilots' status remained
unchanged. In February 1864, the Congress made a desperate attempt to
conscript every available man into military service, expanding the manda-
tory ages from seventeen to fifty years. Again, the exemption for pilots
remained in place.[16] Confederate leaders understood that the pilot's role in

successful blockade-running was more valuable to the war effort than any military service contribution.

Union blockade squadrons also understood the value of local pilots. Squadron leader Samuel F. DuPont encouraged indefinite incarceration of captured pilots, conflating their role with that of supercargo, he recommended that the captain and supercargo/pilot "should not be permitted to be at large." DuPont further opined, "[The Navy Department] can not exercise too much vigilance in preventing the return of such men, who, from their local knowledge of this part of the coast, are the most efficient instruments of the rebels in violating the blockade." Capt. S. W. Godon of the USS *Vermont* informed the Navy Department about William Gladding, "a pilot" recently captured off the coast of Georgia. Godon declared that Gladding was "too dangerous a man to be allowed to be adrift." The pilot's skills, the captain warned, were to be used in the escape of the blockade-runner *Nashville*.[17]

In both cases, the Union blockade officers begged the Lincoln administration to incarcerate these seamen for the rest of the war. In March 1863, DuPont told one of his captains that if he "had any Charleston pilots [he] would send them up [to a Northern prison] with pleasure." DuPont noted that "since the blockade was established" in 1861, he had not captured any pilots, but that "occasionally a coast pilot [had] been onboard some of the vessels." However, these valuable guides soon became "proficient on the outside work" and were hired for oceangoing blockade runs.[18] By 1863, Union blockade squadrons understood that capturing skilled maritime pilots indirectly decreased blockade-running success.

Pilots were also valuable to the blockade squadrons. In May 1863, a captain off the coast of South Carolina requested "a pilot" be sent to his vicinity, stating, "[The seaman] will add to my efficiency as a blockader off here." Squadron leader Samuel DuPont used the pilots as they became available. He informed Gideon Welles that he had two first-class pilots and one third-class pilot ready for blockade service. DuPont also noted that he relied on the "services of certain contraband pilots" and paid them thirty to forty dollars per month for their assistance.[19] In addition to captured or loyal Union pilots, former slaves with maritime knowledge became a valuable source of expertise about Confederate ports. However, since blockade-runners paid such fabulous rates, Union blockade squadrons were usually at a disadvantage in accessing skilled pilots.

The tactics blockade-runners used to avoid capture changed from 1861 to 1865. In 1861 it was possible to feign ignorance, fly deceptive flags, or manipulate cargo manifests to avoid seizure. By 1862, Union squadrons ignored these basic ruses and started to seize all suspicious vessels. In other cases, blockade-runners made no pretense about their intent and used speed to avoid the Union squadrons. The ability to navigate through a hostile fleet to the safety of a Confederate port required great skill and adaptive tactics. It was this cat-and-mouse game between the blockade squadrons and the blockade-runners that witnessed the most tactical innovation and corresponding countermeasures.

The early months of blockade duty produced some confusion on how to identify blockade-runners. For example, a Union squadron seized the schooner *Reform* as it left the Port of Baltimore on July 13, 1861. After much investigation, however, it was discovered that the ship and crew were involved in an elaborate Union spy mission to procure cotton and tobacco seeds from the Confederacy. In effect, the Union blockade had snagged one of its own vessels. The agents and the ship were eventually released from custody, but not until the episode was publicized to the US government's embarrassment. This example highlights the desperate desire to continue wartime cotton and tobacco imports in the North, and the difficulty of forewarning the blockade squadrons about friendly or hostile vessels.[20]

In the first months of the war, blockade-running captains could use the excuse that they had not been notified about the blockade. According to the letter of international blockade law, this was a legitimate reason for ignoring the blockade. Merchant vessels could have been at sea or foreign ports for weeks or months, and thus be completely uninformed about the blockade declaration, before coming to a Confederate port. On May 20, 1861, the British ship *Hiawatha* was stopped by the blockade squadron near Hampton Roads, Virginia. Flag Officer Silas Stringham informed his superiors that the *Hiawatha*'s captain "[offered] the excuse that they did not hear of the blockade" within a reasonable time frame. Stringham was "far from being satisfied with this vessel's" excuse, and he ordered the *Hiawatha* taken to a New York prize court.[21]

Blockade-running in 1861 was a veritable free-for-all with very little chance of capture, but that began to change in 1862 as the Union deployed naval resources. Continued blockade-running success depended on new tactics. The crew of the British schooner *Lion*, which was captured in an episode spanning from February 25 to March 2, resorted to such novel methods. The *Lion* ran out of New Orleans to Havana, where it was purchased and flagged by a British merchant. The ship was later captured on the voyage to Matamoros, and while the Union captain found gunpowder on the vessel, he uncovered "no log book, no letters of instruction . . . no alleged owners, [and] no manifest."[22] However, the *Lion* did have a Confederate flag onboard, so the ship was seized and taken to the prize court at Key West. But before the *Lion* could reach its destination, a gust of wind allowed it to escape from Union captors.

This bizarre episode informs historians of several aspects of blockade-running in 1862. First, while the deception of false flags and inaccurate or missing logbooks and manifests was commonplace, this would fool only the most naïve US captains. Second, the schooner's ease of escape due to a "gust of wind" tells us that the US captain did not hold the *Lion*'s crew as prisoners. Nor did he put his own prize crew aboard the vessel for delivery to the prize court. Why did this occur? According to the Union captain's testimony, it was a legal technicality. He admitted that after its delivery to the prize court, the *Lion* would be released anyway due to its British ownership. The US captain complained about the frustration of blockade duty in which legality restrained him.[23]

In 1862 British blockade-running captains evolved tactics to counter the blockade squadrons. One new tactic was a blockade-running fleet with a decoy ship. When five British steamers left Bermuda bound for the Confederacy in October 1862, two Union vessels cruising nearby pursued until the British ship *Desperate* voluntarily pulled alongside them. With this decoy in place, four other blockade-runners made an easy escape from Bermuda, unnoticed by the distracted Union ships.[24]

Successful blockade-running captains learned new methods to avoid capture. Seasoned captain John Wilkinson believed that "a cordon of fast steamers stationed ten or fifteen miles apart *inside the Gulf Stream*, in the course from Nassau and Bermuda to Wilmington and Charleston, would have been more effectual in stopping blockade-running than the whole United States Navy concentrated off those ports." Wilkinson explained that this strategy would have been more successful because "every experienced captain of a blockade-runner made a point to cross the [Gulf] stream early enough in the afternoon, if possible, to establish a ship's position by chronometer so as to escape the influence of that current upon his dead reckoning."[25] In other words, blockade-runners needed to get their bearings before guiding their ships into port using visible signals. Wilkinson believed that this temporary disorientation was an ideal time for the Union squadrons to pounce. Tactical adaptations by blockade-running captains typically kept them one step ahead of the US fleet in 1861 and 1862. In these early months of blockade-running, the Confederacy relied on captains' strategic edge and risked important foreign missions on their ability.

Blockade-runners also smuggled the intangible cargo of important Confederate personnel on board. Most Civil War audiences are familiar with the story of Confederate diplomats James Mason and John Slidell who were successfully taken by blockade-runner to the Bahamas, and then arrested on board the British packet ship *Trent*. This oft-discussed episode highlights an important point. The rebel envoys were not captured on board the blockade-runner *Theodora* outbound from Charleston. Even after the Charleston newspapers' announcement of Mason and Slidell's departure, the blockade squadron could not capture them. It took a violation of British neutrality, when Capt. Charles Wilkes of the USS *San Jacinto* stopped the *Trent* outbound from Nassau, for the Union navy to catch the men. This was doubly embarrassing for the Lincoln administration. The Union blockade was incapable of capturing the Confederate diplomats on their blockade run from Charleston to Nassau, and then Mason and Slidell's illegal seizure sparked a diplomatic crisis with Great Britain. Other scholars have covered this episode in depth, but the main point is that blockade-runners consistently carried vital intangible cargo that was sometimes as important to interdict as weapons and war materiel.

Matthew Fontaine Maury, both a world-renowned expert on ocean currents and wind and the Confederacy's most internationally recognized scientist, was among the important rebel personnel blockade-runners carried. In the fall of 1862, the *Herald* left Charleston headed for Bermuda with Maury on board. Maury was born in Tennessee, but he made his home in Fredericksburg, Virginia. The scientist had a brief career at sea; he was on board the USS *Vincennes* when it circumnavigated the world in 1829-30, the first US naval vessel to do so. However, Maury's active service career had been cut short due to a stagecoach accident in 1839. This terrible turn of events was both disappointing and serendipitous for him, because his real talents lay in compiling data, studying, analyzing, and writing about the world's oceans. In 1844, Maury had been appointed superintendent of the Naval Observatory in Washington, DC, where, with his staff, he began the massive task of gathering data about ocean currents, winds, and other observations from thousands of ship captains. This task was the foundation for Maury's most famous scientific work, *The Physical Geography of the Sea*

(1855), which brought him international scientific acclaim. In April 1861, Maury decided to resign his position in the US Navy and follow his home state of Virginia out of the Union. As few people had more to lose by joining the rebellion, his scientific reputation never recovered.[26]

In 1862, Maury's mission was to travel via blockade-runner to England and assist Confederate agent James D. Bulloch in purchasing more commerce raiders. It was also hoped that the scientist's international reputation would enhance Confederate sympathies in England. After apparently helping the *Herald*'s captain regain the proper bearing after a storm took the ship off course, Maury landed in Liverpool in November 1862. Maury the scientist was hailed in London, but his reputation could not overcome mounting disapproval from the Confederacy's English opponents. His mission was only partially successful. In aiding Bulloch, Maury could take credit for getting another rebel commerce raider to sea, the CSS *Georgia*, and almost getting a second into operation, the CSS *Rappahannock*. Even so, the scientist's sojourn in England was regarded as largely unsuccessful. He decided to return to the Confederacy, and he left England in May 1865. Maury planned to run the blockade again, but when he reached Havana, Cuba, he was informed there was no longer a Confederacy—the war was over.[27]

One of the most famous Civil War personalities to have her fate linked to blockade-running was Rose O'Neal Greenhow, master spy of the Confederacy. Before the war, Greenhow had successfully navigated the highest social and political circles of Washington, DC, and this proximity to power afforded her the opportunity to spy for the Confederate States. In the summer of 1861, she provided priceless intelligence for the Confederate army in northern Virginia. Thanks to Greenhow's espionage, the rebels knew the timing and strength of the Union army marching toward Manassas. Confederates were thus able to concentrate forces and win the Civil War's first major battle, First Bull Run, on July 21. However, Pinkerton detectives soon uncovered Greenhow's espionage. She was arrested on August 23 and served five months of house arrest. After public defiance of the Lincoln administration, Greenhow was then transferred to the Old Capitol Prison. All the while, she meticulously cultivated the role of martyr for civil liberties—an alleged victim of Lincoln's tyranny. After ten months of detention and widespread publicity, on May 31, 1862, Rose O'Neal Greenhow was released from prison and banished to the Confederacy. Now her saga as an overseas Confederate agent began.[28]

Rose O'Neal Greenhow was among the handful of Confederate person-alities, along with Stonewall Jackson and Robert E. Lee, who were inter-national celebrities. The extensive publicity of her arrest, detention, and unrelenting defiance toward her captors made the rebel spy a heroine in the eyes of Europe's Confederate sympathizers. Jefferson Davis intended to use this notoriety to good effect, and he dispatched Greenhow to England in 1863. As biographer Ann Blackman notes, "It was highly unusual, perhaps unprecedented, for a president to send a woman to represent her country in a foreign land [in the 1860s], even in an unofficial capacity."[29] Greenhow and her nine-year-old daughter, Little Rose, departed from Wilmington on board the blockade-runner *Phantom* on August 5, 1863. Against seem-ingly long odds, and after a dramatic chase by three Union blockaders, the *Phantom* sped toward Bermuda at the uncatchable pace of seventeen knots.[30] Greenhow spent a month in St. George, Bermuda, and then con-tinued on her mission to England on board the Confederate steamer *Har-riett Pinckney.*

Greenhow and Little Rose arrived in Great Britain, and the unofficial Confederate envoy immediately went to work. She traveled to Liverpool, hotbed of Southern sympathizers, to sell the cotton that had also escaped Wilmington on the *Phantom*. Greenhow's next mission was diplomatic. She journeyed to London with official dispatches for James Mason, the Confederacy's unrecognized ambassador, but it was also in London that Greenhow garnered her greatest publicity. She contracted for and wrote a popular memoir, *My Imprisonment and the First Year of Abolition Rule at Washington*, that met with mixed reviews. But whether one agreed with Greenhow's ardent Confederate nationalism or not, she had indisputably developed an international persona. Due in large part to the popularity of her memoir, "Rose met with the highest officials in the British and French governments, dined with top leaders of European society, and buttonholed anyone who would listen to her arguments for [Confederate] recognition and her defense of slavery."[31]

After a year of unofficially representing Confederate interests in Europe, Greenhow departed Britain with two valuable assets. First, her interna-tional fame, or infamy, had vastly expanded, and she was without ques-tion the most famous Confederate woman in international terms. Second, sales from Greenhow's memoir generated an impressive profit, and she was returning to the South with four-hundred gold sovereigns worth about $2,000, which she planned to donate to the war effort. Neither asset would save Greenhow from her fate, and one perhaps even sealed it.

On her way back to the Confederacy, Rose O'Neal Greenhow traveled on board the blockade-runner *Condor*, which departed Britain in August 1864. After stops in both Bermuda and Halifax, Nova Scotia, the *Condor* headed for Wilmington to run the blockade, making its daring attempt to dash through the blockade on October 1, 1864. Union blockaders fired at the runner, and it was almost to the safety of New Inlet when Capt. William Hewett spotted a wreck in the narrow channel ahead. Hewett swerved the *Condor* to starboard—the wrong way, as it turned out—and ran aground. But the ship was too near shore under the protection of Fort Fisher's long-range artillery for the blue-jacketed sailors to capture their prize.

Greenhow now had to decide whether to wait for better conditions and high tide to free the *Condor*, which is what Captain Hewett and his crew did, or to embark into a lifeboat and take her chances rowing to shore three hundred yards away in a pounding surf. She chose the latter. Six passengers, including Greenhow, boarded the lifeboat, which was quickly swamped in the rough surf. But only five souls made it to shore—Rose O'Neal Greenhow was missing. Shortly thereafter, her body was found on the beach near Fort Fisher. Greenhow's body was carried in a funeral procession with military honors through Wilmington and buried in Oakdale Cemetery.[32]

Rose O'Neal Greenhow's major accomplishments and death were inextricably linked to blockade-running. She habitually pierced the Union blockade—whether by smuggling intelligence to Confederate generals through Union lines in 1861, or on board the *Phantom* and the *Condor* during her international mission in 1863-64. The irony is that blockade-running also caused Greenhow's ultimate demise, which is among the most fascinating stories of the Civil War.

Blockade-runners carried internationally recognized intangible cargoes like Matthew Fontaine Maury and Rose O'Neal Greenhow, but they also carried eminent Confederate officials less eager for the public eye. One such relatively unknown but extremely important figure was Colin J. McRae. Antebellum experiences typically predicted the manner and quality of wartime service, and McRae was no exception to this maxim. His father had initiated him into the booming mercantile business of the 1830s in Alabama and Mississippi. When his father died in 1835, McRae had been forced to assume leadership of the family enterprises at only twenty-one years of age. And he capably managed both family and business affairs. The primary mercantile business was based in Mobile, Alabama, and during the cotton boom of the 1840s and 1850s McRae became an important cotton factor, or financial middleman.

McRae profited from being the indispensable go-between for Alabama's cotton planters. Each year, he or a company representative traveled to the interior Black Belt plantations and sold supplies on credit, to be reimbursed when the cotton was harvested later that year. From Mobile, McRae arranged for transshipment of the cotton to the international merchant houses in New York and Boston, from which it was shipped to European markets. These antebellum financial connections to international cotton markets made Colin McRae uniquely suited to assist in matters of overseas Confederate credit and finance. He was among the handful of Confederate leaders who truly understood the complexity of cotton-based international finance, and this expertise caused him to run the blockade.[33]

At the outset of the war, Colin McRae probably did not anticipate having to go abroad. In 1861 and 1862 he served as a provisional congressman from Alabama. McRae helped to jump-start two industrial concerns—the Shelby Iron Company and the Selma Foundry—that greatly enhanced rebel munitions production in the Deep South.[34] However, by 1863 the Confederacy desperately needed McRae's knowledge of cotton-based international finance. The businessman was asked to travel to Europe for a multifaceted mission. Foremost, he was to make sure that proceeds from the Erlanger Loan were being maximized. Second, he was to investigate allegations of corruption by Caleb Huse, a rebel procurer of supplies in London. The Confederate government eventually consolidated all European fundraising and supply purchases under McRae's control. But before he could address Confederate finance in Europe, McRae had to run the blockade out of Mobile. It is unclear which blockade-runner carried him out of Mobile in early 1863, but he arrived in Southampton, England, on May 13.[35]

In 1863 the Confederate States gave Colin McRae control of all government purchases in Europe. And starting in 1864, McRae coordinated blockade-runner cargoes for the Confederate government. In February 1864, the Confederate Congress passed a law that required blockade-runners to reserve 50 percent of their ships' cargo for government supplies. The Ordnance Bureau already owned several blockade-runners—the *Cornubia*, *Eugenie*, *Merrimac*, *Phantom*, and *Robert E. Lee*—as did some individual Southern states. But this statute ensured that privately owned ships also carried portions of their cargoes for the Confederacy instead of the private market. McRae coordinated the purchase and delivery of supplies to be loaded on blockade-runners, and he was also responsible for selling government-owned cotton carried on outbound trips through the Union cordon. In each of these endeavors McRae improved the financial standing of the Confederacy, but it was too little, too late.[36]

Colin McRae's mission to Europe in 1863 took far longer than he anticipated. He probably expected another blockade run on his journey back to the Confederacy, but he never got the opportunity. He remained in Europe when the war ended, and he never returned to the South. In 1867 he moved to Belize, where he died in 1877.[37] Colin McRae's wartime career demonstrated the crucial nature of blockade-running for the Confederacy. McRae improved on the system in which exported cotton, and cotton bonds that promised future delivery, generated desperately needed revenues in Europe to buy weapons, supplies, and even ships. Centralized government coordination of these sales, purchases, and shipments did not develop until 1864 under McRae's oversight, but the results were impressive. The businessman likely had a better understanding of the "big picture" of blockade-running than anyone outside the Confederacy. Among persons inside the Confederacy, McRae possessed knowledge of the subject that was probably second only to that of Ordnance Bureau head Josiah Gorgas. This is why Colin McRae's story is intimately tied to the larger narrative of blockade-running.

The three selected examples of intangible cargo—Matthew Fontaine Maury, Rose O'Neal Greenhow, and Colin J. McRae—each possessed a distinctive link to an international community and a personal link to blockade-running. Maury's prewar oceanographic studies brought him international fame. He charted trade routes that informed Confederate commerce raiders exactly where to look for US merchant shipping. The blockade-runners also benefited from Maury's scientific studies of currents and ocean mapping as they carried their illicit cargoes across the Atlantic Ocean.

Rose O'Neal Greenhow resorted to blockade-running for her Confederate mission abroad. One can imagine that the thrill of outrunning blockade squadrons and snubbing her nose one more time at the Yankees suited her personality. Greenhow's story is among the most fantastic in blockade-running lore, and whether or not one finds her adamant pro-Confederate outlook distasteful, one cannot help but be amazed by her life. Her espionage for the South is forever tied to the larger story of blockade-running.

Colin J. McRae passed through the Union cordon one time, but he had an enormous impact on blockade-running from mid-1863 onward as coordinator of government shipments. He saw the "big picture" of blockade-running and managed it as best he could in the Confederacy's last months. One can only speculate about the beneficial effects to the Confederate war effort had the government initiated stricter management of cargoes before 1864. As noted by these intangible examples, blockade-running touched far more aspects of the war effort than just the typical imports of munitions and exports of cotton.

Had one Southern emissary achieved Confederate recognition, the intangible cargo blockade-runners carried could have been as important as the tangible cargoes of war materiel, if not more so. Smuggled weapons killed Union soldiers, but one successful Confederate mission abroad could have irretrievably tilted the war toward victory for the South. This sense of importance in preventing Confederate diplomacy by interdicting blockade-runners caused the *Trent* affair of 1861. For a blockade squadron, capturing valuable intangible cargo was sometimes just as important as stanching the flow of guns and cotton. The Confederacy depended on surreptitious overseas transport to conduct international communication and diplomacy. The fact that the rebels operated any semblance of organized foreign diplomacy and international finance via blockade-runners is noteworthy.

Great Britain and Blockade-Running

Blockade diplomacy was a major aspect in the foreign policy of Great Britain, the United States, and the Confederacy. Again, Great Britain's first foreign policy goal in the Civil War was to avoid war with the United States. Britain wanted to diplomatically ensure a legal blockade that all nations respected. The second main goal of British foreign policy was to continue the flow of cotton from the Confederacy. This meant that despite its neutrality, Great Britain indirectly supported blockade-running. The nation's policy toward the blockade was a diplomatic one buttressed by Lord Russell and Lord Lyons and based on international law (see chapter 1), but Britain unofficially allowed for active support of blockade-running and turned a blind eye to blockade violations. Is it any wonder that the country's duplicitous actions caused American complaint and legal action in the postwar years? In hypocritical contradiction of foreign policy, some British officials actively assisted blockade-runners throughout the war.

British consulates around the Atlantic basin reported on blockade-runners after the blockade declaration in April 1861. Consuls in Bermuda, the Bahamas, St. John's, Cuba, Honduras, and Mexico all dispatched information to Lord Russell. At this early stage the official did not consider these ships blockade-runners, stating instead that they carried "bona fide" British goods. In accordance with the Declaration of Paris, the vessels were not blockade-runners since they flew a neutral flag and did not carry contraband. Also, if runners safely arrived at a Confederate port without being stopped, then the blockade was legally "null" per the Declaration of Paris. On May 30, 1861, the British government confidentially instructed Royal Navy officers to intervene on behalf of the nation's merchant ships should the US blockading force not be sufficient. On June 5 Robert Bunch, British consul in Charleston, observed six ships, three of them British, that had arrived since the blockade's declaration. The Union vessels' deep draft prevented navigation in the shallow channels, and Bunch reported a steady flow of merchant traffic. In New Orleans, the British consul noted in July that local newspapers decried the "paper blockade."[38] In the early months of the war, British consulate reports implied that vessels broke the blockade with ease and regularity.

Great Britain was not the only foreign power that hoped to benefit from wartime shipping. Port cities like Charleston, Mobile, and New Orleans had the most diverse populations in the Confederacy. Merchants, government officials, privateers, and sailors from all around the Atlantic world lived and worked in these blockaded areas. In addition to the Americans and British, Norwegians, Germans, and Russians were all eager to profit from illicit wartime trade.

Between May 28 and July 25, 1861, at least fifty-one vessels arrived in Charleston. Schooners, steamers, and sloops carried a variety of cargoes like rice, Sea Island cotton, upland cotton, turpentine, naval stores, sugar, cattle, sheep, iron, and liquor. Not one of these ships was approached by a Union blockader; rather, they entered and left Charleston unmolested. On July 23 a British vice-consul reported he sailed up and down the Carolina coast from Charleston to Hatteras without encountering a Union vessel. Charleston consul Robert Bunch declared, "It remains to be seen whether or no[t] a really effective blockade will now be established." At Wilmington, North Carolina, at least ninety-three vessels arrived and cleared between May 1 and July 25, 1861, bound for ports like Liverpool, Rio de Janeiro, London, Martinique, and Nassau. Steamship captains stated that three-hundred-ton vessels with less than eight feet of draft could easily navigate the channels into the Cape Fear River—one such ship cleared Wilmington on July 23 with 1,700 bales of cotton.[39] At this early stage the blockade thus appeared to be a sham.

It should not be surprising that in this early stage of the blockade British vessels came and went with such regularity. Union squadrons were arriving on station, vessels' availability was increasing, and US officers were learning the intricacies of local weather, shoals, and tides. It is noteworthy that British ships routinely traveled to and from Confederate ports in the spring and summer of 1861 without ever seeing a Union blockader. Captains filed affidavits to this effect in order to determine the blockade's legality—in terms of the Declaration of Paris, a blockade must be effective enough to prevent access in order to be binding. On August 5, Capt. Charles Grantham aboard the *William Seabrook* chronicled the absence of Union ships on his journey from Charleston to Fernandina, Florida. This was almost four months since the blockade's declaration, and Grantham noted where he expected to see Union squadrons but found none.[40] Reports of an absentee blockade provided the British Foreign Office with leverage in blockade diplomacy.

British consulates compiled information from blockade-running captains. These statements indicated easy access from April through July 1861, but reports dating from the late summer began to acknowledge a stronger Union naval presence. The full deployment of Union squadrons meant vessels could be notified of the blockade. However, Charleston consul Robert Bunch noted that British vessels passed the blockade undeterred and he believed the cordon to be "a laughing stock."[41] There is little doubt that Bunch's opinion was biased, since he was eager to inform the Foreign Office that the blockade was a farce for diplomatic purposes. Despite these prejudiced observations, the blockade was gradually being enforced.

August and September 1861 brought new developments for British officials and merchants. Steam-powered ships that had earlier passed through the blockade unmolested were now occasionally captured or forced to change destinations. In September the steamer *Gordon* and the sloop *Dixie* were able to run into Charleston, but the schooner *H. Middleton* was taken. Each successful vessel provided detailed information about the blockade's status to the British consulate. Reports implied that the Union blockade was proving difficult to enforce. According to observers, the blockaders' main problem was their size and their inability to pursue runners into shallower waters.[42]

As the contest between squadrons and runners intensified, British officials balanced diplomatic relations with America and continuation of cotton exports. This balancing act led to numerous reports about the Union blockade and blockade-runners. A great deal was at stake; detailed information regarding the blockade's effectiveness was critical to British mercantile success. Algernon Lyons, commander of the British ship *Racer*, performed a naval reconnaissance mission for Great Britain's government. Scouting the inlets of the southeastern coast from Charleston to Havana while commanding a British-flagged vessel, Lyons proceeded unchecked. He even held informal conversations with Union blockade ships along his route.

Lyons met with a Captain Green aboard the USS *Jamestown*, who told him that in two months on station "no vessel of any sort" had attempted to run out of Savannah. Lyons also met with a Captain Mercer of the USS *Wabash*, who informed him that in forty-five days only two vessels had tested the blockade, and both of them "were made prizes of."[43] Other than these two Union ships, Lyons and the *Racer* encountered no other blockaders while cruising the Southern coast for over a week. The captain concluded that a legal blockade existed at Charleston and Savannah but nowhere else. He also emphasized to his superiors that his conversations with Union captains were always private and confidential—in other words, off the record.

Lyons's detailed report illuminates two key points. Throughout May, June, and July, the British consulates were busy creating tables and lists of the vessels that successfully ran the blockade. However, Lyons's confidential conversations with blockading captains yielded a different picture— the US captains anecdotally supported claims of an effective blockade. Which set of data had greater credibility? Each view was distorted by the purposes of the messenger. British consuls hoped to show merchant shippers that trade continued despite the blockade, while blockade commanders wanted to demonstrate the opposite. In 1861 the British knew that vessels were disembarking from ports like Havana, Nassau, St. George, and Matamoros. As the war dragged on, Union blockade captains had indirect access to this type of information. US consuls usually forwarded it to them in a lengthy and time-consuming process during which the intelligence was passed through the State Department, then to the Navy Department, and finally to the blockade squadron leaders.

In the early stages of the war, the British government had a better "big picture" understanding of blockade-running than the Union squadrons. US fleets simply could not know the unknown, like the number of vessels leaving British ports, or the number of runners slipping through unseen. A second key point of Lyons's report was that blockade commanders' grandiose claims of success could be interpreted as a form of intimidation through misinformation. But given the British informational advantage in the Atlantic ports, making false claims could be a risky choice. Captains Green and Mercer most likely believed their arguments about an effective blockade. Significantly, even at the blockade's earliest and weakest deployment, blockade commanders were eager to declare their efforts effective.

Information was central to maintaining British trading operations in Atlantic ports. Great Britain collected intelligence on blockade squadrons and their tactics and chain of command. British records are replete with correspondence between captains exchanging information about the blockade. One of the many details gleaned was the discovery, by Capt. Algernon Lyons, that the captains of smaller US vessels did not have authority to pursue blockade-runners on their own.[44] This circumstance made shallow-water tactics even more effective. Once the runners evaded larger US ships, the smaller Union ships might not be authorized to pursue them. If this information was accurate, a blockade-runner could in theory steam right past a small Union vessel knowing it would sit idle.

In June, July, and August 1861 Great Britain gathered an intelligence table for the coast of Virginia and North Carolina. British vessels made as many as four runs each into the entrances of Cape Henry, Oregon Inlet, New Inlet, Cape Hatteras, Ocracoke Inlet, Cape Lookout, Beaufort, and the Cape Fear inlets. In those thirty-six voyages, the majority of the ships proceeded to Confederate ports without encountering the blockade squadrons. In the ten instances where runners made contact with the blockade, British commanders chatted informally with US captains, while British observers, judging from the breadth of their reports, made copious notes about Union ship types, sizes, and number of guns.[45] From this and other similar tables, British captains could reasonably deduce blockade squadron dispositions, movements, and tactics. Early in the war the US fleets were stretched thin and unable to cover every inlet. This collection of information allowed British captains to create an updateable map that could be used to slip through the cordon.

During August 1861, shipping into Confederate ports continued with little harassment from the blockade squadrons. In the North Carolina ports of Beaufort and Wilmington, British vessels arrived and cleared with regularity. At Beaufort, the 600-ton ship *Alliance* traveled from St. John and delivered lead and pig iron. Along the way she witnessed the *Pearl* arriving from the West Indies. In addition, the 778-ton vessel *Gondar* traveled direct from Liverpool with salt and iron. Eleven schooners and two steamers arrived safely in Wilmington as well.[46] These early months proved to be the heyday of blockade-running, and the British were rightly worried that the blockade would become stronger.

Great Britain's consul in Charleston, Robert Bunch, informed his superiors about the status of the blockade at the end of September 1861. Bunch noted that he had performed his duties, "the absolute necessity of . . . procuring and transmitting all possible particulars respecting the blockade of this coast." He also noted several interesting facts about the early blockade. While the Union squadrons were not allowing ingress to foreign-flagged vessels, they were allowing ingress to those flagged as Confederate—presumably to pin them in rebel ports. Foreign-flagged ships were not allowed into port if they contained "guns, men, and stores." Bunch could not account for why the blockade fleets left their stations at different intervals, except that it was not due to weather. He speculated that the departures were related to orders, but they likely owed to a combination of changing assignments, coal resupply, and repairs.

Bunch further reported that smaller British vessels between 50 and 330 tons, like the *Rowena* (330) and *John Welch* (250), were safely running between Charleston and Savannah and then on to the West Indies. So many ships arrived in Charleston in August and September 1861 that Bunch made a full-page table to summarize the voyages. During those months, British steamers, schooners, and sloops entered the port almost daily. Several steamers were among them: the *William Seabrook* (two arrivals); the *General Clinch*, *John Randolph*, *Chesterfield*, and *Dixie* (three arrivals each); and the *Telegraph*. These ships brought cattle, hides, coal, corn, sugar, molasses, fruit, cigars, and coffee, and they hailed from a variety of American and foreign ports, including Savannah, Beaufort, Fernandina, Havana, Rio de Janeiro, Trinidad de Cuba, Puerto Cabello, and many others.[47] Even as late as September 1861, Charleston was virtually an open port despite the blockade declaration.

In the Gulf of Mexico, the British kept a close watch on shipping into and out of Galveston and particularly New Orleans. The British consul in Galveston, Arthur T. Lynn, reported that no fewer than thirteen vessels entered and left New Orleans in July. However, these ships were smaller, the largest being *Texas Ranger* (237 tons) and the others being schooners between 30 and 60 tons. Lynn correctly pointed out that July shipping was immaterial, since the key month for exporting cotton was September. In this respect, the Union blockade benefited from timing, since it allowed

several months to implement an interdiction of New Orleans. Lynn estimated that 260,000 bales of cotton could be exported in September if the
blockade could be circumvented.[48]

Blockade-runners in the Gulf of Mexico had several advantages over
those operating in the Atlantic, including more predictable waters, greater
proximity to Mexico and Honduras, and ample hiding places around Cuba.
Lynn admitted his goal was to get cotton "off the plantations" and out to
sea. Galveston was not properly blockaded until after September, and Lynn
observed that, small ships willing to "run under the guns" of the USS
Santee were arriving in port as late as October 19. In fact, October 1861
was an important month because all major Confederate ports from Norfolk
to Galveston now had a Union blockade presence for the first time. The
wide-open blockade-running of April through September ebbed. George
Coppell, acting British consul in New Orleans, described the new situation.
US forces seized a telegraph station and forced the mouth of the Mississippi River with shallow-draft vessels. These actions hampered Great Britain's consular communication and shipping, and they were the harbingers
of a more vigilant Union blockade of New Orleans.[49]

In the fall of 1861, the British Admiralty and Foreign Office assembled a
set of tables listing vessels that had run the blockade—in either direction—
at all of its Atlantic and Caribbean ports. One table showed that at least
fifty-five vessels, including repeat runs by several ships, entered and exited Wilmington in May, June, and July, but most of these ships were sail
powered. By comparison, at least twenty-eight vessels entered Charleston between May and August, but nine were steam-powered and flying
Confederate flags. In the period between August 29 and September 16,
blockade-runners made it into, or out of, Charleston a total of sixteen
times—a rate of almost once per day.[50]

Blockade-running also continued to and from Savannah despite British
reports that this port was effectively blockaded. Between May and August,
twenty-four blockade runs were made to or from Savannah. Along the Gulf
Coast, at least fifty-six violations occurred at Mobile in the months of June,
July, and August. So many vessels arrived in New Orleans in the summer
of 1861 that the British tables identifying them ran on for several pages.
At least one hundred ships ran into and out of New Orleans in May and
June, but in July that number plummeted to fifteen, and in August only
seventeen vessels cleared the Crescent City. Shipping from New Orleans
was curtailed at the beginning of July 1861.[51]

By the fall of 1861, British reports of blockade-running continued, but they were now noting some captures. British consul in New York Edward Archibald, described the high-profile runners *Bermuda* and *Fingal*, whose fate was highly publicized in the Union and Confederacy. He noted that the *Bermuda* successfully ran to Liverpool, but the *Fingal* was bottled up in Savannah. The latter vessel was eventually converted into an ironclad, the CSS *Atlanta*, and captured by Union blockaders in 1863. However, Archibald stated that the *Bermuda* not only ran to Liverpool and back again with "guns, rifles, [and] shot and shell," but it also encountered no Union blockade ships on any of its voyages. The consul further claimed that smaller vessels ran the blockade with regularity throughout 1861.[52] The blockade was indeed tightening in late 1861, but only selectively, with re-spect to sail-powered ships and the largest steam-powered vessels.

Britain's consul in Savannah, A. Fullarton, described how the runners adapted to a more stringent blockade in the fall of 1861. He noted that "high prices . . . stimulated the people to greater exertions in procuring a larger supply." To avoid the attention of the Union blockade squadron, the locals "[outfitted] a number of small vessels suitable for the West Indies trade and the peculiarities of this coast." In other words, until the Union could implement an inside, or close, blockade in Georgia's intracoastal waters, small blockade-runners could slip out unmolested past the US squadron stationed off the mouth of the Savannah River. This adaptation created a robust trade between Savannah and the West Indies starting in September 1861. With respect to Savannah, Fullarton sarcastically declared, "So much for the blockade of this port."[53] As seen in the narrative of the blockade-runner *Standard*, the Union navy eventually plugged this loophole in the blockade around Savannah starting in early 1862. However, the issues con-cerning the port's blockade provide a perfect example of the measures and countermeasures both squadrons and runners took throughout the war.

Consul Fullarton also described the blockade presence at Savannah's main entrance via the river. Although two large Union ships could block the main channel, Fullarton stated, smaller vessels still got through using that route. He noted that the blockade would mysteriously lift, and not be-cause of foul weather or pursuit of a runner, but by a commander's order. The consul therefore concluded, that "The blockade . . . is maintained in a very ineffective manner, the vessels being too few in number, and not suit-able in class for the purpose of preventing access." This assessment fit with Confederate arguments concerning a paper blockade, and other British consuls repeated Fullarton's opinion. He described a porous blockade at best, calling it one in which "vessels merely cruise up and down, visiting for a few days . . . one harbor or another." The consul recommended that full "advantage . . . be taken of this," since there were "numerous vessels successfully running the blockade to and from the West Indies, in most cases without seeing the blockading vessels at all."[54]

Fullarton's description of conditions around Savannah is a microcosm of the immense importance of blockade diplomacy in the fall of 1861 into the winter of 1862. If the Union navy could not manage to scrape together a legitimate blockade in early 1862, Great Britain was poised to ignore it altogether. If one adds the inflammatory conditions of the *Trent* affair to this diplomatic situation, then one can appreciate Gideon Welles's ability to press ships into service and create a genuine blockade.

British consular reports had a twofold mission. Foremost, consuls were to report accurate information about trade conditions, but a secondary goal was to provide evidence to refute the blockade's legal standing—to protect British diplomatic interests. The British consul in Savannah, Edward Molyneux, contributed to this collection of intelligence. In November 1861, he lamented the Union capture of Port Royal, analyzing the event in a peculiar way. He did not understand that the US Navy wanted the port as a supply base to maintain blockade squadrons. Instead, he believed Port Royal was seized because of blockade-running in the area. In other words, Molyneux thought the Union capture of Port Royal proved the blockade was ineffective. The consul understood, however, that the loss of Port Royal and Tybee Island would "effectively blockade" the Savannah River in the future. He pointed to the "bitter" response of Southern landowners in the area as proof of strong "determination for their independence," and he believed this attitude was prevalent throughout all the "Southern states."[55] Molyneux peppered his consular reports with rebel-leaning analysis. This seemingly pro-Confederate attitude was not unusual among consular dispatches since consuls thought the blockade's damage to British commerce was a serious offense.

Back in Charleston, consul Robert Bunch reported that October and November 1861 had been good months for British shipping, observing, "The blockade can scarcely be considered effective." In the role of legal posturing, Bunch produced affidavits signed by ship captains claiming no blockade was in effect. When they encountered the Union squadron in late 1861, captains reported seeing two to four vessels. Bunch noted that

British ships entered and cleared Charleston at the rate of one per day in October, including the *Cecile* and *John A. Moore*. In November he listed thirty-five ships that arrived in Charleston, but these were mainly small, sail-powered vessels that carried between 1,000 and 3,900 bushels of rice or 20 to 100 bales of cotton.[56] It is difficult to gauge the true effectiveness of the Union blockade from such reports, since Bunch was among those trying to discredit the blockade's legal standing.

Confederate diplomats were eager to reinforce British consular reports of a weak blockade. In early 1862, James M. Mason, Confederate commissioner to Great Britain, hoped to prove the blockade was a farce. Mason argued to Lord Russell that large vessels continued to violate the blockade through main channels, and "wishing to be perfectly frank," he contended that the smaller vessels arriving by inland channels proved the blockade was legally null. As per the Declaration of Paris, Mason argued the blockade was pierced so consistently that it should not be recognized. The commissioner noted the long list of arrivals and departures from Confederate ports in the last three months of 1861, and he hoped to nudge Britain toward outright refutation of the blockade's legality.[57]

This was the ideal time for Confederate envoys to attack the blockade's legitimacy. The *Trent* affair had soured relations between the US and Great Britain, and Her Majesty's government was formulating arguments for and against Confederate recognition. If Great Britain was going to declare the blockade illegal, it would do so in early 1862 for a couple of reasons. First, throughout 1861 the Union blockade had been more of a de jure deployment than a de facto cordon of naval ships. The number of blockade violations in 1861 was embarrassing for the US Navy. However, in 1862 deployment of ships was making the blockade a reality. If Great Britain wanted to declare the Union blockade illegal, it needed to do so before the US capacity to purchase, build, and deploy sufficient blockade vessels came to fruition. The second reason early 1862 was the ideal time for British refutation of the blockade was that the Union appeared to be losing the war. An ineffectual blockade was only one problem among several mortifying aspects of the Union war effort. The Confederates won most major battles of 1861, and U. S. Grant's success in the Tennessee River valley at Fort Donelson and Shiloh still lay in the not-too-distant future.

Several British government departments associated with foreign policy collected information about blockade-running. Consular tabulations of blockade violations in late 1861 differed from the data compiled by the

British Admiralty. Admiralty records dating from August through October 1861 show a slightly different set of ships and cargoes. For example, according to the British Admiralty reports in Havana, the average blockade-runner size was 131 tons, with the largest steamer, the *Theodora*, topping the list at 578 tons. Most of the schooners were between 100 and 150 tons.[58] Vessels using Havana as a transshipment point ran the blockade into Mobile, New Orleans, or Galveston. The variance of shipping information between the Foreign Office and the Admiralty showed that the consulates were only seeing a small portion of the overall blockade-running picture. These consular snapshots provided one portion of intelligence about the interdiction, but back in London, Lord Russell in the Foreign Office could compare these reports with the Admiralty's intelligence to develop a more holistic analysis of the Union blockade.

The winter of 1861–62 witnessed a decrease in the number of blockade violations. The Union blockade squadrons were increasing in numbers. Britain's consul in Savannah, Edward Molyneux, noted that only three vessels escaped that port in February 1862, all through the southern passage used by smaller runners. The steamer *Kate*, however, delivered ten thousand Enfield rifles and forty thousand pounds of gunpowder, and continued to travel back and forth between Nassau and Confederate ports.[59]

In the spring of 1862, a new pattern emerged for British blockade-running in the Gulf of Mexico. In the early months of 1862, Lord Russell worried about British ships being interdicted in Mexican territorial waters. Lord Russell requested the Admiralty provide a stronger naval presence as a deterrent. This was a precursor to the legal entanglement over British shipping in Matamoros, Mexico. The *Labuan* affair (see chapter 1) was one such episode that occurred at the disputed zone at the mouth of the Rio Grande. Britain's continued trade through Matamoros became a sore spot for the Lincoln administration. In 1862 British schooners and steamers were stopped and harassed in the waters between Cuba and the Florida Keys. British consuls recorded every detail of these encounters for legal purposes, and it was usually necessary, as in the case of the British ship *Lion*, which was seized by the US Navy. Lord Lyons assured the Lincoln administration that the *Lion* "had nothing contraband onboard."[60] This was just one of the numerous examples of the British government pushing for the release of seized British ships.

In 1861 the British navy collected intelligence about the blockade, but in 1862 the Royal Navy transitioned to a policy of *friendly intimidation*. In April 1862, Lord Lyons suggested to Lord Russell that Britain "send instructions to the United States' blockading ships . . . to promote harmony . . . between the British and American squadrons." Lyons sought a blockade détente, but he also noted, "[The US blockaders] appear to be exercising a right of visit" or, in less diplomatic terms, illegal searching "that is unauthorized by international law."[61] In some instances, the British representative contacted the rear admiral of the blockade squadron to complain. This tactic warrants some analysis. Whether a British ship's passage was legal or not, Britain used government officials and naval officers to confront Union blockade squadron commanders, either to question their actions or to remind them of international law. As we have seen, US squadron commanders were briefed on the details of international law, but they were ordered to avoid any legal arguments. This detail was significant because the Royal Navy and its diplomats challenged the blockade's legality at the point of contention—where blockaders were stopping runners—instead of solely in the diplomatic arena.

This friendly intimidation continued and was part of an unwritten grand bargain between the United States and Great Britain. The delicate balance of blockade diplomacy using friendly intimidation might be summarized thus: Great Britain could argue blockade legality through diplomats or resort to naval firepower if necessary, but the US and Britain had to reach a mutual understanding that some amount of British shipping to and from the Confederacy could occur. Likewise, while Union squadrons might resort to a show of force to deter British naval vessels from interfering in blockade duties, most US captains were naturally hesitant to fire on a British vessel. Evidence shows that most warning shots were just that, and not acts of war.[62] Britain's friendly intimidation continued throughout 1862 but waned as the war transitioned into 1863 and 1864.

Blockade-running disrupted normal trade conditions in the Atlantic maritime economic system. Due to the large number of blockade-runners using Nassau as a transshipment point, the governor of the Bahamas, C. J. Bayley, was caught in a predicament. Nassau's regular trade with New York now involved cargoes of Southern cotton brought out by British blockade-runners. However, the United States protested that items sent from New York to Nassau, especially coal, should be banned. Technically this was all legitimate commerce, but according to Bayley, the US wanted to have its proverbial cake and eat it too. The governor protested in May 1862, "The Custom House authorities in New York have taken measures to impede or prevent the shipment of ordinary supplies from that city to this port. . . . As it is known that this port has been the resort of vessels from the Confederate

States of America, and as it may be presumed that cargoes shipped in New York for this port are really intended for the ports of the Southern Confederacy, it is just possible that the officers of the Custom House in that city may have taken upon themselves the responsibility of forbidding the exportation of goods and articles of consumption in Nassau."[63]

Bayley implored Lord Lyons to oppose trade restrictions between New York and Nassau, but the Union customhouse officials were correct—the additional coal was being used to power blockade-runners. Owners of the coal-transport vessel *Time* stated that the vast amounts of imported coal owed to "increased steam communication between [the Bahamas] and the mother country." But Union authorities were not fooled. In a series of rulings relayed to the British, US treasury secretary Salmon P. Chase declared that the embargo of goods suspected of reaching Confederate ports was legal. Despite some pushback, Lord Lyons admitted to Lord Russell, "It could hardly be a matter of surprise that the Custom-House officials should look with some suspicion on the extraordinarily large exports to the Bahamas of articles which happened to be in particular request in the States blockaded by the Federal cruisers."[64]

Even if the British wanted to stop the illegal trade—which they did not—it was nearly impossible to do so in the Bahamas. A British vice admiral informed his superiors that he was not "disposed to scrutinize too minutely . . . the vast contraband trade of which these islands [were] the focus." The type and sheer volume of goods coming in and out of Nassau due to blockade-running caused a diplomatic reassessment of trade relations. In June 1862, US and British officials reached an agreement resuming trade between New York and Nassau unless specific intelligence proved a commodity was directly bound for the Confederacy.[65]

British officials around the Atlantic littoral argued against trade restrictions. They contended that legitimate goods, even necessities, could be denied based on the Union argument that they aided the Confederacy. Representatives of Great Britain calculated exactly how many tons of commodities were required, and some US officials implied that by doing so, they were involved in a blockade-running conspiracy. Officially, British harbor masters were engaged in nothing of the sort, and it was not their duty to confirm the destination of every ship leaving a British-controlled port. Blockade-runners provided false destination information in any case, but everyone in port, including high-ranking British officials, knew which ships were bound for the Confederacy. This British knowledge of blockade-running was explained away by technicalities, but this reality re-flected economic demand and a unique profit opportunity that was not to be wasted.[66]

In August 1862, US secretary of state William Seward alleged that Brit-ish officials encouraged blockade-running. He noted that trade to Nassau had increased in 1862 out of proportion to previous years, and he believed the types of goods traded had changed to those "not suited to the wants of the inhabitants." Seward claimed that Great Britain performed no over-sight of the illicit trade in Nassau. In one instance, "the British schooner *Time* . . . discharged her entire cargo [of coal] into the rebel steamer *Cecile* then lying in the harbor." Seized letters proved that merchant houses in London, Nassau, and Charleston conspired to facilitate contraband trans-port through the Bahamas, and even provided backup plans in case run-ning the blockade proved more difficult than anticipated.[67] So despite of-ficial British statements to the contrary, the US fully understood that in 1862 local British leaders were complicit in aiding blockade-runners.

William Stuart, British chargés d'affaires in Washington, replied to Seward's complaint in September 1862. He reminded the secretary of state that international law was on Britain's side because British ships carried normal trade goods, not contraband. Stuart declared that if the US at-tempted to restrict Great Britain's legitimate trade in the Americas, then the US was choosing to enter a state of "quasi-hostility." The implication was clear—there was a line intentionally shielding both legal and illegal trade that the United States must not cross. Stuart explained that any instances of illegal trade were accidents of geography that could not be eliminated by British controls. In summation, the chargés d'affaires frankly told Seward, "A neutral ship having succeeded in evading a blockade af-fords no ground for international complaint." From the British perspec-tive, blockade-runners capable of escaping Union squadrons were the US Navy's problem, not Great Britain's. Lord Russell supported Stuart's re-sponse to Seward, and he reaffirmed that the "notorious existence of an extensive trade . . . between the so-styled Confederate States and Nassau" was irrelevant to larger arguments of blockade diplomacy.[68]

Great Britain's Foreign Office and Admiralty knew full well the extent of blockade-running, and in specific cases the British government even provided support. One such example was Matamoros. British merchants in Matamoros submitted reports to the Foreign Office describing how the US blockade off the Rio Grande diminished their trade. From the British standpoint, Matamoros was a neutral Mexican port, but from the American perspective, Matamoros was a conduit for Texas contraband. In October 1862, a representative of Stolterfoht & Sons, a Liverpool merchant house, informed Lord Russell about a "great movement" of cotton out of Texas through Matamoros. The representative expected "over 100,000 bales" to be exported that quarter alone, and the merchant offered to lessen any diplomatic troubles by excluding other contraband. "It was a matter of great importance" to British traders to know whether the British Admiralty might station any warships near Matamoros to protect their shipping. This merchant's request was granted; the British warships *Orlando*, *Greyhound*, and *Immortalite* were posted off the mouth of the Rio Grande to protect the rights of British traders in Matamoros.[69]

In some respects, however, the British Foreign Office and Admiralty were not fully aware of the depth of British subjects' participation in blockade-running. In 1863, an investigation disclosed that British port officials, commanders, and merchants were complicit in this shadowy business. In this case, the inquiry focused on ports in England itself—not far-flung colonial harbors with less oversight. Its findings were not a revelation to British leaders, but these officials nevertheless received a wake-up-call of sorts to be more careful in their forbearance. At many English ports, ads solicited what appeared to be legitimate work on a ship's crew. However, once the ship was at sea, the crew discussed the real contractual arrangements for blockade-running. Some crew members were doubtless surprised to learn they were working on a blockade-runner, but some knew the unspoken terms before embarkation.

Would-be blockade-runners were sometimes exposed when they were forced back to British ports for repairs. The *Agrippina* carried 148 cases of rifles, 400 barrels of gunpowder, and 1,840 cases of cartridges, but it was compelled to return to Plymouth harbor. The *Harriet Pinckney* was also forced back to safe harbor in Plymouth with a cargo of 11,340 rifles. British customs officials would never have known about these departures or cargoes had the ships not had to return to port. A typical conclusion to these types of investigations read as follows: "No communication was made to the [customhouse] collector . . . and when [the vessel] disappeared it was supposed she had merely run out to try her machinery. . . . There does not appear to be any neglect of duty on the part of the Customs officer on this matter."[70] In the cases of the *Agrippina* and the *Harriet Pinckney*, both ships were bound for Bermuda, where their cargoes would have been transferred to a blockade-runner. British port officials could not prevent the front end of blockade-running out of England itself, and it was doubtful whether British colonial officials in the Bahamas or Bermuda could have done so either—even if they had wanted to.

According to British reports, blockade-running activity increased in 1863. Statistical data shows the average number of successful runs by steam-powered blockade-runners rose from 2.8 in 1862 to 5.1 in 1863, and the number of steam-powered vessels making at least one blockade run increased from 114 in 1862 to 152 in 1863 (see chapter 5—Price data). British reports also detailed the purchase of new blockade-running ships, spare parts, and engines sold to the Confederacy. According to both British records and available statistical data, steam-powered blockade-runners made an estimated 780 runs in 1863. The average capacity of those vessels was 451 tons, so up to 352,000 tons of goods were transported through the blockade. This was a significant increase over 1862, which witnessed an approximate total of 183,000 tons of cargo smuggled through the Union cordon.[71]

In June 1863, US consul to the Bahamas S. C. Hawley wrote to Secretary of State Seward about the continued profitability of blockade-running. Hawley had previously told Seward that the business was waning, but he now believed otherwise. The consul listed the blockade-runners operating out of Nassau and correctly, as it turned out, estimated that the smugglers completed about "4 1/3 voyages" before capture by the Union blockaders. At that rate, the profits to be made still outweighed the risk of loss. Hawley worried that profitability was attracting more blockade-runners. "The number [of runners] engaged is as great as ever," he warned, "and I do not expect to see it reduced until our blockade is made more effective." Hawley rhetorically asked his superior, "Suppose a foreign power should allege that our blockade is null and void for want of force or vigilance, would a reply that our blockade had defeated or captured 1 in 10 or 12 of the ventures satisfy the requirements of the law of blockade?"[72] Hawley understood the basic economics—so long as blockade-running remained profitable and ships violated it several times before capture, investors and crews would always be willing to take the risk.

By the end of 1863, Great Britain curtailed its support of blockade-running. For example, in November 1863, communication between London and Bermuda became conveniently difficult. The British dockyard manager was lax in submitting reports, or he was intentionally mute about his country's continued furtherance of blockade-running. Shortly thereafter, a new dockyard manager was assigned to Bermuda, and Admiral Milne informed him of the official British position on blockade runners. If asked, the manager was to answer that he "was not aware" of any blockade-running steamers under repair in Bermuda. The next day, Milne admitted to "many repairs" of such vessels in Bermuda. He also noted that the term "repairs" extended to the provisioning of coal for blockade-runners. The new dockyard manager responded "[Surely] it must have been obvious what was the nature of the vessel's employment." The admiral's official reply was that he "was not aware of [the ships'] character." Milne expected the new dockyard manager to continue Great Britain's covert assistance to blockade-runners in Bermuda. The pattern was simple—British colonial ports facilitated blockade-running with full knowledge of the trade but with only a thin veil of plausible deniability.

Admiral Milne finally resorted to a strained definition of culpability. He admitted, "These steamers are blockade runners carrying arms and munitions to [the] southern states . . . [but] we don't know exactly when they ran the blockade." According to Milne, if the ships in question had broken through the cordon three months prior to coming to Bermuda, then they were no longer considered blockade-runners.[73] It is unclear how the admiral arrived at this calculation, but he reaffirmed Britain's maritime responsibility to take in damaged vessels in the mid-Atlantic. In reality, Great Britain was eagerly assisting in coaling blockade-runners in its colonial ports, including Nassau in the Bahamas, St. George in Bermuda, and Halifax in Nova Scotia, Canada.

Events in 1863 showed that the Union was winning the war, and as a result, British assistance to blockade-runners became less visible thereafter. Once British officials realized the Confederacy would likely be defeated, they became less egregious in supporting the illegal trade. In early 1864, the Foreign Ministry received a stern warning from Seward concerning the blockade-runner *Banshee*. The vessel was captured trying to enter Wilmington, and most of the crew were British subjects. In 1861 or 1862 this incident would have been handled with diplomatic delicacy, but now Seward had the upper hand, and he listed the British subjects' names and summarized their testimony. Thirty-four British subjects were captured, and they attested to a total of eighty-nine blockade runs among them—an average of 2.6 runs per man. One Irish crew member had run the blockade sixteen times! This was obviously a veteran, mostly British crew and the secretary of state demanded they be prevented from future service.[74] By 1864 evidence of Great Britain's complicity in blockade running was firmly established. In the war's final year, British officials constructed a stronger legal defense to be used in any postwar court battles.

British policy toward blockade-running in 1864 and 1865 was based on silent consent instead of active participation. British subjects continued to break through the Union cordon, and there was little that could be done to stop them, but now Great Britain's government was less likely to offer them protection. As historian Amanda Foreman notes, in 1864 "the cost of shipping supplies to the Confederacy and the increasing likelihood of capture were wiping out the profits of blockade running." On both ends of the supply chain—in Great Britain and outside Confederate ports—the booming business of contraband smuggling was being curtailed. Part of this equation was the Confederacy's inability to procure credit in British markets. The Erlanger Loan of 1863, in which cotton bonds were sold on European financial markets, was trading below par. The promise of exported cotton held less value as the Confederacy's chances of independence diminished in 1864. British merchants were less eager to advance the capital needed for blockade-running ventures—although some still did.[75]

For its part in blockade-running, the British government could only look the other way for so long. As the reality of Union victory became obvious in 1864, British officials could no longer afford to antagonize the United States over blockade legalities. In fact, by 1864 British policy had shifted from aggressive pursuit of maritime rights to a defensive posture. It was clear that the world's preeminent naval power—Great Britain—would have to coexist with the world's emergent naval power—the United States. However, prior British complicity in blockade-running and commerce raiding complicated diplomatic relations between the two nations.

British documentation of blockade-running from 1861 to 1865 offers a study in contrasts. First, when a British ship was harassed, fired on, or captured, British officials generated a flood of documentation—testimonies, enclosures, and affidavits—to build a legal case against the Union interdiction. On the other hand, when a dozen or more British ships successfully ran the blockade, officials simply summarized the runs on a one-page table. Thus, the British treated their nation's harassed vessels as victims of US aggression, and they treated blockade-running as regular commerce. But Great Britain's legal position eroded in 1863 once the Union forged a path to victory. Britain's open and contemptuous support of blockade running in 1861 and 1862 was tempered by the increasing reality of Union victory after 1863. British officials had to reckon with the postwar emergence of a United States that harbored ill will toward Great Britain.

Commerce Raiders and the Blockade

Commerce raiders achieved some of the Confederacy's greatest naval successes, indirectly affecting the Union blockade as a result. At least nine vessels operated as Confederate commerce raiders—the *Sumter, Nashville, Shenandoah, Georgia, Tallahassee, Rappahannock, Chickamauga, Florida,* and *Alabama.* However, not all of these ships had an equal opportunity to prey on the US merchant fleet due to factors like construction timing and the progress of the war. It was much easier for rebel raiders to destroy Union shipping from 1861 to 1863 than in the last two years of the war. Built in England specifically for predation of the US merchant fleet, the CSS *Alabama* and the CSS *Florida* were the two most important Confederate commerce raiders. The ships' exploits filled Northern and Southern newspapers, giving the vessels legendary status and creating notoriety for their captains, John Newland Maffitt on the CSS *Florida* and Raphael Semmes on the CSS *Alabama.*[76] The commerce raiders and the blockade were inextricably linked as components of the Union and Confederate naval strategies.

The CSS *Florida* ran the blockade twice, coming into Mobile, Alabama, in broad daylight on September 4, 1862, and leaving again on January 16, 1863. John Newland Maffitt was an experienced blockade-runner and among the most knowledgeable naval officers, Union or Confederate, about the entrances to Confederate ports. He earned fame for his daring daytime blockade breach in September 1862, which seriously damaged his vessel. Upon departing from Mobile in January 1863, Maffitt escaped the USS *Cuyler,* one of the fastest ships in the blockade squadron, and commanded the *Florida* on a successful commerce-raiding cruise down to South America, across the Central Atlantic, into the Northern Atlantic, and finally to port in France. Maffitt relinquished command in September 1863, but the *Florida* attacked merchantmen until US forces captured it in a Brazilian port in October 1864. Maffitt's successful blockade run into Mobile, where he oversaw the *Florida*'s repair, resupply, and refitting, and his breach of the cordons again in January 1863 gave the CSS *Florida* an opportunity to devastate US merchant shipping. In its career the *Florida* destroyed forty-three US ships valued at over $4 million, and it captured or bonded another fourteen vessels.[77] The inability of the blockade squadron outside Mobile to capture or destroy the *Florida* in either 1862 or 1863 had dire consequences for US merchant shipping.

The most infamous Confederate commerce raider was the CSS *Alabama,* commanded by Raphael Semmes. Both the *Alabama* and its captain attained legendary status in the transatlantic popular mind. Newspapers in the North, the South, Great Britain, and around the world heard tales of the raider's exploits—some exaggerated. But there was no need for hyperbole when it came to the *Alabama*'s devastation of the US merchant fleet. The vessel never had to run the Union blockade, although it did sink a Union blockader, the USS *Hatteras*, off Galveston, Texas, in January 1863.[78]

The main long-term effect of the *Alabama*'s cruise was to divert naval resources away from the blockade. In December 1862, Gideon Welles admitted his displeasure at being forced to "detach so many of [the navy's] best craft, on the fruitless errand of searching the wide ocean for" the *Alabama*. The allocation of resources to catch the commerce raider directly impacted the blockade. In the weeks leading up to the naval assault on Charleston in April 1863, Secretary Welles informed the mastermind of the pending assault, Samuel DuPont, "A large number of our best wooden vessels, necessary for the blockade . . . are unfortunately required in the West Indies to pursue the *Florida* and *Alabama*."[79] The lack of anticipation and coordination among the Union fleet kept the *Alabama* one step ahead of its pursuers. The vessel wreaked havoc on US merchant shipping until the USS *Kearsarge* finally destroyed it off the coast of Cherbourg, France, in August 1864. Details of the *Alabama*'s English origins ruptured relations between the US and Great Britain, and this grievance was not resolved until 1872 by an international court in the *Alabama* claims.

The construction of Confederate commerce raiders depended on covert support in Great Britain. Official British policy prevented building warships for either side of the Civil War, but investigators uncovered a network of British subjects who supported rebel commerce raiders. Recruiters in London filled the crews of Confederate ships. At the Crown and Shears pub in London, two men called Champion and the Dutchman recruited sailors. In the case of the CSS *Rappahannock*, the recruiters paid prospective seamen's passage to Calais to board the Confederate ship. Some recruits were tricked into signing on, and once the true nature of their mission was discovered they opted out. The captain attempted to rally the would-be crew members with a rousing speech: "You men know what you are engaged to do; you are now on your own hook, and whatever you can make at sea, the better for you. You are now going privateering, the same as the 'Alabama' and the 'Florida.' You men are going to fight for money, and I am going to fight for glory." But in many cases, British crew members stayed on, presumably for a sense of adventure and the potential for profits.

The CSS *Rappahannock* was exceptional because it had formerly been a

British-owned vessel named the *Victor*. At some point, Confederate agents in Calais purchased the ship and converted it into a commerce raider. The British government found this egregious act illegal, but British lawyers advised Lord Russell that an indictment of the shipowners should be delayed until they "received and considered further evidence."[80] This episode was just one more piece of evidence proving Great Britain's complicity in Confederate commerce raiding.

In the fall of 1864, some Confederate leaders believed commerce raiders were unintentionally refocusing Union blockade strategy. The CSS *Tallahassee* ran out of Wilmington on August 6, 1864, and successfully destroyed over thirty ships before its return. In addition, the CSS *Chickamauga* made a successful sortie out of Wilmington in late October 1864. Maj. Gen. W.H. Chase Whiting, commander of the Cape Fear area Confederate defenses, believed the commerce raiders made Union blockade strategists target Wilmington. However, Whiting begged the Confederate high command to leave the raiders in the vicinity for defensive purposes. President Davis wanted the *Tallahassee* and *Chickamauga* to run out of Wilmington and prey on Yankee merchantmen, and he noted the potential alleviating benefits of the "withdrawal of a portion of the blockading force from Wilmington" to hunt them. Stating, "[The] presence of these vessels in [Wilmington] . . . increases the rigor of the blockade," the Confederate president contended that if they ran out to attack merchant shipping, then the Wilmington blockade would be weakened.[81]

Union blockade leaders were concerned about the presence of the *Tallahassee* and the *Chickamauga*, but it is unclear whether the ships' presence altered blockade strategy. If anything, the successful raids only further showed the Union high command that Wilmington needed to be captured outright. Had it increased the Cape Fear blockade in direct response to the commerce raiders' activities, the US Navy would have provided a brief example of an offensive blockade in an attempt to suppress the enemy's capital ships.

Rebel commerce raiders occasionally confronted the Union blockade, and they indirectly affected American blockade policy. The US merchant fleet lost 110,000 tons of shipping to Confederate commerce raiders and sustained an estimated $25 million in losses. But lasting damage came when American owners switched registry by selling their vessels to parties from neutral countries. An estimated 800,000 tons of shipping was reflagged to avoid destruction. According to some historians, this "flight from the flag" had devastating long-term consequences for the American merchant marine. British buyers benefited from desperate American sellers as British purchases of US ships increased from 71,673 tons in 1861 to 252,579 tons in 1863. Rebel commerce raiders crippled the US merchant fleet, as did the actions taken to avoid destruction. Historian George Dalzell speculates that Confederate raiders "did greater and more permanent damage to the entire nation than the blockaders inflicted on the South." That is questionable, but it is remarkable that of the 237 merchant ships Confederate commerce raiders destroyed, not one fatality occurred![82] Unfortunately, that record of humane treatment would not be repeated in twentieth-century commerce raiding.

Conclusion

Blockade-running was a lot like other short-lived boom economies in the nineteenth century; it attracted a wide assortment of characters from around the globe looking to get rich quick. The main factor was the short time frame for making money. The profit window for blockade running was only open for an undeterminable period, and that window began to gradually close after 1861. Unlike other boom economies, however, such as the 1849 California gold rush, wartime blockade-running was not the foundation for any future economic development. If the South had won the war, one might argue that blockade-running would have become the basis for a southern postwar merchant marine—a major development, since the South was dependent on northern shipping up to 1860. But this did not occur. If there was a successful economic aspect of blockade-running, it was that the activity attracted great sums of outside capital put to use on behalf of the Confederate war effort. So long as profits could be made by smuggling materiel into the Confederacy, capitalists, primarily in Great Britain, would be willing to finance such expeditions—whether they were technically legal or not. Blockade-running was among the most lucrative boom economies in the Civil War, and it remains one of the most fascinating episodes in American history.

CHAPTER 4

———— ★ ————

The Psychology of the Blockade

THE UNION BLOCKADE OF Confederate ports was more than just another military campaign. Lincoln's April 1861 blockade proclamation was a symbolic announcement of strength—a powerful statement of the naval resources to be used against the Confederacy. Thus, from the outset, the Union blockade was a psychological weapon used to the Union's advantage. The theme of this chapter is psychology. Subtopics include the blockade's psychological effect on home-front Confederates, its role as a deterrent to shipping, and historiography.

The Union blockade of Confederate ports was a constant factor in contemporaries' views of the war. Naval interdiction involved a continuous military campaign, and this persistence gave it a special psychological aspect in the Confederate mind-set. The Union cordon of ships was a daily reminder of the South's inferior resources. The blockade's existence spurred the Confederacy's most ambitious weapons programs—ironclads and submersibles—in an attempt to lessen its power. But the Union blockade was not only a military advantage. Hungry, resource deprived Southern civilians knew that the Union blockade was responsible for abnormal economic conditions. Some Confederate commentators never actually encountered a Union ship, but they still attributed the deteriorating conditions around them to the blockade. In so doing, these individuals personified the blockade's psychological effectiveness against the Confederacy.

The mere existence of a blockade demoralized the Confederacy. Unlike Union armies that could be temporarily repelled, the blockade was the one aspect of the US war effort that never went away. In fact, it appeared to only grow stronger as the war dragged on, and the Confederacy could do little to relieve the stranglehold. This is why Southerners placed so much hope on Great Britain's intervention—they knew they were virtually powerless to disrupt the blockade. The growing cordon of US ships gripped the Confederate psyche and took on a persona of its own, no less than other symbolic entities. Confederates referred to the blockade as a leviathan-like presence that could not be dispersed, a never-ceasing reminder of ultimate failure. The blockade's effect on the Confederate mind-set was an intangible advantage for the Union war effort.

The blockade's psychological impact on those engaged in maritime trade with the Confederacy was immediate, and it was sustained throughout the war. Historian Stephen Wise argues that "as early as May 1861, the reduction of goods in the South was beginning to have an effect on the Southern economy." Wise notes that the "mere announcement of the blockade had a profound effect on businesses."[1] Conducting illicit trade with the Confederacy had serious ramifications like the loss of a ship or the imprisonment of captain and crew. Each shipping firm and crew had to weigh the risks against the potential profits. The Union blockade deterred some, but fantastic profits ensured someone would always be willing to endure the hazards of blockade-running. One fundamental question, however, needs to be addressed: Did the blockade act as a psychological deterrent to shipping firms and crews?

The final psychological element to be discussed focuses on historians and their blockade analysis. After 150 years, one might expect scholars to have reached some consensus about the Union prohibition of Confederate trade, but that is not the case. One type of analysis predominates, and as a result some historians who analyze the blockade might be influenced by a psycho-historiographic effect.

Psychological Effect on Southerners

The Union blockade was the topic of countless Southern newspaper articles, official proclamations, and military reports. But many of these sources discussed the blockade with a predetermined agenda, often in an attempt to prove its ineffectiveness. If today's readers take these materials at face value, they might be convinced the Union blockade was a sham—an ineffective farce perpetrated by the despotic Lincoln administration. Therefore, to understand how the blockade affected the Confederate psyche, one must turn to Southern diarists. In reflective moments while writing in their journals, Southerners revealed their internalized fears, analyses, and criticisms of the Union interdiction.

Wartime diarists analyzed the visible evidence and attributed their declining living standards to the interdiction of Southern trade. From the

earliest days of the war, the Union blockade gripped the Confederate imagination, despite the fact that in 1861 it was not fully implemented. However, the blockade's psychological effect began with Lincoln's declaration
on April 19, 1861. Some Southerners dismissed the blockade in the first
months of the war, and this was consistent with the optimistic spirit of
Confederate nationalism at the time.

Diarist and outspoken Confederate nationalist Edmund Ruffin inherited
a Tidewater Virginia plantation at a young age and was a respected pro-
ponent of agricultural management and improvement. Ruffin championed
the use of marl to improve crop productivity, and he gained acclaim as
editor of the *Farmer's Register*. When his capability for running profitable
plantations became a much-copied model across the South, his success allowed him to distribute his estates to heirs in the 1850s and embark on his
other passion—political exhortation. Ruffin himself was far too impolitic
and abrasive for elective office, but his abilities as a political agitator were
considerable. Alongside John C. Calhoun and the South Carolina nullifiers
of the 1830s, Edmund Ruffin was among the first to advocate for Southern
secession.[2]

The most important factor in Ruffin's secessionist mind-set was the protection of slavery, and he held white supremacy as a bedrock principle. For
Ruffin, the South's labor system could only be protected outside the Union,
not inside it with feckless political compromises. In the 1850s he advocated
tirelessly for secession, communicating with numerous Southern political
elites, particularly in South Carolina. Ruffin's deep affinity for the Palmetto
State brought him there in December 1860 to be present for the advent of
secession. In a nod to his lifelong obsession with Southern independence,
on April 12, 1861, the sixty-seven-year-old was given the honor of firing the
first shot at Fort Sumter.[3]

Edmund Ruffin kept a detailed diary from 1856 to 1865, and the Union
blockade was among the many topics he analyzed therein. Shortly after
Lincoln's April 19, 1861, blockade proclamation, Ruffin noted the blockade's
potential psychological effectiveness. He stated that the "general blockade of southern ports [was] not yet carried into effect strictly anywhere,"
but ships were "afraid to attempt passing out" of Virginia's ports because
"the enemy's vessels [were] near enough to capture them." On May 3,
Ruffin admitted that Virginia was effectively shut off from maritime trade.[4]
Virginia was the easiest Confederate state to isolate from maritime traffic
due to the Chesapeake Bay's centrality to waterborne commerce. The US

Navy only needed to patrol the entrance to Chesapeake Bay from Cape Henry to Norfolk to seal off most of the state's ocean-based commerce.

Ruffin understood the stakes of trilateral blockade diplomacy in the early months of the war. He stated, "The blockade of southern ports will not be recognized unless it is 'effective," adding "[I do not] believe that a general blockade, operating to prevent the exportation of cotton to Europe will be permitted, even if it could be made 'effective." Like other misguided Confederate policymakers, Ruffin accepted the tenets of King Cotton Diplomacy. As late as September 1861, Ruffin trusted that blockade diplomacy was working in the Confederacy's favor. He opined, "Spain, France, & England will not long delay recognizing the independent nationality of the [Confederate] [States]," and he hoped these nations would begin "refusing to recognize the legality of the Yankee blockade of [rebel] ports, where a real blockade [had] not been maintained." Ruffin was incorrect on all counts.

Although 1861 ended with high diplomatic hopes for the Confederacy due to the *Trent* affair, in the end, the advantage in blockade diplomacy shifted to the Union in 1862. As late as October 1863, Ruffin complained of British perfidy on "the law of blockade," which he believed had "been ignored & disregarded to prevent the otherwise necessary . . . abrogation of the illegal & ineffective Yankee blockade."[5] Much like Confederate leaders who clamored about the blockade's ineffectiveness based on the Declaration of Paris, Ruffin was an early forerunner of the geopolitical ineffectiveness interpretation.

Ruffin's optimism in 1861 about an ineffectual blockade reversed in 1862, and he eventually developed a pessimistic outlook by 1864. In response to the Union sinking of a stone fleet off Charleston in 1861, Ruffin commented that the action did "not say much for the efficiency of the Yankee blockade." In early January 1862 he noted, "Even with this novel aid . . . 4 vessels from foreign ports . . . passed the blockade in one week . . . [and] reached Charleston safely." However, by mid-February of that year, he had changed his opinion. Worrying that the recent success of the Union army and navy boded ill for Confederate hopes, Ruffin remarked, "[I would feel] much less uneasiness . . . if we were but sufficiently supplied with arms and gunpowder, but both are deficient, & made & kept so by the blockade of our sea-ports." In April 1862, Ruffin displayed the blockade's psychological effect on Southerners: "The continuation of the Yankee blockade threatens more danger to our cause, by the consequent scarcity & high prices . . . than do the Yankee arms & armies & fleets."[6]

By October 1862, Ruffin ruminated on European acquiescence to the blockade. "If the powers of Europe still continue to permit the blockade of our ports," he said, "[I do] not see how [the Confederate] government can continue to find means to wage war." Ruffin reiterated this sentiment in early 1863. In early 1864 he frankly admitted, "The Yankees have . . . made their blockade effective."[7] Although Ruffin commented on many aspects of the war, the blockade was ever present in his mind-set concerning the diminishing hopes of Confederate victory.

Feeling the need to record the momentous events occurring in her hometown of Charleston, South Carolina, twenty-two-year-old Emma Holmes started a diary in February 1861. After the surrender of Fort Sumter, Holmes learned of Lincoln's intention to cut off Confederate ports. She expressed little concern on May 9, 1861, but acknowledged, "Old Abe has at last fulfilled his threats of blockading us by sending the [USS] *Niagara* here." Holmes complimented the *Niagara*'s modern equipment and noted it was "probably the fastest ship in the U.S. Navy." But she also remarked at this early stage of war, "[President Lincoln's] whole fleet does not consist of more than 24 vessels." On May 18, after the USS *Niagara*'s departure, Holmes naïvely believed the blockade was over. She remarked, "The much talked about blockade is at an end, not having done us any harm, but plenty to Old Abe, who will have to answer to the English government for interruption to her trades." Like many other Southerners in early 1861, Holmes believed in the power of King Cotton Diplomacy. She assumed that any Union blockade would cause Great Britain "to lose their valuable freight of King Cotton."[8]

On October 2, Holmes penned remarks about the two Confederate diplomats—James Mason and John Slidell—who were waiting to run the blockade out of Charleston on their way to Europe. The envoys sought an opportune moment to break through the cordon aboard the *Nashville*, a time when they would find "only one or two [Union] vessels off the bar." After Mason and Slidell waited several weeks in Charleston, Holmes concluded, "Some traitor has signaled [the Union blockade squadron]." The diplomats eventually ran the blockade out of Charleston, only to be taken off a British ship by a US vessel, resulting in the *Trent* affair.

In 1861, Emma Holmes was unimpressed with the Union blockade. Although the squadron off Charleston was clearly stronger by that fall, Holmes still had little respect for its potency. In July 1862 she noted the arrival of a blockade-runner in Charleston "& others expected," but this was her last comment about the blockade or blockade-runners.[9] Emma Holmes did not confide any analysis about the blockade's effectiveness to her diary for the remainder of the war. There is no written proof that the blockade had a psychological effect on Miss Holmes, but she is among the few Southern diarists who could see the Union blockade squadron every day. It is possible the Union blockade became such a normal presence for her that she did not deem it worthy of further comment after 1862.

Mary Boykin Chesnut's diary is rightly considered among the finest produced during the Civil War, and she, too, devoted some of her entries to the Union blockade. Raised amid South Carolina's aristocracy, Mary was educated in Charleston, but her family's plantation was near Camden. By her middle teenage years, she had traveled across the South to Mississippi, and had visited Mobile and New Orleans. Mary had no shortage of suitors for her hand, but it was James Chesnut Jr., scion of one of South Carolina's wealthiest families, who won her favor. Mary and James were married in 1840. Mary Boykin Chesnut was thirty-eight years old when the Civil War erupted in 1861. She had unique access to the highest levels of Confederate policymaking, since her husband was a prominent politician turned adviser to Pres. Jefferson Davis. But this access was not Mary Chesnut's greatest asset—it was her writing ability.[10]

In 1861 Mary Chesnut described, analyzed, and was psychologically affected by the Union blockade in a variety of ways. In July of that year, she declared, "Every day we grow weaker and [Union forces] stronger. . . . Already [Confederate armies] begin to cry for more ammunition, and already the blockade is beginning to shut it out." Although this was a premature reaction to blockade-caused shortages, it was an excellent example of the blockade's psychological effect. The next month Chesnut heard a dinner-party rumor that a high-ranking British lord had "pronounced the blockade incomplete," but a reasonable guest believed "such a speech would only make the Yankees stricter and cause them to double the ships on guard duty."[11] Chesnut was aware of the blockade's implications for international diplomacy.

Even in its earliest stages, the blockade affected the Confederate psyche. Chesnut was worried in July 1861, but by September she noted, "An iron steamer has run the blockade at Savannah," remarking that this event allowed Confederates to "raise [their] wilted heads like flowers after a shower." In cities blockaded by the US Navy, the psychological effect could be increased. In October 1861, Chesnut informed her husband of conditions in Charleston and stated, "Little is heard of except the blockading fleet" and the increase in the number of Union vessels. Chesnut's "prayers [were] answered" in November, when "another ship with ammunition and arms . . . slipped into Savannah." She declared, "If our prayers are to be so effective, let us all spend our days and nights on our knees." In December "a furious windstorm" slammed Charleston, and Chesnut exclaimed that she "rather enjoyed it—in the interest of the fleet outside the bar." She commented "as the blast howled . . . 'How now, blockaders?'" Opining about the Union squadrons ill intent, she added, "Evil thoughts are like chickens come home to roost."[12] Throughout 1861 Mary Chesnut displayed a wide variety of emotions—both optimistic and pessimistic—about the Union blockade.

Mary Chesnut's diary entries reveal her capacity for historical analogy, as well as her wit and perception. In March 1862, Chesnut compared the Union blockade of the Confederacy to the Roman siege of Utica, an important port city for Carthage, in the Second Punic War. She displayed the blockade's psychological effect when she noted the Yankees did not fret over Confederate naval capability. "No pent-up Utica contracts their powers," she declared. Chesnut glumly perceived the Union forces' advantage, observing, "The whole boundless world is theirs to recruit in." Meanwhile, the Confederates were limited to "only this one little spot of ground." The cumulative result of these thoughts led Chesnut to a depressing conclusion: "The blockade or stockade which hems us in," she wrote, leaves the Confederacy with "only the sky open to us."[13] The analogy that the Union interdiction was a prison, or stockade, that confined the Confederacy was a telling sign of Chesnut's mental response.

Chesnut's psychological state regarding the blockade was not always pessimistic, but it did tend to return to a sense of gloom. In March 1862, Chesnut rejoiced and declared, "Thank God for a ship. . . . It has run the blockade with arms and ammunition." In November 1863, she described "a charming picnic at Mulberry," at the family plantation near Camden, South Carolina. Mary Chesnut boasted of "as good a dinner as mortal appetite could crave—the best of fish, fowl, and game—a cellar that cannot be excelled," concluding, "In spite of the blockade, Mulberry does the honors nobly yet." By November 1864, she acknowledged the Union's "stringent blockade at Wilmington," the last major Confederate port open to blockade running.[14] Someone as well-informed as Chesnut recognized the dreaded ramifications of the Union blockade's four-year campaign that, in conjunction with Union armies, was squeezing the life from the Confederacy.

For Mary Chesnut, the Union blockade was an ever-present reminder

of the obstacles to Confederate independence. She devoted fewer diary en-
tries to the blockade in the war's later years, but that is probably because
it was already a constant in her psyche. However, in the war's early years,
Chesnut's ability to convey the psychological effect of the blockade on the
Confederate mind-set was one of the most powerful commentaries among
Southern diarists.

Catherine Ann Devereux Edmondston, a diarist in northeastern North
Carolina, also analyzed the Union blockade. Edmondston started her diary
during the momentous events of 1860, and she was thirty-seven years old
when the Civil War broke out. In July 1861, she traveled to Charleston,
South Carolina. She recounted her disturbing experience on a Sunday
morning: "[As we were] rounding a point where we could look past [Fort]
Sumter down the channel, out to sea, a black object struck our eyes in
the dim distance." She asked about the dark object, and someone replied,
"The Blockading Squadron, Madam!" Edmondston's visceral psychological reaction was intense: "I cannot describe the rage which instantly seized
me. The revulsion of feeling was greater than I ever recollect to have un-
dergone. I felt strong enough in my own single person to head the boat
sea-wards & seize, grapple, and sink them! There they lay, three vessels
insolently barring our way from the great God-given highway! O! for a navy
that could cope with them! . . . They robbed me of my Sabbath peace . . .
tho they do not so effectually shut us out as they suppose, for Privateermen
slip past them every dark night both to & from the West Indies."[15]

For many Confederates the Union interdiction was an abstract notion. Most Southerners never personally saw a Union blockader like
Edmondston did, but the fact that the blockade existed at all was a psychological advantage for the North. Edmondston's anger upon seeing a blockade vessel is an excellent example of the psychological transition that oc-
curs when abstractions are corroborated by visible proof. The fact that the
Union maintained an uninterrupted blockade for four years was a constant
visual reminder—and for those who did not live in Southern port cities, a
theoretical reminder—of the Confederacy's vulnerability.

As the war progressed and supplies dwindled, some Confederates blamed
the increased effectiveness of the blockade. Catherine Edmondston was
among those who believed that the blockade was ineffective, but over time
she begrudgingly acknowledged its efficacy. In August 1861, Edmondston
noted that blockade-runners were successful, but she also confessed, "The
fear of a dearth of them . . . caused us serious uneasiness." In November,

she admitted that the Confederacy looked to England with "feverish anxiety," explaining, "From [Great Britain] was confidently expected a deliverance from the inconveniences we now began to suffer from the blockade." By April 1862, high prices of commodities forced Edmondston to admit, "Such is the success of the blockade that it will go far to teach us economy & self denial!"[16] The blockade was an important component of Confederate inflation since it choked off normal trade with the outside world. On July 21, 1862, Catherine Edmondston reflected on the one-year anniversary of the rebel victory at Bull Run and asked, "Who would have thought one year ago that this war would still be raging and blockade unraised?" She commented that Southerners had learned to do without luxuries and were adapting to the realities of life under blockade.[17]

Edmondston rarely commented on the blockade after 1862, but her entries up to that point indicated a psychological concern about its potency. Edmondston was among those who observed the Union squadrons in person, and she responded with virulent anger. Most Confederates only read about the blockade in newspapers, or heard repeated stories about the Union cordon and the blockade-runners on which the Confederacy had become so dependent. Edmondston's reaction was an excellent example of the how the Union blockade psychologically affected home-front Confederates.

Diarist John Beauchamp Jones worked as a clerk in the War Department in Richmond and had access to abundant information about the Confederate war effort on all fronts. He analyzed many aspects of the Civil War in his journal entries, and he assessed the Union blockade from the outset. In April 1861, Jones told an "incredulous" Gov. Henry Wise that the Lincoln administration intended to "subjugate the South," declaring, "[The president will] blockade our ports, and endeavor to cut off our supplies." Governor Wise believed Union naval interdiction violated international law, but Jones thought that was a minor impediment to Northern strategy.

In late May 1861 Jones boasted, "It will be impossible for Lincoln to keep all our ports hermetically sealed." Less than a week later, however, he worried about the blockade's effect on inflation after purchasing some clothes. "What will be the price of such commodities a year hence if the blockade continues?" he wondered. "It is fearful to contemplate!" Jones's concerns vacillated in 1861, but this assessment of inflation reflected the blockade's psychological impact on prescient Southerners. In December 1861, the clerk penned a passport for captured US congressman Alfred Ely on makeshift brown paper. Ely mocked the Southern-made paper, and

Jones replied that it was a "necessity imposed . . . by the blockade." Ely kindly responded that he hoped Jones would one day again have "the dignity of white paper."[18] Even in 1861, basic items, like paper, were in short supply in the Confederacy.

In 1862 and 1863 J. B. Jones continued to mention the blockade in both optimistic and pessimistic tones. In October 1862, he noted that his wife had "obviated one of the difficulties of the blockade" by substituting regular coffee with roasted cornmeal. Ersatz measures were also a constant reminder of the blockade's presence. In January 1863, Jones worried that rebel newspapers overly celebrated the exploits of blockade-runners. Although such reports were part of a larger strategy to delegitimize the blockade in international eyes, he believed they would "increase the vigilance of the blockading fleet." Jones noted in March 1863 that a man told him, "If the Yankees only knew it, they might derive all the benefits they seek . . . without the expenditure of human life, by simply redoubling the blockade of our ports." Commentary about the blockade among Confederate citizens and newspaper editors shows the public perception of the Yankee naval squadrons hovering off Confederate ports. In August 1863, Jones stated, "[The runners] go and come every week in spite of the [Union] cruisers, and . . . so long as this continues, the war can be maintained." He believed in a thriving blockade-running conspiracy in which vessels bribed their way through the Union squadrons, but these allegations were unfounded, and Jones saw alleged conspiracies in other aspects of the war as well.[19]

By 1865, Jones was well informed enough about the Confederacy's dire situation to mock an optimistic newspaper article about blockade-running success. On January 3, 1865, he copied a "seemingly well authenticated" story that declared Confederate "armies [were] in no danger of immediately becoming destitute of supplies." The Pollyanna-like article stated, "The alleged ceaseless vigilance of the Yankee navy in watching blockade-runners . . . has amounted to comparatively little . . . [and] the proceeds of the blockade have been very great." As a War Department clerk with access to ample information about the South's circumstances in 1865, Jones knew better. If the Yankees believed the Southern press, he noted with biting sarcasm, "The publication itself may cause the immediate fall of Wilmington."[20] From 1861 on, J. B. Jones understood the importance of the blockade in Union strategy, and although he was not as demoralized as other Confederate diarists, the blockade remained a constant factor in his perception of the war. One could argue that his proximity to the high command shifted his concern to other demoralizing aspects of the Confederate war effort—and there was no shortage of those after mid-1863.

Still another diarist who commented on the Union blockade was Ella Gertrude Clanton Thomas. Twenty-seven years old in 1861, Thomas hailed from an affluent family of aristocratic planters near Augusta, Georgia. She received a superb education and periodically recorded her views on the war and society. In July 1861, Thomas calmly noted, "Lincoln has blockaded our ports," and she pondered how this Union naval campaign might affect her daily life. She complained about an inability to obtain books, saying that she had "read nothing new for some time." Thomas believed that the Union "blockade [had] prevented the importation of new books," and that this could "prove to be a serious inconvenience." Such frivolity in 1861 became an afterthought by 1864, as Southerners were deprived of life's basic necessities.

By 1863 the Union blockade had evolved into an ever-present aspect of the Confederate social psyche. In one particularly poignant episode during an 1863 Christmas party, Thomas informed the children they were having a party "in lieu of . . . Santa Claus presents." The reason, she told the children, they were not receiving gifts was because "Santa Claus has not been able to run the blockade." At least in this instance, the psychological effect of the blockade intruded on the holiday wishes of Southern children.

In August 1864, Thomas worried about the Union invasion of Georgia and the possible fall of Atlanta. She addressed rumors of an armistice, believing that "it would be a suicidal move" since the Confederate "ports would still continue blockaded." The cumulative psychological effect of the blockade was evident in Thomas's outlook. By March 1865 she finally reached a point of complete demoralization and lamented, "I feel the restraint of the blockade and as port after port becomes blockaded I feel shut up, pent up."[21] Ella Gertrude Clanton Thomas is an excellent example of a home-front diarist who never saw a Union blockading vessel in person, but who felt the psychological pressure of their presence just the same. She was increasingly worn down by the blockade's existence.

Teenager Emma LeConte recorded events in Columbia, South Carolina, from January to August 1865. LeConte is most known for her narrative of Sherman's occupation and alleged destruction of Columbia in February 1865, but she also had a keen eye for economic and diplomatic developments. She described a Confederate fundraising bazaar in January and stated, "To go in there one would scarce believe it was war times." She noted, "The tables are loaded with fancy articles—brought through the blockade, or manufactured by the ladies." In addition to the fine edible goods, LeConte observed "some beautiful imported wax dolls . . . raffled for five-hundred dollars."

After surviving the Columbia conflagration, LeConte addressed the rumored peace talks of March 1865. She tried to sift through "a thousand unfounded and conflicting rumors" as she held out hope "for intervention." In a nod to the Union blockade's psychological effectiveness, LeConte declared, "If recognition meant the opening of our ports only, that would be all we would ask." On April 20, 1865, she pondered the sudden disintegration of the Confederacy. Bemoaning the meaningless sacrifice of rebel soldiers, she observed that not long ago, Confederates had "had every reason to hope for success." LeConte wondered, "[What is] the cause of this sudden crushing collapse? I cannot understand it."[22] LeConte's diary does not allow for a long-term analysis of the blockade's psychological effect on Southerners, but she acknowledged the Union blockade's role in Confederate defeat.

Southern diarists periodically commented about the Union blockade, and one can assume that the same commentary can be found in private correspondence. The cumulative psychological toll of the blockade is impossible to quantify, but it is clear that the never-ending existence of the naval squadrons was an intangible advantage for the Union war effort. The blockade did not cause Confederates to give up, nor was it the main catalyst for Union victory, but it was a constant military campaign that eroded the Confederate spirit from 1861 to 1865. To be sure, some rebels mocked the interdiction as a farce. Some Confederates defiantly refused to believe it was little more than an affront to foreign powers, but by 1865 these biased observers lived in a state of denial. The psychological strain of four years of blockade complemented the string of Union battlefield victories, creating a foundation for the pervasive sense of doom that shadowed the Confederacy by 1865.

The failure of King Cotton Diplomacy also enhanced the Union blockade's psychological power. Confederates had invested great hope in the strength of this diplomacy; the intentional withholding of Southern cotton in 1861 was expected to force Great Britain into the war on the seceded states' behalf. Instead, this self-imposed embargo was the biggest diplomatic and economic blunder in the Confederacy's brief existence. The South could have shipped large quantities of cotton to England in 1861 before the blockade was fully implemented. In so doing, Confederate officials could have amassed considerable cash and credit to finance the war effort. When the Confederates finally realized that withholding cotton could not sway Great Britain into intervention, it was too late. Beginning in 1862, the South attempted to export as much cotton as possible, but the blockade was becoming fully operational. At the time, however, King Cotton Diplomacy seemed like the only economic tool to leverage outside intervention. The blockade could have been an extremely embarrassing fiasco for the Lincoln administration in 1861, if only Confederates had not abided by the strictures of King Cotton Diplomacy.

Some Confederates brushed aside the blockade because King Cotton Diplomacy made it seem superfluous—an annoyance that British naval power would quickly disperse. In April 1861, Catherine Ann Devereux Edmondston derided Lincoln's blockade as an essentially meaningless gesture. "Let them try their boasted blockade! Who cares?" she declared. "Who will be most hurt—us? Themselves? or England?" Edmondston, like many other naïve Confederates in 1861, believed cotton would carry the rebellion to victory. Answering her own question of who would be most harmed by the Union blockade, she concluded, "Not us, for we make the necessaries of life. . . . But what will England do for cotton when her looms are idle? What her starving population for bread? King Cotton will raise his own blockade in his own time." After a year Edmonston still harbored great hopes in King Cotton Diplomacy. In March 1862, she wrote, "Ah! Mother England! You little know the misery in store for you! You think you can raise the blockade when you will & relieve your suffering children, but . . . what will you do when there is no cotton for your ships to carry to your idle factories[?]"[23] The policy's failure wounded Confederate pride since so much confidence had been attached to it.

The nefarious psychological impact of King Cotton Diplomacy was that Confederates tended to believe the blockade grew more effective the longer it lasted. This notion turned out to be false. The Union blockade had a similar influence on the Confederate mind-set, except in reverse; the blockade's psychological effectiveness grew each year. In fact, the failure of King Cotton Diplomacy and the increasing power of the Union interdiction can be viewed as two sides of the same coin—both being symbols and reminders of the Confederacy's fundamental economic weakness. By 1863 Southern trust in King Cotton Diplomacy had dissipated, and by then, King Cotton's nemesis, the Union blockade, was in full operation systematically interdicting Confederate cotton exports.

The Blockade as a Psychological Deterrent to Shipping

A corollary of the psychological effectiveness argument is the deterrent effect. How many ships decided against blockade-running due to the US Navy's presence? Historian Craig L. Symonds argues that "though hundreds of blockade-runners successfully ran through the blockade, far more were deterred from ever trying to run it at all."[24] How many ships were too intimidated to approach Confederate ports? This question is difficult to answer because historical actors rarely left documented evidence of abandoned plans.

The deterrent effect has become axiomatic for some blockade historians, and a few examples will suffice to show that the concept has been an enduring aspect of blockade historiography. In 1949 two scholars firmly established the deterrence argument. In "The Civil War Blockade Reconsidered," Edwin B. Coddington remarked that "by 1863 the Federal Government had established a tight enough cordon around the Southern coast to require extraordinary efforts and an unusual outlay of capital on the part of those who risked sending vessels through it."[25] That same year, historian Marcus Price argued that the Union blockade's: "effectiveness lay not so much in the ships and cargoes captured as in the ships and cargoes its mere existence kept away from Southern ports . . . scores of vessels that would have piled their merchandise high on Carolina wharves had there been no blockade simply did not choose to incur the risk of capture."[26]

The deterrent argument has been reaffirmed in other blockade analyses. In his Pulitzer Prize-winning history of the Civil War, James M. McPherson notes, "While it is true that five out of six runners got through, that is not the crucial statistic. . . . Rather, one must ask how many ships carrying how much freight *would have* entered southern ports if there had been no blockade."[27] In C. L. Webster's detailed 2010 study of blockade-running, he contends that "the Federal blockade effectively discouraged the vast majority of available ship owners and shipping firms from even attempting to run into Southern ports."[28] The assumption that the blockade deterred many more ships than it interdicted remains a powerful argument. But is it accurate?

Difference of opinion about the deterrence theory stems from an imprecise definition of the term. Large cargo vessels lumbering into Confederate ports, as well as many sailing vessels, were deterred from blockade-running because they were easily captured. It is also true that blockade-runners were forced to adapt to wartime circumstances by limiting cargo capacity

TABLE I.[29]

Year	Total Number of Steamer Ships running that year
1861	71
1862	86
1863	118
1864	127
1865	50

in exchange for speed, but these specialized ships were not deterred from breaking through Union cordons. Many crews, especially foreign nationals who were not permanently imprisoned in Union jails, deemed the risk of blockade-running acceptable due to fabulous profits. In fact, the number of steam-powered blockade-running ships actually increased from 1861 to 1864 (see Table 1).

Irrefutable statistical evidence indicates that steam-powered vessels were willing to risk running the blockade in ever-increasing numbers up to 1865. As a potential counter to this data, historians who continue to support the deterrent argument have failed to provide any statistical, or even anecdotal, evidence to support their claims. The blockade-as-a-deterrent argument is rational, but it has one insurmountable flaw—it cannot be proved. Fantastic profits coupled with the neutral protections of foreign nationals ensured that the reward for blockade-running far outweighed the risks. Crew members could be exposed to bodily injury if a ship was fired on or sunk, but Union squadrons much preferred to capture a vessel for the pecuniary prize benefits. The greatest argument against the deterrent effect is the increased number of blockade-running attempts as the war progressed, despite the gradual loss of available Confederate ports. Although logical, the case for the blockade as a deterrent cannot be supported by documentary or statistical evidence and thus should be considered speculative.

Psycho-Historiographic Effect

The deterrent theory is just one aspect of a larger psychological issue in blockade historiography. Another inherently psychological aspect of this scholarship is the point of departure from which historians analyze the blockade's contribution to Union victory or Confederate defeat. This last phrase seems redundant, but it is not. Union victory and Confederate defeat are similar topics, but one can come up with drastically different analyses depending on which phrase is used. Historians tend to approach blockade analysis from one of these two starting points—Union victory or Confederate defeat. It is important to understand this point of departure because it greatly influences the analysis.

The blockade is a factor in the two fundamental questions of Civil War history: Why did the North win the war? Why did the South lose the war? The first question is the most important in this chapter, and it is typically answered in the following manner: the blockade assisted Union armies in a gradual but complete reduction of Southern economic and military resources. The overwhelming majority of historians analyze the blockade in this contributory manner, thereby supporting the contributory effectiveness argument. A full-scale analysis of the blockade's efficacy over time will be saved for the next chapter. However, it is worth discussing contributory effectiveness here, because of its central importance to the psychohistoriographic effect on scholars.

The most common effectiveness argument focuses on the blockade's contribution to Union victory. The contributory effectiveness model stops short of claiming the blockade won the war for the Union, but it insists that supply interdiction caused crippling industrial shortages and exacerbated inflation in the Confederacy. Historians who argue for contributory effectiveness point out that the Union did not need to completely shut off trade for a successful blockade. Instead, the North only needed to minimize the South's access to outside resources—which it did. This analysis of the Union blockade's effectiveness is powerful. Rare is the Civil War historian who would argue that the naval interdiction did not contribute to Union victory in some way.

One specific example of contributory effectiveness is the blockade's role in the deterioration of the Confederate rail system. Due to the Union maritime trade interdiction, Southern railroad companies experienced serious equipment shortages, and insufficient domestic iron production eventually caused the collapse of railways. Confederate railroad companies confronted numerous obstacles, "such as lack of man power, continued use of the facilities to capacity, and destructive raids of the enemy." But according to historian Edwin Coddington, "the blockade remained the primary cause" of rail-system collapse.[30]

Other economic sectors struggled to maintain production in the face of widespread shortages. Coddington points out that Southern "textile manufacturers not only suffered from deterioration of machinery but lacked sufficient quantities of oils and other items used in production." According to scholars who pursue the contributory-effectiveness interpretation, enough materials were denied importation to stifle full industrial production. Thus, as Coddington and others argue, "even an imperfect blockade was an important element in weakening [the] Southern economy under the stress of war."[31] There is little doubt that the Union blockade caused shortages of vital industrial equipment and hampered Confederate transportation and industrial production.

The naval interdiction also prevented full-scale imports of personal goods like food, clothing, and luxury items. A primary tenet of the contributory model, as identified by historian James McPherson, declared that the blockade advanced the "ruinous inflation that reduced the Confederate dollar to one percent of its original value by the end of the war." This aspect of the contributory-effectiveness argument points to the decreased availability of goods as the primary reason for Confederate inflation. However, inflation is a more complicated concept than just the scarcity of goods. The Confederacy's monetary policy and failure to collect taxes also created a crippling inflationary environment. As economic historian Eugene Lerner observes, the Confederate "stock of money rose more than in any comparable period of American history since the Revolutionary War," and by "October, 1864, almost 60 [percent] of all money received by the Confederacy had come from the printing press."[32]

In addition, Lerner contends that while the blockade affected prices for "commodities entirely imported" that ersatz could not replace, it "did not affect the home production of partly imported goods, and their prices rose less." He further notes that the inflationary scale depended on the commodity. For example, "the price of wheat, corn, and other products produced in limited quantities in the Confederacy simply did not rise fast enough" to justify significant cargo space aboard blockade-runners. In conclusion, Lerner asserts that "the blockade was felt in every corner of the southern economy," but that most Confederate used innovation and substitution to ensure that "the effect of the blockade was greatest in the short run." Though the interdiction exacerbated Southern shortages across a spectrum of commodities, it was not necessarily a decisive factor in the rapid rise of Confederate inflation.

The Union blockade was without question a key component in the inflation cycle. Yet to claim that it was the most important component minimizes the significance of misguided Confederate financial policies that caused hyperinflation. Both Treasury Secretary Christopher Memminger, who eventually stepped down in mid-1864, and the Confederate Congress deserve blame for the shortsighted measures that caused price increases. However, as Eugene Lerner remarks, had "southerners attacked the most basic cause—the increase in the stock of money per unit of real income—with more vigor and understanding, they might have mitigated some of their hardships."[33] The Union blockade made Confederate inflation worse, but claiming that the blockade was the primary reason for this inflation overlooks other important factors.

One important unintended effect of the blockade was the scarcity of salt. Antebellum Southerners relied on imported salt despite underutilized deposits that existed in the region. As in so many other economic sectors during the prewar years, the Southern states were overly dependent on foreign imports. Salt came into Southern ports as ballast on ships that typically left loaded with cotton. For example, New Orleans alone unloaded 350 tons of salt per day from 1857 to 1860.[34] Thus the price of salt remained low in the South, and entrepreneurs lacked motivation to mine deposits. When the blockade was established, however, inbound vessels no longer used salt for ballast, instead bringing in guns, munitions, and more profitable items. The scarcity of cheap salt meant that the South diverted precious manpower and industrial resources to domestic salt production. Historian Ella Lonn notes this was yet another shortsighted lack of preparation by Confederate leaders that contributed to defeat. However, a great deal of credit should go to the Union blockade for this inadvertent yet critical contribution that caused a salt shortage in the Confederacy.

The contributory-effectiveness argument can also be applied to other aspects of Union victory. This interpretation highlights the continual, grinding pressure of the blockade over time. Historian Bern Anderson summarizes this aspect of contributory effectiveness, noting "It is significant . . . that the Union army's major victories did not occur until the South was suffering from shortages imposed by the Union blockade. By creating these shortages, the Union navy ensured the ultimate victory of its cause."[35] The case for contributory effectiveness links an effective blockade to diminishing Confederate military capabilities. For historians in this analytical camp, scarcity of military supplies, and not a declining will to fight, was the primary cause of the South's collapse. The contributory-effectiveness argument is a powerful and logical component of the blockade's role in Union victory.

Contributory effectiveness analysis has become sacrosanct among most Civil War historians. There is much to admire in this interpretation, but it has also encouraged the tendency to presume the blockade's increased potency over time. The psycho-historiographic effect does not detract from Civil War scholarship, but a detailed study of effectiveness is needed. We, the authors, did not expect the catalyst that drove us to undertake a new investigation of the blockade's efficacy over time.

A lecture on Civil War naval history sparked a curious question in our minds that shattered our previous conceptions about blockade historiography. After this experience, we could never return to the standard interpretation of the blockade's effectiveness over time. The statement in question deserves detailed scrutiny. A renowned Civil War historian, after briefly analyzing the blockade's effectiveness, flatly declared, "I will never be convinced by any statistical evidence that the Union blockade was not effective." No reaction emanated from the audience after this authoritative statement. But after hearing these words, our first reaction was that this respected scholar had spent decades thinking about the subject and had reached this conclusion after careful consideration of a preponderance of evidence. "Who are we to question this renowned historian's interpretation?" we asked ourselves.

However, the question that we discussed next forever changed the way we thought about the blockade: "If statistical evidence could never be convincing, then what kind of evidence could be convincing—Anecdotal?" As we mulled over this matter, it struck us that some blockade historians may have developed what could be termed a psycho-historiographic effect. In other words, we wondered whether historians have been overly swayed by previous interpretations without having done their own due diligence. Do some historians believe the blockade was effective simply because it existed? The next question we asked ourselves was, "Have previous blockade studies psychologically influenced historians into a presumption of increasing effectiveness?" A detailed development of the relevant historiography may help determine whether there has indeed been a psycho-historiographic effect on historians. In addition, we endeavored to compile and analyze the available statistical evidence to see whether it either supported or refuted the standard interpretation of the blockade's increasing effectiveness over time (see chapter 5).

Conclusion

The Union blockade was the one constant military campaign of the Civil War from April 1861 to May 1865, the US Navy consistently interdicted trade at Confederate ports. Historians have debated whether that interdiction was successful. Yet it is clear that the mere existence of the blockade provided a psychological edge to the Union. From the outset, both sides understood the North's material advantage, and the Union interdiction was a persistent reminder that, even if Confederate armies won numerous battles, the rebels could never match Union naval superiority. This important mental advantage increased as the war dragged on, contributing to Confederates' demoralization.

However, this psychological effect cannot be measured in statistical terms. It is a logical assumption that the Union blockade created an advantage for the North and assisted its war effort. During the war and ever since, this notion has also influenced historians' analysis of the blockade. For example, scholars have accepted that the Union blockade was a serious deterrent to import and export of goods. This is true to a degree if one is discussing normal trade relations and large cargo ships, but as we have seen, the number of steam-powered ships willing to risk the blockade actually increased during the war. Another aspect of blockade psychology is linked to the historical debate over effectiveness. In addition, though historical interpretations make a good case for both the blockade's effectiveness and ineffectiveness, the prevailing tendency is to highlight the interdiction's contributions in grinding down the Confederacy's ability to wage war. As a result, after decades of accumulated historiography that supports the contributory-effectiveness argument, a psycho-historiographic effect may have taken hold among some Civil War historians.

CHAPTER 5

---★---

The Blockade's Effectiveness

SERIOUS STUDENTS OF Civil War history are obligated to analyze the extent to which the blockade assisted Union victory. The question of the blockade's effectiveness has prompted interpretive disagreements among historians for decades, and this debate remains one of the enduring controversies of Civil War scholarship. One might expect this dispute to have been resolved, as numerous scholars have exhaustively researched and analyzed the subject. However, a fresh interpretation of the blockade's effectiveness is still possible if one asks new questions of the evidence. But first, let us take a brief look at how historians have evaluated the Union blockade's effectiveness.

Civil War historians have interpreted and analyzed the Union blockade's effectiveness, or lack thereof, in a variety of ways. Reorganizing the interpretive models into subcategories can encourage better understanding of the effectiveness debate. Those who argue for the blockade's effectiveness can be divided into three main schools: psychological, contributory, and cost-benefit scholars. We have already discussed the main points of the psychological and contributory-effectiveness arguments (see chapter 4)— the blockade's deterrent effect, the reduction of Confederate home-front morale, and historians' examination of contributory effectiveness—so let us turn to cost-benefit effectiveness.

The cost-benefit interpretation of the Union blockade is a detailed analysis of the relationship between the Union interdiction's success and the Confederate economy. This interpretation seeks to answer a fundamental question: Was the Union blockade effective enough to justify the North's allocation of resources to the task? Advocates of cost-benefit effectiveness argue that the Union resource outlay was justified by the interdiction's contribution to Union victory. Historian James McPherson supports this analysis stating, "Naval personnel constituted only 5 percent of the Union armed forces, [but] their contribution to the outcome of the war was much larger."[1]

Economic historian David Surdam also details the cost-benefit argument, and he contends that previous scholars were "asking the wrong questions." According to Surdam, "The effectiveness of the blockade cannot be measured solely by how much material was smuggled through it or by the success rate of blockade runners piercing it." Importation of military supplies was obviously vital to Confederate survival, but Surdam argues, "The focus upon imports has almost been myopic and also misses what may have been two of the blockade's most important achievements: disrupting intraregional trade and denying the Confederacy badly needed revenue from exporting raw cotton and other staple products."[2]

Surdam's study provides detailed analyses of the blockade's effect on a variety of Confederate economic sectors, including railroads, beef and pork supplies, and cotton markets. He concludes, "The blockade diminished the purchasing power of Southern staples . . . [and] also contributed to the collapse of the Southern logistical system. . . . [Thus] the Federal navy's efforts appear to have been judicious . . . [and] for the resources expended, the blockade appears to have been a worthwhile investment."[3] David Surdam's cost-benefit argument is among the strongest of the effectiveness arguments because its analysis of the blockade relies on statistical methods.

A corollary of the cost-benefit argument might be the called the adaptation effect. The Union blockade forced shipowners to build blockade-runners for maximum speed, thus reducing their cargo capacity. New shipbuilding technology used to construct state-of-the-art blockade-runners, like the twin-screw propeller, lower profiles, lower drafts, and larger engines amidships, inevitably curtailed cargo capacity. Rear Adm. S. P. Lee, who oversaw the blockade of Wilmington, admitted the runners' technological superiority. In July 1864, Lee regretted to report that his fastest blockaders were being outmatched by a "new class of steamers now employed in blockade running." He stated that this "great revolution in the blockade running business" could only be countered by speedier blockade vessels.[4]

In August 1864, Rear Admiral Lee informed Navy Secretary Gideon Welles, "[Blockade-runners have] facilities . . . which they never had before." According to Lee, these runners traveled at "great speed and . . . very low in the water," and most of them were "commanded by officers belonging to the British navy, on account of their superiority in skill and boldness."

The rear admiral hoped to capture or sink all such vessels, but he acknowl-edged, "The experience of this war shows that it is impracticable to make a perfect blockade against steamers built expressly for the purpose of breaking the blockade."[5] Although this point was likely lost on Lee at the time, even if his squadron could not easily catch the technologically superior blockade-runners, the blockade's very existence forced these ships to adapt for speed, thereby limiting their cargo capacities. In hindsight, this was an important, but often overlooked, unintended aspect of the interdiction's operations.

Ineffectiveness Arguments

Some historians have contended that the Union blockade was ineffective. These arguments can be separated into three main interpretive models: geopolitical, material, and statistical ineffectiveness. The geopolitical model is a legalistic argument based on a one-sided interpretation of the Dec-laration of Paris (1856). The material-ineffectiveness argument lists the quantity of goods successfully imported into the Confederacy, and the statistical-ineffectiveness model uses empirical evidence of successful runs through the blockade to show the blockade's weakness. Each interpretation must be examined in detail to formulate a comprehensive analysis of the Union blockade's effectiveness.

Confederate leaders and diplomats declared geopolitical ineffective-ness immediately after Lincoln's blockade proclamation on April 19, 1861. Rebel leaders fully understood the Declaration of Paris's legal importance to Great Britain. Confederate foreign-policy formulators also appreciated the notion of might makes right, and this view of the diplomatic situation between Great Britain, the United States, and the Confederacy governed the Southern argument of geopolitical ineffectiveness. It made sense that the nation with the most to lose in maritime law—Great Britain—was the arbiter of the Declaration of Paris, which decreed "that blockades to be binding must be effective—that is, maintained by a force really sufficient to prevent access to the enemy's coast" (see appendix 1). Britain upheld this legal blockade standard despite contrivances from both sides of the conflict, but Confederates insisted the Union blockade was illegitimate because it was not completely effective.

The United States was not a signatory to the Declaration of Paris, but it needed to respect this international law to successfully navigate diplomacy with Great Britain. Confederate officials used the declaration's terminology to construct a one-sided definition of the blockade's ineffectiveness. This was a blatant attempt to coax British intervention. On August 13, 1861, the Confederate Congress passed a resolution mainly in agreement with the Declaration of Paris, and legislators posed as willing adherents to international law governing naval interdictions. Since the high-seas rebel navy consisted primarily of commerce raiders, the Confederate Congress continued "the right of privateering" but conformed to the other articles.[6] Federal and rebel diplomats were not technically bound to the limits of the Declaration of Paris, but they were wrapped up in its de facto legal ramifications as imposed by British naval power.

Confederate politicians and newspaper editors made every effort to proclaim the blockade ineffectual. They understood that if their ineffectiveness argument swayed international observers, then the blockade might be declared non-binding. European condemnation and perhaps even military intervention to break the blockade might follow. On November 29, 1861, Confederate commissioners in London, headed by William Lowndes Yancey, wrote to British foreign secretary, Lord John Russell, "If . . . we can prove the blockade to have been ineffectual, we . . . have a right to expect that the nations assenting to this declaration . . . will not consider it to be binding." The envoys further pleaded, "The great interests of neutral commerce of the world imperatively demand that her Majesty's Government should take decisive action in declaring the blockade ineffective."[7]

Southern newspapers listed successful runs into Confederate ports as evidence of the blockade's porousness. However, these attempts to publicize the blockade's ineffectiveness, and thus highlight international illegality, did not convince Great Britain to intervene. Lord Russell summed up the British position on the blockade when he declared to Lord Lyon on February 15, 1862, that "the blockade was duly notified . . . [and] sufficient really to prevent access . . . [which did] create an evident danger of entering or leaving it." Lord Russell flatly refuted the geopolitical-ineffectiveness argument when he further stated, "The fact that various ships may have successfully escaped through [the blockade] . . . will not, of itself, prevent the blockade from being an effectual one, by international law."[8]

After the war, Confederate president Jefferson Davis asserted that "the so-called blockade . . . policy of European powers was so shaped as to cause the greatest injury to the Confederacy." Davis complained that "neutral Europe remained passive when the United States, with a naval force insufficient to blockade effectively the coast of a single state, proclaimed a paper blockade of thousands of miles of coast."[9] Throughout the war, Confederate leaders interpreted runners' intermittent success as concrete proof that the Union interdiction was ineffective and thus nonbinding, but to no avail.

The American Civil War occurred in the same era as several precedent-setting events for the codification of modern warfare. German-born American Francis Lieber played a pivotal role in this international process with his publication of *Code of the Government of Armies in the Field* (1863). Lieber's code was developed alongside other initiatives in Europe that chartered new international laws. The initial Geneva Conventions, signed by twelve nations in 1864 and ratified by the US in 1882, followed by the Hague Conventions in 1899 and 1907, attempted to standardize rules for war. Although the Civil War largely predated the codification movement, the Confederate government grounded its attempted refutation of the blockade's legitimacy in this worldwide movement to define the regulations of warfare.

Most historians remain unconvinced by the case for geopolitical ineffectiveness. Confederate leaders developed a clever example of legal legerdemain, but they based their semantic attack on a biased definition of international law, a standard to which they did not even fully subscribe. The fact that some ships got through the Union cordons did not mean the blockade was inadequate. Confederates who utilized the geopolitical argument can be accused of one-sided denial of the interdiction's capability. In blockade historiography, postwar Confederate leaders typically deployed the geopolitical-ineffectiveness argument as part of the Lost Cause paradigm.

Another method to analyze the blockade's effectiveness is a quantitative calculation of how much war materiel was brought through the blockade. Historians who use the material-ineffectiveness interpretation argue that enough supplies slipped past US blockaders to allow the Confederacy to protract the war into 1865. By implication, then, the blockade was not a major factor in Confederate defeat. Union blockade officers admitted that a substantial quantity of contraband slipped through the blockade. In August 1862, squadron commander Samuel F. DuPont remarked to Gideon Welles that he was "fairly oppressed by . . . the insufficiency of the blockade," and that one of his subordinates acknowledged, "That the violations have been frequent." DuPont also informed Welles, "Some two million sterling of arms and merchandise have gone [through the blockade] in the last ten days."[10] Apparently, high-ranking Union and Confederate officers believed enough materiel pierced the blockade to render its overall efficacy doubtful.

Historians who argue for material ineffectiveness highlight military imports and minimize the blockade's effect on the Confederate economy. Historian William Still insists, "Considerable evidence indicates that the blockade did not represent a major factor in the Confederacy's economic exhaustion." According to historian Frank Owsley, "the economic difficulties in the Confederacy . . . resulted from internal problems such as interruptions of transportation and inadequate manpower resources." Scholars who support the material-ineffectiveness theory maintain that the "Confederates could get whatever they wanted or needed through the blockade, if they wanted it badly enough." In basic economic terms, so the argument goes: "Had Confederates been willing to pay more for cargo space, they would have gotten more [imports but] that they did not pay more . . . argues that they had sufficient domestic supply available to preclude the necessity of draconian measures to increase foreign supply."[11]

This aspect of the material-ineffectiveness argument is counterintuitive. It reasons that more materiel did not make it through the blockade because Confederates believed they had enough supplies, not because the Union blockade was effective! However, this corollary of the material-ineffectiveness argument is an overstatement that other evidence does not support. The written record overwhelmingly shows that Confederate leaders were never content with their supply situation, and that the war effort constantly required more commodities of all types—munitions, machines, and food.

The material-ineffectiveness interpretation is best supported by the sheer numbers and amount of contraband brought through the blockade. Historian Stephen Wise, author of the most comprehensive study of blockade-running, supports this view. Wise does not explicitly argue that the blockade was ineffective, but he does note the following: "In terms of basic military necessities, the South imported at least 400,000 rifles, or more than 60 percent of the nation's modern arms. About 3 million pounds of lead came through the blockade, which by [Ordnance Bureau chief, Josiah] Gorgas's estimate amounted to one-third of the army's requirements. Besides these items, over 2,250,000 pounds of saltpeter, or two-thirds of this vital ingredient for powder, came from overseas. Without blockade-running the nation's military would have been without proper supplies of arms, bullets, and powder."[12] When one compares the amount of munitions smuggled through the Union blockade with the amount produced domestically in the Confederacy, it is arguable that rebel armies could not have continued the war past 1863 without blockade-running. This reasonable assertion about reliance on blockade-running gives potency to the material-ineffectiveness argument.

These examples have focused on material aggregation and can only partially show the Union blockade's weakness. However, the material-ineffectiveness interpretation poses other questions that might be unanswerable. Did enough supplies get through the blockade to deem it ineffective? If so, how much smuggled materiel was required to determine ineffective status? Historians run the risk of endlessly disputing these questions.

Historian Robert Browning Jr. constructs a corollary of the material-ineffectiveness argument focusing on the logistical problems of maintaining blockade squadrons. He describes the North Atlantic Blockading Squadron's unprecedented problems of bureaucracy and supply, in essence discussing an aspect of material ineffectiveness from the Union perspective. According to Browning, logistical obstacles "prevented the quick implementation and enforcement of the blockade, restrained the efforts of the squadron during the entire war, and touched on nearly every aspect of its performance." Poor-quality steamships hampered Union efforts, and as a result, "the blockade suffered greatly because of the inefficiency of the gunboats that patrolled the coast."[13] Blockaders' absences from patrol due to repairs and re-coaling prevented squadrons from operating at full capacity.

Though Browning notes that these logistical issues "virtually crippled the effectiveness of the blockade," he ultimately qualifies his conclusion admitting that "the blockade did not effectively keep contraband out of the Confederacy." But he clarifies this point: "It is equally clear that the blockade severely damaged the Confederate war effort in several ways." In a nod to the consensus interpretation of contributory effectiveness, Browning concludes "that the Union was an important factor in the destruction of the South's ability to wage war."[14]

Browning's well-researched interpretations straddle the arguments for both material ineffectiveness and contributory effectiveness. As for historians who would statistically tabulate blockade-runners, he notes, "Steamers evaded the blockade virtually at will [and] it is not necessary to make a complete list to make that point."[15] Browning highlights several important interpretations of both the blockade's effectiveness and ineffectiveness. This is an important point. Some historians use a variety of arguments and interpretations to arrive at their conclusions, and at times they simultaneously argue for the blockade's strengths and weaknesses.

The material-ineffectiveness argument, much like its opposite—the contributory-effectiveness model—suffers from the historical pitfall of assumption. Arguing that the Union interdiction was materially ineffectual assumes that Confederate leaders conducted a well-thought-out blockade-running policy. This argument also presumes that domestic sources could supply what did not come through the blockade. Neither of these assumptions is entirely accurate. The Confederate government did not make an effort to control runners' cargoes until 1864. To be sure, the Confederacy paid high prices for war materiel, and the Ordnance Department became adept at procuring specific items, but, for the most part, the Confederate government purchased whatever military goods happened to be imported. Most cases for material ineffectiveness cite impressive lists of imported goods, but falter when applying those numbers to a larger analytical framework of Confederate needs. While importation statistics prove that some supplies got through the blockade, the material-ineffectiveness interpretation does not resolve the debate about the blockade's effectiveness.

As the historiography indicates, it may be impossible to create an agreeable definition of the Union blockade's overall effectiveness. However, it is possible to address the long-standing assertion that the blockade's effectiveness increased over time from 1861 to 1865. This sacrosanct interpretation has been a steadfast foundation of blockade scholarship since the 1930s. The first major study to claim the blockade's increased effectiveness over time was Frank Owsley's *King Cotton Diplomacy* (1931). Owsley was also the first scholar to estimate blockade-runner captures, and as a result, his work has greatly influenced the debate about the blockade's effectiveness. He declared, "It seems from all the evidence that the captures ran about thus: 1861, not more than 1 in 10; 1862, not more than 1 in 8; 1863, not more than 1 in 4; 1864, not more than 1 in 3; 1865, after most of the ports were captured and fleet concentrated about the gulf, 1 in 2." Owsley concluded that the increased annual effectiveness of the Union blockade resulted in "an average for the war of about 1 capture in 6."[16]

These numbers continue to serve as a yardstick for other studies, and they are still cited as proof of the blockade's ever-increasing potency. However, there is one problem—Owsley made these claims without compiling statistical data about blockade-runners. Instead, he simply cited James Soley's 1883 book *The Blockade and the Cruisers*. To be fair, this was the best account of the blockade and blockade-running up to the time of Owsley's work, and it is still a valuable source. However, since Owsley's publication of *King Cotton Diplomacy*, far too many historians have repeated his evidence for the blockade's growing effectiveness without performing their own due diligence. Fortunately for Civil War historians, two scholars of blockade-running, Marcus Price and Stephen Wise, compiled impressive statistical data sets that allow for an updated analysis of blockade efficacy throughout the war.

Statistical analysis of successful runs and captures is the most precise way to determine the blockade's effectiveness over time from 1861 to 1865. Statistical effectiveness, or ineffectiveness, is the final interpretation to be examined. The first detailed study of blockade successes and captures based on numerical data was the seminal work of Marcus Price. In a series of articles published in the late 1940s and 1950s, Price used records from the National Archives to create a comprehensive list of blockade-runners. He identified the vessels' type—whether steamer or sloop—as well as their tonnage and crew size. Price also listed crucial information like the ships' known successful runs and, if applicable, the location of their capture or destruction. In addition, he organized his data geographically, providing blockade-running statistics from North Carolina, South Carolina, Georgia, Florida, and the entire Gulf Coast.[17] This organizational method provides readers a glimpse into the blockade's effectiveness at specific Confederate ports.

However, Price's data suffers from two pivotal omissions. First, the data set lists blockade-runners as they traveled "for" and "from" Confederate ports, and Price assumed that each of these vessels successfully violated the blockade. But some ships could travel inter- or intra-coastally and reach a Confederate port. For example, it was possible to travel between Mobile and New Orleans without going into the Gulf of Mexico and confronting the Union blockade. Likewise, it was possible to travel between Charleston and Savannah with limited exposure to the offshore Union blockaders. These inter- and intra-coastal routes were eventually hampered by the close, or inside, blockade, but Price did not make this distinction in his list of blockade-runners.[18] Second, while Price's data lists the number of known successful runs during each year, it does not provide readers with the number of attempts—and this information is extremely important when trying to determine the blockade's effectiveness. Price's work contains some limitations, but it remains one of the most detailed compilations of statistical data on blockade-running during the Civil War.

However, in order to perform a comprehensive statistical study of the interdiction's effectiveness over time, scholars need crucial data on the number of attempts to break through the blockade. Fortunately, historian

Stephen Wise's statistics complement Price's data and allow for deeper analysis. Wise compiled the most comprehensive set of statistical data in *Lifeline of the Confederacy: Blockade Running during the Civil War* (1988), consulting a wider array of primary sources to achieve his goal of putting "together the entire story" of blockade-running. His superb collection of appendices fills in the gaps of Price's work. Appendices 5 through 15 in particular allow historians to assess the number of captures and successes, but more importantly, Wise's data provides the number of blockade-running *attempts*. Whereas the Price data only notes "Place and Date Captured or Destroyed" for each vessel, the Wise information shows the date and location of *each run* through the blockade, including particulars about capture or destruction. Wise's extra layer of detail allows for a more comprehensive analysis of the blockade's effectiveness over time.[19]

The combination of the Price and the Wise data sets makes a new statistical analysis possible. The primary goal is to answer this question: Did the effectiveness of the Union blockade increase, decrease, or remain static during the Civil War? The methods used in this study are designed to achieve the most objective assessment possible. (see appendix 4 on methodology) Wise, like Price, organized the data geographically. To show the relative accuracy of their data sets, both historians arrived at roughly equal numbers of steam-powered blockade-runners that were captured or destroyed: Wise estimates 221 and Price 223. This relative replication of the number indicates that both data sets are robust. We dropped the two additional vessels from the Price data and created a combined data set that could be cross-referenced for information on each steam-powered blockade-runner.

To achieve maximum objectivity concerning both the blockade squadrons and the blockade-runners, several different methods were used. First, this study only calculates statistics for steam-powered runners. Sail-powered blockade-running on all but very small vessels was drastically curtailed in 1862 (see chapter 3). It is worth noting, however, that blockade-runners at times resorted to a combination of sail and steam power to maximize speed. Steam-powered vessels formed Union cordons, so sailing ships reliant on wind power were easy prey. For this reason, this study only considers statistics for the steam-powered runners to provide a level playing field between blockaders and runners. This capture/destruction data for steamers allows for a more unbiased statistical assessment of the blockade's effectiveness.

Second, this study uses a standard incremental timetable to allow an equal opportunity to determine effectiveness or ineffectiveness. If incremental time periods are established, then the blockade's effectiveness can be measured over time. In the interest of fairness to both the Union squadrons and the blockade-runners, we have eliminated the first and last six months of blockade service from the calculation. After Lincoln's blockade declaration in April 1861, the US Navy spent the next six months building and deploying the squadrons. US fleets could hardly be expected to be effective during this early period. Indeed, the first vessels posted outside Confederate ports were woefully insufficient to interdict rebel supplies. Therefore, this period from April to October 1861 should be excluded in a fair study of the blockade's effectiveness.

Likewise, in the final six months of the war from October 1864 to April 1865, blockade-runners had fewer Confederate ports to enter. Options were particularly limited after Mobile Bay fell to Union forces in August 1864 and Wilmington, North Carolina, was closed off to runners in January 1865. We refer to the first and last six months of the blockade as the preliminary phase (April 1861 to October 1861) and the final phase (October 1864 to April 1865). In summation, we omitted the preliminary phase from this study for yielding inferior data since the blockade was not yet fully established. Likewise, the final phase coincided with the Confederacy's collapse and the Union capture of the remaining rebel-held blockade-running ports, so we excluded data from that period as well. In effect, we have removed the outlying statistics to allow equal opportunity of success for both the Union squadrons and the blockade-runners.

Third, instead of breaking up the blockade results into geographic regions, like Price and Wise did, we divided the statistical table for gauging effectiveness into time increments to search for periodic changes in capture rates. Thus, each phase corresponds to a ninety-one-day or ninety-two-day blockade-running cycle beginning on October 19, 1861, and ending on October 18, 1864.[20] This method allows scholars to assess capture rates over time for the Union squadrons and blockade-runners when both sides had an equal opportunity for success.

The Price data (see Table 2, Chart 1) shows that the Union blockade maintained a relatively steady capture/destruction rate over the course of the war. Blockade squadrons captured or destroyed 187 blockade-running steamers throughout the twelve phases from October 1861 to October 1864. The only aberrations in this pattern of blockade-squadron success are phase one (October 1861 to January 1862), when only one runner was captured or destroyed, and phase five (October 1862 to January 1863), when

TABLE 2. Capture/Destruction Rates by Union Blockade[21]

Phase	Days in Phase	Steamers: Number Captured/ Destroyed	Deviation from Median	Percentage of Total Captured or Destroyed
Preliminary Phase 4/19/61-10/18/61	183	3	NA	NA
Phase 1: 10/19/61-1/17/62	91	1	-15.5	0.45%
Phase 2: 1/18/62-4/18/62	91	14	-2.5	6.28%
Phase 3: 4/19/62-7/19/62	92	21	4.5	9.42%
Phase 4: 7/20/62-10/18/62	91	12	-4.5	5.38%
Phase 5: 10/19/62-1/17/63	91	5	-11.5	2.24%
Phase 6: 1/18/63-4/18/63	91	13	-3.5	5.83%
Phase 7: 4/19/63-7/19/63	92	20	3.5	8.97%
Phase 8: 7/20/63-10/18/63	91	26	9.5	11.66%
Phase 9: 10/19/63-1/17/64	91	20	3.5	8.97%
Phase 10: 1/18/64-4/18/64	92	18	1.5	8.07%
Phase 11: 4/19/64-7/19/64	92	22	5.5	9.87%
Phase 12: 7/20/64-10/18/64	91	15	-1.5	6.73%
Final Phase: 10/19/64-4/18/65	182	33	NA	NA
TOTALS:	1461	223		
Median result for 91/92 day phases		16.5		

five runners were captured or destroyed. Other than these two statistically less successful periods, the US fleets consistently seized or destroyed an average of 15.6 blockade-runners during each of the twelve phases from October 1861 to October 1864—or about 5 vessels per month. This is credible statistical evidence of the Union interdiction's capability.

However, the Price data also points out the ebb and flow of the runners' success and failure. In phases one through six, from October 1861 to April 1863, with the exception of phase three, the runners appeared to have a high success rate since the number of captures and destructions was relatively low. By contrast, the Union blockade squadrons achieved their highest capture and destruction rates in phases seven through eleven, from April 1863 to July 1864.

How did the number of captured and destroyed vessels affect the overall

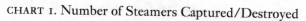

CHART I. Number of Steamers Captured/Destroyed

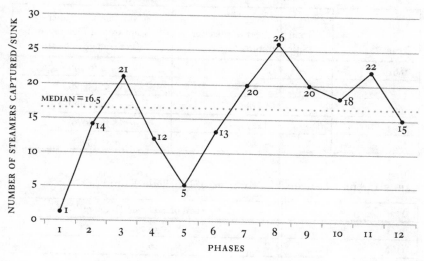

business of blockade-running? In other words, did the attrition of ships curtail efforts to penetrate the Union cordon? US squadrons seized or laid waste to almost 7 percent of the steam-powered blockade-running fleet in each phase. However, replacement ships prevented the attritional destruction of these vessels. With the exception of the truncated year of 1865, the Confederacy managed to attract an increasing number of steam-powered runners into its remaining ports from 1861 to 1864 (see Table 2).[22] This annual increase of steamships counters the oft-argued deterrent argument, in which historians assert that the mere existence of the blockade scared away potential blockade-runners. In fact, the opposite is true. Increasing numbers of steam-powered blockade-runners became involved in the trade up to 1865.

On the other hand, according to Table 2, Union blockade squadrons performed admirably. They consistently captured or destroyed about 60 percent of the yearly blockade-runner fleets from 1862 to 1864. But continued opportunity for high profits and improved technologies for ships meant there would be no shortage of entrepreneurs attempting to violate the blockade. Technologically advanced blockade-runners sacrificed cargo space in exchange for larger engines, shallower drafts, and increased speeds. It is legitimate to argue that by forcing this design change, Union

TABLE 3. Percentage of Steamers Captured/Destroyed[23]

Year	Total Number of Steamer Ships running that year	Number of Steamers Captured or Destroyed (Percentage of total)
1861	71	4 (6%)
1862	86	51 (59%)
1863	118	74 (62%)
1864	127	76 (60%)
1865	50	18 (36%)

TABLE 4. Annual Steamship Tonnage of Blockade-Runners[24]

Year	Total of Steamer Tonnage
1861	36,030
1862	40,554
1863	49,471
1864	52,301
1865	20,246
TOTAL	198,602

fleets diminished the total amount of war materiel brought through the blockade.

However, unlike Confederate armies that were decimated by attrition, the blockade-running fleet replaced its losses by entering new ships into the trade. The ability to attract new steam-powered vessels, combined with the presence of the surviving ships, meant that the blockade-running fleet's replenishment outpaced its losses for four straight years. As a result, despite the number of captured and destroyed vessels, the total tonnage of blockade-running steamers increased annually from 1861 to 1864 (see Table 4). Price's data shows that the Union blockade maintained a steady effectiveness over time beginning in 1862, but increased blockade-runner participation offset this improvement in the capture/destruction rate.

The statistical data displayed up to this point provides an excellent understanding of the Union blockade's performance, but it does not allow for calculating the periodic percentage of captured/destroyed vessels or

TABLE 5. Percentage of Steamers Captured/Destroyed by Phase

Phase	Days in Phase	No. of Steamers Captured/ Destroyed	Total Blockade Attempts	Percentage Captured/ Destroyed	Deviation from Median
Preliminary Phase: 04/19/61–10/18/61	183				
Phase 1: 10/19/61–01/17/62	91	1	14	7.14%	-10.62%
Phase 2: 01/18/62–04/18/62	91	14	41	34.14%	16.38%
Phase 3: 04/19/62–07/19/62	92	21	31	67.74%	49.98%
Phase 4: 07/20/62–10/18/62	91	12	35	34.28%	16.52%
Phase 5: 10/19/62–01/17/63	91	5	24	20.83%	3.07%
Phase 6: 01/18/63–04/18/63	91	13	72	18.05%	0.29%
Phase 7: 04/19/63–07/19/63	92	20	143	13.98%	-3.78%
Phase 8: 07/20/63–10/18/63	91	26	109	23.85%	6.09%
Phase 9: 10/19/63–01/17/64	91	20	118	16.94%	-0.82%
Phase 10: 01/18/64–04/18/64	92	18	103	17.47%	-0.29%
Phase 11: 04/19/64–07/19/64	92	22	141	15.60%	-2.16%
Phase 12: 07/20/64–10/18/64	91	15	118	12.71%	-5.05%
TOTALS (Phases 1-12)	1096	187	949	19.70%	
Avg. (Phases 1-12)	–	15.6	79.08		
Final Phase: 10/19/64–04/18/65	182				
TOTALS	1461	223	–	100%	–
Median result for 91/92 day phases	–	16.5	–	17.76%	–

analyzing the blockade's effectiveness over time. The one missing element in this examination has been the number of blockade-running attempts, and for this information we need to delve deeper into Stephen Wise's detailed data set. The Wise data provides the total number of steam-powered blockade-running attempts.

We can now calculate the *percentage* of steamers captured or destroyed in each three-month phase (see Table 5). This calculation highlights the blockade's effectiveness over time from October 1861 to October 1864. The

CHART 2. Percentage of Steamers Captured/Destroyed by Phase

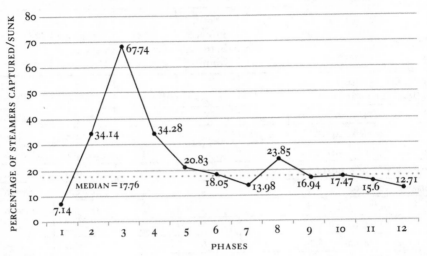

median percentage of blockade-running steamers seized or destroyed per phase is 17.76 percent. Over the entire twelve-phase period, an average of 19.70 percent of steam-powered runners were taken or destroyed. After a poor showing in phase one, Union blockade squadrons performed admirably in phases two, three, and four, with captured/destroyed percentages of 34.14 percent, 67.74 percent, and 34.28 percent respectively. However, contrary to previous historical analysis—put forth by Owsley and numerous others who have argued for increased effectiveness over time—Union squadrons actually captured or destroyed lower percentages of steam-powered blockade runners from October 1862 to October 1864, with the exception of a slight uptick in phase eight in the summer of 1863.

The Union squadrons' ability to capture or destroy steam-powered blockade-runners dropped from an all-time high effectiveness rate 67.74 percent in phase three (April–July 1862) to a low effectiveness rate of 12.71 percent in phase twelve (July–October 1864). (See Chart 2 for further relevant information.) With the exception of phase eight's (July–October 1863) rate increase up to 23.85 percent, the remainder of the phases from five through twelve witnessed captured/destroyed percentages of roughly 20 percent or lower. The statistical evidence also shows, contrary to conventional historical assumptions, that from July 1862 to October 1864, with the exception of one three-month period in 1863 and a miniscule increase from phase nine (16.94 percent) to phase ten (17.47 percent), the Union blockade's effectiveness at capturing or destroying steam-powered runners actually decreased over time.

It is important to note that although Frank Owsley was incorrect about the blockade's increasing success with regard to steam-powered vessels, he was remarkably accurate about the overall percentage of steam-powered blockade-runners captured or destroyed. The statistical evidence shows that a median 17.76 percent of steamships attempting to break the blockade were captured or destroyed per phase, and this figure is remarkably close to Owsley's assertion of "1 capture in 6," or approximately 16.66 percent. Statistical evidence reaffirms the general historical consensus that, on average, the Union squadrons caught every sixth blockade-runner—Owsley established this position in in *King Cotton Diplomacy* (1931). However, the same cannot be argued for the consensus historical interpretation that the blockade's effectiveness against steam-powered vessels increased from October 1861 through October 1864. In fact, numerical data proves that the Union blockade actually captured or destroyed an increasingly lower percentage of steam-powered blockade-runners during that period.

Based on statistical evidence over standardized time increments in which both the Union squadrons and runners possessed equal chances of success, the blockade's effectiveness against steam-powered vessels decreased from 1862 to 1864. After a pitifully low capture rate of 7.14 percent between October 18, 1861, and January 17, 1862, the interdiction's effectiveness against these same vessels increased to an impressive 67.74 percent capture rate by July 19, 1862. After that, the blockade's effectiveness plummeted, and with the exception of one small improvement between July 20 and October 17, 1863, capture rates for steamers consistently hovered around 20 percent and declined to a low of 12.71 percent in October 1864. According to the statistical evidence from October 1861 to October 1864, steam-powered blockade-runners succeeded on roughly four out of five attempts, and they actually stood a greater statistical chance of piercing the blockade as the war dragged on into 1863 and 1864.[25] This data contradicts previous historical interpretations that argued the Union blockade's effectiveness increased over time.

The conventional analysis of the blockade's efficacy during the four years of war is a bedrock of Civil War historiography. In 1931 Frank Owsley set the standard interpretation of this subject in his impressive work *King*

Cotton Diplomacy. Historian Bern Anderson reinforced this theme when he declared that "by 1863 there was a very real and definite risk in running the blockade." Anderson logically concluded, "By then [1863] the Union Navy had ships with sufficient speed to catch most runners and the efficiency of the blockade improved with experience."[26] Both Owsley and Anderson, and most historians since, have assumed that the Union blockade's period of increased effectiveness at catching steam-powered runners in 1862 and 1863 carried over into 1864. It did not. The specialized, technologically superior ships continued to successfully penetrate the US squadrons in 1864 at higher rates than in either 1862 or 1863. In fact, with regard to steam-powered blockade-runners, statistical evidence reveals that the blockade's effectiveness actually decreased from 1863 through 1864.

Conclusion

The Union blockade's effectiveness remains ambiguous, and historians may never completely agree on the subject. However, sufficient statistical evidence supports several assertions and a fundamental analysis of the blockade's effectiveness. First, the Union blockade was no doubt effective in preventing large cargo ships from entering the Confederacy. Likewise, ships with lessened cargo capacities carried out Southern cotton exports, thus severely limiting the Confederate economy. Also, by the end of 1862, the blockade was so effective at capturing sail ships that very few vessels continued in that aspect of the trade. In all of these statistical categories, the Union blockade's indisputable efficacy conforms to previous historical analysis.

But there is one aspect of the Union blockade's effectiveness that does not match conventional wisdom—the increased ability over time to capture or destroy steam-powered blockade-runners. Statistical evidence proves that the Union blockade was most effective in 1862, and that it became less so throughout 1864. This evidence counters previous historical assumptions about the blockade's increased effectiveness during the war, as claimed by Frank Owsley and cited by many other historians ever since. The statistical fact that, given an equal chance of success between early 1862 and late 1864, Union blockade squadrons were less capable of apprehending steamships than previously assumed does not negate the blockade's overall effectiveness. In fact, one could explain this phenomenon using anecdotal evidence from the squadron leaders themselves. The seamen openly admitted in 1863 and

1864 that the new class of specially designed blockade-runners outclassed ships in the Union squadrons. It was through sheer force of numbers and the improved tactics of port saturation—with inside and outside blockade lines—that the US fleets compensated for this gap in maritime innovation. The effectiveness debate will likely continue, but one statistically proven fact should not be ignored. Union blockade squadrons' ability to capture or destroy steam-powered blockade runners did not increase from 1862 to 1864 as previously assumed; instead it actually decreased.

Conclusion

——————★——————

ROM THE UNION BLOCKADE'S inception in April 1861 to its conclusion in May 1865, a daily battle ensued between blockade
squadrons and blockade-runners. The US Navy's interdiction of
Confederate commerce was the longest continual military campaign of the
Civil War. This undertaking used up vast quantities of manpower, food,
coal, and materials required to construct and maintain the armada. During
the war, land-based military campaigns received more publicity, and perhaps this was deserved. However, it is regrettable that the blockade's pivotal
importance to the Civil War's development and outcome was largely under-
appreciated during the conflict—and it has been ever since. Historians have
written a handful of stand-alone studies about the blockade and blockade-
runners, but academic works typically cover the Union interdiction as a
secondary campaign in the Civil War. This dearth of scholarly treatment
is not in keeping with the blockade's importance as the longest-running
military campaign, and as the only uninterrupted Union wartime strategy.

One aspect of the blockade's strategic origins was its boosting of Union
morale in April 1861. It is easy to overlook the fact that the Confederacy
temporarily held the upper hand in the first year of the war. The Lincoln
administration needed time to recruit, train, and equip Union armies and
build up the US Navy. In April 1861, Union military power was unprepared
to wage an offensive war against the Confederacy. The rebel attack on Fort
Sumter provided the Lincoln administration with the momentum to begin
large-scale recruitment, but these armies could not be trained and put into
offensive campaigns for several months. In the interim, Lincoln had to act.
He decided to use one of his greatest advantages—the US Navy. Lincoln
knew the navy was not prepared for a full-scale blockade in April 1861,
but he proclaimed the interdiction anyway as a promise of future naval
dominance. The interdiction of rebel supplies did not seriously hinder the
Confederacy until 1862, but Lincoln's projection of naval power was an
important psychological boost for the Union in the war's early stages.

The April 1861 blockade declaration was calculated to bolster Union hopes. Lincoln knew that his announcement hazarded a diplomatic tussle with Great Britain, but it was among the few readily available options to counter the rebellion in its first month. Much like the Emancipation Proclamations of 1862-3 did not immediately free any slaves, the president's 1861 blockade declaration did not immediately close off the Confederacy. Instead, it promised to develop a formidable naval interdiction, and in both instances—emancipation and the blockade—Lincoln masterfully guided his promises to fruition.

Great Britain loomed large over the Union blockade. The Royal Navy was the most powerful in the world, and British economic interests were deeply tied to Southern cotton. Lincoln needed to tread softly lest Her Majesty's government come fully into the war—not necessarily on the Confederate side, but to protect British economic prerogatives. While British intervention could have tipped the scales in the South's favor, this never occurred for a variety of reasons. First, in 1861 and 1862 Lincoln adroitly managed foreign affairs with Great Britain. He skillfully navigated several serious crises, including the issue of blockade declaration versus port closures, the *Trent* affair, and the use of emancipation as a diplomatic weapon in late 1862. The Confederacy's disastrous policy of King Cotton Diplomacy helped the Lincoln administration, but it was the president's mastery, and Seward's maturation, that kept Great Britain at bay. This is not to say that the British did not extract concessions from both sides—they did, in the form of contraband cotton exports and a willingness to sell supplies to Northerners and Southerners. In addition, Great Britain managed to get both Union and Confederate administrations to respect the Declaration of Paris, and this successfully continued British maritime primacy.

Union blockade squadrons grew in number and capability after 1861. Navy Secretary Gideon Welles admirably coordinated, constructed, and implemented the interdiction. From the outset, his sagacity in empaneling the Blockade Strategy Board and—more importantly—in abiding by its recommendations, put the Union blockade on a firm strategic foundation. In fact, the Union blockade involved the only enduring strategic plan from 1861 to 1865. The blockade was a component of the Anaconda Plan, but Welles ensured that the interdiction strategy was carried out. Gideon Welles oversaw a massive expansion of the US Navy from about forty ships in 1861 to over six hundred vessels in 1865—many of them guarding Confederate ports. From 1862 to 1864, each blockade squadron increased the number of ships on duty, continuing to strengthen the cordon of vessels along the Southern coast. This ceaseless naval pressure played a key role in interdicting vital military supplies and perpetually demoralized Confederate nationalists. The existence, performance, and sheer scale of the blockade was an important factor in Union victory.

Blockade-runners adapted to the strategy and tactics of the US squadrons and continued to arrive in Confederate ports well into 1864. In 1861, blockade-running was a veritable free-for-all with very little chance of seizure by the few Union blockade vessels. That changed in 1862, when runners' capture rates dramatically increased—the cat-and-mouse game had begun. For the rest of the war, blockade-running captains tested US fleets' tactics with countermeasures. Smuggling continued to be profitable, but by 1864 Union blockaders were omnipresent, and only the most technologically advanced runners—those with a veteran captain and some good luck— had a decent chance to arrive safely in the remaining Confederate ports.

Blockade-running was an illicit but highly lucrative sector of transatlantic maritime commerce that sparked boom economies in transshipment points like the Bahamas, Bermuda, and Cuba. In addition, the Confederate government relied on blockade-running to conduct international diplomacy and finance, and the Union blockade's diminution of these aspects of the southern war effort has been typically overlooked. Government ownership of blockade-runners—for example, the Confederate Ordnance Department and the State of North Carolina both owned vessels—proved the vital nature of the trade. The Confederate government was overly dependent on the cargo decisions of blockade-running entrepreneurs, and it did not regulate cargoes until 1864. By then it was too little, too late. Without question, the Confederate war effort could not have lasted as long as it did without the crucial supplies carried through the blockade. In early 1865, when every major Confederate port was in Union hands and Confederate armies were cut off from foreign supplies, rebel hopes were completely dashed.

The blockade also provided intangible advantages to the Union war effort. Lincoln's declaration in April 1861 might not have frightened Confederates since runners came and went almost at will. But blockade squadrons increased their numbers in 1862, and the reality of a ceaseless, ever-multiplying blockade became a psychological weapon for the Union. Confederate naval sorties attempted to disrupt the interdiction, but to no avail. However, the Union cordons did not deter entrepreneurs from attempting the trip into Confederate ports. From 1861 through 1864, more steam-powered blockade-runners entered the trade each year.

But the psychological aspects of the blockade did not just affect wartime contemporaries. One could argue that a psycho-historiographic effect has influenced some historians such that they argue for the blockade's effectiveness simply because it existed. The blockade certainly contributed to Union victory and caught many smugglers, but it is dubious to repeat the effectiveness interpretation without deeper investigation, and to cite "Union victory" as evidence that the blockade was effectual. Ultimate victory does not prove whether a military strategy is successful—there have been plenty of effective military strategies on the losing sides of wars, and plenty of ineffective military strategies on winning sides. Civil War historians should be careful not to conflate Union victory with the blockade's effectiveness—the two topics are related, but each has a myriad of underlying factors that contribute to the final interpretation.

Was the Union blockade effective? In many ways the answer is an emphatic "yes!" The number of vessels in Union blockade squadrons ballooned after 1861, and runners could no longer come and go with ease. In 1862 several facts became evident: Sail-powered ships were easily captured, and only smaller sailing vessels continued in the blockade-running trade. But more importantly, starting in April 1862, US squadrons proved their capability of catching blockade-runners. This improvement was slightly offset by the runners' new tactics and improved technology, but from 1862 to the end of the war, the Union interdiction was a formidable obstacle to Confederate commerce. The average career of a steam-powered blockade-runner was only two round trips, beyond which statistics indicate they would be captured or destroyed by the Union fleet. Some ships beat the odds and made numerous successful runs, and others were captured on the first attempt, but regardless of individual runners' narratives, Union blockade squadrons eventually caught their prey.

This general description of the never-ending mission to interdict blockade-running may be the greatest argument for the blockade's efficacy. However, historians have overstated the blockade's increasing effectiveness from 1862 to 1864 with respect to steam-powered runners. This does not mean the US Navy was ineffective. It simply means that catching state-of-the-art blockade-runners was difficult. Union squadrons made up for this disadvantage by increasing the number of vessels off Confederate ports, but a purpose-built runner with a veteran captain, an experienced pilot, and a protected entrance to a rebel port always had a chance of success, no matter the numbers arrayed against it. In this respect, the blockade was not as successful as historians have led us to believe.

Was the blockade an important component of Union victory? Yes. To pose the same question another way, was implementing a Union blockade better than having no blockade at all? The obvious answer is yes—of course it was. But that does not help us understand the blockade's effectiveness. The opposite question must also be asked: Was the blockade effective at catching steam-powered blockade-runners from mid-1862 to late 1864? The answer to that question is "not very effective." In fact, statistical evidence shows that the percentage of steam-powered blockade-runners that the Union captured/destroyed actually declined from July 1862 to October 1864, with one miniscule exception.

Almost from the moment of the Confederacy's creation, the Union blockade was a shadow that loomed over the rebellion. This naval penumbra cast a pall of inevitable doom over Confederate nationalists' psyche mainly because astute Southerners realized they could do little to remove the blockade. Like an eclipse, the shadow grew darker as the war progressed, as the Union navy deployed the full might of its maritime resources. But, just like an eclipse does not eliminate all light, the blockade did not completely block out all shipping to the Confederacy. Another apt analogy is that the Union blockade was like a massive boulder that falls into a small stream—a serious impediment to the natural watercourse, but incapable of completely preventing the water from finding a less direct route. However, the fact that all blockade-running was not stamped out does not mean the blockade was ineffective, since some of its power lay in its effect on Confederate morale.

The only surefire way to completely shut down blockade-running was for Union armies to capture Confederate ports. Historian Stephen Wise notes that "as long as there were ports that steamers could utilize, the Confederacy survived." Wise also understands the importance of port captures, stating "Once the seaports were captured the [Confederate] nation was destined to die."[1] Stationing land forces in Southern ports and their environs was the Union's only certain method for halting attempts to break the blockade. In some cases, control of vital entry points like Fort Pulaski downriver from Savannah, Fort Fisher at the entrance to Wilmington, and Forts Morgan and Gaines at the mouth of Mobile Bay prevented access to Confederate ports.

Which side won the four-year-long blockade campaign? The answer depends on how one asks the question, and who is asked. From the Union perspective, the blockade was a key contributory component in preventing the Confederacy's unhindered importation of war materiel, and in interdicting its outbound cotton to Europe. By 1864, it was obvious to all that the Confederacy was being gradually starved of resources in almost every category. This paucity of supplies, along with shortsighted monetary policy, sparked Southern hyperinflation in 1863, which further eroded the rebel war effort from within. There is no doubt the Union blockade was a major factor in the Confederacy's failure to obtain enough resources to prosecute the war to its fullest extent.

From the Confederate perspective, the Union blockade was a hindrance, but not the most important factor in rebel defeat. The basic argument for this view is that blockade-runners imported enough military supplies to sustain the Confederate war effort. One simple statement sums up this point. Did rebel armies ever lose a battle because they lacked arms and ammunition? The answer is no. Proponents of this sufficient-military-supply argument note that Confederate armies lost battles due to poor generalship and an ever-worsening manpower disadvantage, but a lack of weapons and munitions was not the main reason for the South's defeat. So which side is right? Both arguments are correct. These two interpretations of the blockade's effect on the overall outcome of the Civil War are both accurate, and they are not necessarily mutually exclusive. Historians, however, must argue about something, and this will continue to be a point of contentious debate.

APPENDIX 1
The Declaration of Paris,
April 16, 1856

The Plenipotentiaries who signed the Treaty of Paris of March 30, 1856, assembled in conference,

Considering: That maritime law in time of war has long been the subject of deplorable disputes;

That the uncertainty of the law and of the duties in such a matter gives rise to differences of opinion between neutrals and belligerents which may occasion serious difficulties, and even conflicts; that it is consequently advantageous to establish a uniform doctrine on so important a point;

That the Plenipotentiaries assembled in Congress at Paris cannot better respond to the intentions by which their Governments are animated than by seeking to introduce into International relations fixed principles in this respect.

The above-mentioned Plenipotentiaries, being duly authorized, resolved to concert among themselves as to the means of attaining this object; and having come to an agreement, have adopted the following solemn declaration:

1. Privateering is and remains abolished;
2. The neutral flag covers enemy's goods, with the exception of contraband of war;
3. Neutral goods, with the exception of contraband of war, are not liable to capture under the enemy's flag;
4. Blockades, in order to be binding, must be effective — that is to say, maintained by a force sufficient really to prevent access to the coast of the enemy.

The Governments of the undersigned Plenipotentiaries engage to bring the present declaration to the knowledge of the States which have not taken part in the Congress of Paris, and to invite them to accede.

Convinced that the maxims which they now proclaim cannot but be received with gratitude by the whole world, the undersigned Plenipotentiaries doubt not that the efforts of their Governments to obtain the general adoption thereof will be crowned with full success.

The present Declaration is not and shall not be binding, except between those Powers who have acceded, or shall accede, to it.

APPENDIX 2

President Lincoln's Blockade Proclamation, April 19, 1861

Whereas an insurrection against the Government of the United States has broken out in the States of South Carolina, Georgia, Alabama, Florida, Mississippi, Louisiana, and Texas, and the laws of the United States for collection of the revenue can not be effectually executed therein, conformably to that provision of the Constitution which requires duties to be uniform throughout the United States; and

Whereas a combination of persons engaged in such insurrection has threatened to grant pretended letters of marque to authorize the bearers thereof to commit assaults on the lives, vessels, and property of good citizens of the country lawfully engaged in commerce on the high seas and in the waters of the United States; and

Whereas an Executive proclamation has already been issued requiring the persons engaged in these disorderly proceedings to desist therefrom, calling out a militia force for the purpose of repressing the same, and convening Congress in extraordinary session to deliberate and determine thereon;

Now, therefore, I, Abraham Lincoln, President of the United States, with a view to the same purposes before mentioned, and to the protection of the public peace and lives and property of quiet and orderly citizens pursuing their lawful occupations until Congress shall have assembled and deliberated on the said lawful proceedings, or until the same shall have ceased, have further deemed it advisable to set on foot a blockade of the ports within the States aforesaid, in pursuance of the laws of the United States and of the law of nations is such case provided. For this purpose, a competent force will be posted so as to prevent entrance and exit of vessels from the ports aforesaid. If, therefore, with a view to violate such blockade a vessel shall approach or shall attempt to leave either of the said ports, she will be duly warned by the commander of one of the blockading vessels, who will endorse on her register the fact and date of such warning, and if the same vessel shall again attempt to enter or leave the blockaded port she will be captured and sent to the nearest convenient port for such proceedings against her and her cargo as prize as may be deemed advisable.

And I hereby proclaim and declare that if any person, under the pretended authority of the said States, or under any other pretense, shall molest a vessel of the United States, or the persons or cargo on board of her, such person shall be held amenable to the laws of the United States for the prevention and punishment of piracy.

In witness whereof I have hereunto set my hand and caused the seal of the United States to be affixed.

Done at the city Washington this 19th day of April A.D. 1861, and of the Independence of the United States the eighty-fifth.

                                                              Abraham Lincoln

Official Records of the Union and Confederate Navies in the War of the Rebellion (Washington, DC: Government Printing Office, 1915) series 1, vol. 5, p. 620. (hereafter cited in the following format: *ORN*, ser. 1, vol. 5, p. 620).

APPENDIX 3

Lincoln's Blockade Extension to Virginia and North Carolina, April 27, 1861

Whereas, for reasons assigned in my proclamation of the 19th instant, a blockade of the ports of the States of South Carolina, Georgia, Florida, Alabama, Louisiana, Mississippi, and Texas was ordered to be established; and whereas, since that date public property of the United States has been seized, the collection of revenue obstructed, and duly commissioned officers of the United States, while engaged in executing orders of their superiors, have been arrested and held in custody as prisoners, or have been impeded in the discharge of their official duties without due legal process by persons claiming to act under the authority of the States of Virginia and North Carolina, an efficient blockade of the ports of those States will therefore also be established.

In witness thereof I have hereunto set my hand and caused the seal of the United States to be affixed.

Done at the city of Washington this 27th day of April, A.D. 1861, and of the Independence of the United States the eighty-fifth.

ORN, ser. 1, vol. 5, p. 621.

APPENDIX 4
Methodology for Statistical Analysis of Effectiveness over Time

The data for our statistical analysis comes from two sources—Marcus Price and Stephen Wise. Let us explain how we combined the two data sets. First, we tabulated all entries from Price's "The Ships That Tested the Blockade" series of articles in *American Neptune*. Second, we tabulated all the appendices in Wise's authoritative work *Lifeline of the Confederacy: Blockade Running during the Civil War* (1988). The Price data appears in the following volumes of *American Neptune*: 8 (1948), pp. 196–241; 9 (1949), pp. 31–62; 11 (1951), pp. 262–90; 12 (1952), pp. 52–59, 154–61, 229–38; and 15 (1955), pp. 97–132. From the Price data we tabulated steamers captured/destroyed (or otherwise "foundered") by location and date.

From the Wise figures we tabulated the number of runs each steamer attempted, successfully or otherwise, and distinguished between inbound and outbound trips. However, we noted that Wise's appendices are not complete with respect to his findings. Wise states that 221 steamers were captured/destroyed (*Lifeline of the Confederacy*, 221), but when we recorded all the captured/destroyed (including all varieties of losses) vessels from the appendices, only 188 entries appeared. Thirty-three steamers are unaccounted for, which we assumed was due either to space limitations or the appendix formats' exclusion of the missing ships. For example, the dates used for outbound journeys cover the entire war, while the inbound runs do not.

Wise's total of 221 seized or wrecked steamers is roughly consistent with Price's findings, which indicate that 223 steamers were lost. The difference of two ships might result from Price's admission that he could not fully account for all the steamers' name changes. In any case, the difference between both data sets is within an acceptable margin of error, and it accounts for less than 1 percent of the total number. To correct for the thirty-three missing steamers in our calculations, we assumed that Wise's outbound data was complete, but that the inbound data was incomplete for reasons explained above.

Thus, we deduced the inbound data for captured/destroyed steamers by comparing Wise's and Price's findings. Using this method, 66 ships were apprehended or laid waste to on outbound runs, and 157 were lost on inbound runs. The same methodology applies to our phase-analysis data.

NOTES

Introduction

1. For a more detailed discussion of the blockade runner *Fingal*, see Stephen R. Wise, *Lifeline of the Confederacy: Blockade Running during the Civil War* (Columbia: University of South Carolina Press, 1988), 53–55. The *Fingal*, trapped in Savannah after the Union capture of Fort Pulaski in April 1862, was converted into an ironclad and renamed the *CSS Atlanta*. In June 1863 the *Atlanta* attempted to break the blockade and was captured by US naval forces.

2. For general information about the size of Union blockade squadrons, see Craig L. Symonds, *The Civil War at Sea* (Oxford: Oxford University Press, 2009), 39–44. The approximate size of U. S. Grant's Army of the Potomac in May 1864 was 115,000 troops, and in May 1864 William T. Sherman's force—the Army of the Ohio, the Army of the Cumberland, and the Army of the Tennessee—combined for 98,000 men.

3. Symonds, *Civil War at Sea*, 61.

4. For a more detailed description of the total amount of supplies smuggled through the blockade, see Wise, *Lifeline of the Confederacy*, 221–26.

5. John A. Dahlgren, *Memoir of John A. Dahlgren* (Boston: James R. Osgood, 1882), 614–17.

6. Jefferson Davis, *The Rise and Fall of the Confederate Government* (New York: D. Appleton, 1881), 2: 371–82.

7. Wise, *Lifeline of the Confederacy*, 24.

8. Lance E. Davis and Stanley L. Engerman, *Naval Blockades in Peace and War: An Economic History since 1750* (Cambridge: Cambridge University Press, 2006), 109.

9. Davis and Engerman, *Naval Blockades, 103*.

10. For a more complete discussion and comparative analysis of the British and American blockades, see Davis and Engerman, *Naval Blockades*, 53–158.

11. Davis and Engerman, *Naval Blockades*, 239. As described by Davis and Engerman, several close blockades "characterized warfare from the English-French continental wars of the eighteenth century through at least the American Civil War." (239). The historians argue that by World War I a distant blockade strategy was required in order to protect blockading squadrons from the improved technologies of longer-range artillery, sea mines, and submarine threats.

12. One nineteenth-century blockade strategy prioritized interdiction; the British

effort to stifle the transatlantic slave trade. In 1807 Great Britain ended its involvement in the transatlantic slave trade and led a coalition that vowed to eradicate the inhumane trafficking of slaves, particularly in the Atlantic basin. The Preventive Squadron was created in 1819 to enforce antitrafficking provisions agreed to by the various signatories. The task of patrolling the coast of West Africa and the Atlantic trade routes was daunting, but in six decades of service, the Preventive Squadron liberated about 160,000 slaves, caused around 17,000 British sailors to perish (mainly due to disease), and cost the British government at least £20 million. For more information on the Preventive Squadron, see Sian Rees, *Sweet Water and Bitter: The Ships That Stopped the Slave Trade* (Durham: University of New Hampshire Press, 2011).

Chapter 1

1. Donald R. Hickey, *The War of 1812: A Forgotten Conflict* (Urbana: University of Illinois Press, 2012), 12, 15, 40, 152–54, 184, 199–200.
2. K. Jack Bauer, *Surfboats and Horse Marines: U.S. Operations in the Mexican War, 1846 - 1848*, (Annapolis, MD: United States Naval Institute Press, 1969), 43.
3. Bauer, *Surfboats and Horse Marines*, 205.
4. For more discussion of the US blockade in the larger context of Anglo-American relations, see Wilbur Devereux Jones, *The American Problem in British Diplomacy, 1841–1861* (London: Macmillan Press, 1974), 60–61.
5. Historian K. Jack Bauer states, "There is no complete listing of the number of blockade-runners taken, but there is every reason to believe that the blockade was effective—to exactly what degree, it is impossible to determine." *Surfboats and Horse Marines*, 236.
6. One goal of British Near East policy was to protect and further develop trade with the Ottoman Empire. This eventually resulted in the Treaty of Balta Liman in 1838, which undermined trade relations between the Ottoman Empire and Russia. For more detailed information on the economic reasons behind Britain's Near East policy, see Frank E. Bailey, "The Economics of British Foreign Policy, 1825–1850," *Journal of Modern History* 12, no. 4 (December 1940): 449–84.
7. For a general discussion of the *Vixen* affair within the larger context of British Near Eastern policy, see Jasper Ridley, *Lord Palmerston* (New York: E. P. Dutton, 1970), 215.
8. Hansard, *House of Commons Debates*, March 17, 1837, 37: 621–56.
9. Hansard, *House of Commons Debates*, March 17, 1837, 37: 621–56.
10. The causes of the Crimean War represent one of the starkest examples of failed international diplomacy. According to historian A. J. P. Taylor, by the outbreak of war on March 30, 1854, the Russians had already performed three of the

Four Points that the Western allies required them to satisfy. So why did these nations go to war in 1854? According to Taylor, "The French had tried diplomacy in order to avoid military action; the British now pressed for military action in order to escape diplomacy." The momentum of the situation carried the nations headlong into war, as Taylor notes: "Since the allies were at war, they had to start fighting." *The Struggle for Mastery in Europe, 1848–1918* (Oxford: Oxford University Press, 1954), 65–67.

11. The Declaration of Paris, in *Conventions and Declarations between the Powers Concerning War, Arbitration and Neutrality* (The Hague, Netherlands: Martinus Nijhoff, 1915). Please see appendix 1 for the full text.

12. The Declaration of Paris, *Ibid.*

13. Great Britain utilized a secretary of state for commonwealth affairs as the head administrator for colonial possessions, and the secretary of state for foreign affairs dealt with relations with other nations. For more detailed information about the British Foreign Service, see Eugene H. Berwanger, *The British Foreign Service and the American Civil War* (Lexington: University Press of Kentucky, 1994), 1–36.

14. Berwanger, *British Foreign Service*, 1–7, 91.

15. Lord Lyons to Lord Russell, January 10, 1861, PRO 30/22/35. The British National Archives, Kew (hereafter cited as TNA).

16. Lord Lyons to Lord Russell, January 10, 1861.

17. Lord Lyons to Lord Russell, January 10, 1861.

18. Lord Russell to Lord Lyons, February 16, 1861, PRO 30/22/96, TNA; Russell to Lyons, March 9, 1861, PRO 30/22/96, TNA.

19. Lord Lyons to Lord Russell, March 29, 1861, PRO 30/22/35, TNA; Russell to Lyons, April 6, 1861, PRO 30/22/96, TNA.

20. Amanda Foreman, *A World on Fire: Britain's Crucial Role in the American Civil War* (New York: Random House, 2010), 69–70.

21. William Howard Russell, *My Diary North and South*, ed. Eugene H. Berwanger (New York: Alfred A. Knopf, 1988), 38. The term Orders in Council refers to the maritime policies instituted in the late eighteenth and early nineteenth centuries. Orders in Council were intended to disrupt trade or deny resources to Great Britain's enemies, and perhaps the most famous example was the Order in Council of 1807 directed against France.

22. Lord Lyons to Lord Russell, April 15, 1861, TNA.

23. Lord Lyons to Lord Russell, April 12, 1861, PRO 30/22/35, TNA; Lyons to Russell, April 15, 1861, PRO 30/22/35, TNA.

24. Historian Amanda Foreman doubts whether Seward "truly understood the difference between a blockade and a port closure, or why it mattered in international law." *World on Fire*, 80; Lyons to Russell, April 23, April 27, 1861, PRO 30/22/35, TNA.

25. Russell, *My Diary North and South*, 130, 171.

26. Russell, *My Diary North and South*, 130, 171.
27. Gavin Wright, *The Political Economy of the Cotton South: Households, Markets, and Wealth in the Nineteenth Century* (New York, W. W. Norton, 1978), 91. In 1861 British officials could not have predicted that the booming economic relationship of Southern cotton and British textile manufacturing was coming to a close. As Gavin Wright points out, "In 1860 the textiles industry stood on the crest of a major overproduction, which would have ushered in this era of stagnation had it not been overshadowed by the Cotton Famine of the 1860s" (96).
28. Sven Beckert, *Empire of Cotton: A Global History* (New York, Alfred A. Knopf, 2014), 242–43.
29. Lord Lyons to Lord Russell, May 6, May 21, 1861, PRO 30/22/35, TNA.
30. Frank L. Owsley, *King Cotton Diplomacy: Foreign Relations of the Confederate States of America* (Chicago: University of Chicago Press, 1931), 134, 136–38.
31. Lord Lyons to Lord Russell, May 2, May 23, 1861, PRO 30/22/35, TNA.
32. Lord Lyons to Lord Russell, June 14, 1861, PRO 30/22/35, TNA. Please see appendix 1 for the specific articles of the Declaration of Paris.
33. FO 881/1049, p. 73–74, TNA; Lord Lyons to Lord Russell, May 23, June 4, June 10, 1861, PRO 30/22/35, TNA. Privateering was common among nations that did not have extant naval fleets as a way to get citizens to join the war effort through profit motive. The privateers' main incentive was money. If an enemy merchant vessel was captured it could be auctioned at a prize court. The main deterrent to Confederate privateering was the lack of prize courts to which a captured vessel could be taken and sold. For an excellent discussion of the privateering issue, see Symonds, *The Civil War at Sea*, 77–80.
34. Lord Lyons to Lord Russell, May 23, June 4, June 10, 1861, PRO 30/22/35, TNA.
35. Lord Lyons to Lord Russell, June 14, 1861.
36. Lord Russell and Lord Lyons were careful to make no implied recognition of the Confederacy during conversations with Northern and Southern diplomats by always referring to the rebels as the "so-called Confederate States."
37. For more detailed information on Britain's neutrality declaration, see Foreman, *World on Fire*, 92–93; Lord Lyons to Lord Russell, June 14, June 18, June 21, 1861, PRO 30/22/35, TNA.
38. Lord Lyons to Lord Russell, June 24, 1861, PRO 30/22/97, TNA.
39. Lord Lyons to Lord Russell, June 24, 1861, PRO 30/22/97, TNA.
40. Lord Lyons to Lord Russell, July 2, 1861, PRO 30/22/97, TNA; House of Representatives, 37th Congress, 1st Session, *The Congressional Globe: A Century of Lawmaking for a New Nation; U.S. Congressional Documents and Debates, 1774-1875*, July 10, 1861, pp. 54–55. (hereafter cited as *Congressional Globe*).

41. Senate, 37th Congress, 1st Session, *Congressional Globe*, July 12, 1861, pp. 83–84, July 24, 1861, p. 234. The only amendment was to change the word "bill" to "act." In late July, both houses passed additional clarification of executive powers dealing with Section 5 of the law. See *Congressional Globe*, 297, 331, 365.
42. Lord Lyons to Lord Russell, July 20, 1861, PRO 30/22/97, TNA.
43. Gideon Welles to Abraham Lincoln, August 5, 18681, *Official Records of the Union and Confederate Navies in the War of the Rebellion* (Washington, DC: Government Printing Office, 1897) series 1, 6, p. 53–55 (hereafter cited in the following format: *ORN, ser. 1. Vol. 5, p. 53–55).*
44. Gideon Welles to Abraham Lincoln, August 5, 1861, *ORN,* series 1, vol. 6, p. 53–55.
45. Lord Lyons to Lord Russell, August 1, August 13, August 16, September 13, 1861, PRO 30/22/97, TNA.
46. Lord Cobden to Charles Sumner, November 29, 1861, in John Morley, *Life of Cobden* (London: Thomas Nelson, 1903), 2: 386.
47. Shelby Foote eloquently describes the real potential for war in late 1861 as follows: "Public men on both sides of the ocean lost their heads, and England and the United States came closer to war than they had ever come without war following." *The Civil War: A Narrative; Fort Sumter to Perryville* (New York: Random House, 1958), 156. James McPherson further develops Lincoln's handling of American public sentiment, and he points out the critical issue of Union saltpeter imports from Britain, an aspect unknown to newspaper readers in 1861. *Battle Cry of Freedom: The Civil War Era* (New York: Ballantine Books, 1989), 389–91. An excellent analysis of the *Trent* affair from the British perspective is Foreman, *World on Fire,* 172–98.
48. Louis Blacker to Joseph T. Crawford, February 9, 1862, ADM 128/58, Series 5, TNA; Crawford to Sir Alexander Milne, March 12, 1862, ADM 128/58, Series 4, TNA; Stuart L. Bernath, *Squall across the Atlantic: American Civil War Prize Cases and Diplomacy* (Berkeley: University of California Press, 1970), 36.
49. Louis Blacker to Joseph T. Crawford, February 9, 1862.
50. Louis Blacker to Joseph T. Crawford, February 9, 1862.
51. Joseph Crawford to Lord Lyons, February 28, 1862, ADM 128/58, Series 4, TNA; Crawford to Commodore Dunlop, March 1, 1862, ADM 128/58, Series 4, TNA; Crawford to Sir Alexander Milne, March 12, 1862.
52. For the increased volume of wartime illicit trade at Matamoros, see Philip Leigh, *Trading with the Enemy: The Covert Economy during the Civil War* (Yardley, PA: Westholme, 2014), 47–49; Joseph T. Crawford to Sir Alexander Milne, March 12, 1862; Crawford to Commodore Dunlop, March 1, 1862.
53. Louis Blacker to Joseph Crawford, February 9, 1862.
54. Louis Blacker to Joseph Crawford, February 9, 1862; Crawford to Lord Lyons,

February 28, 1862; Lord Russell to Lyons, March 28, 1862, ADM 128/58, Series 1, TNA; William Seward to Lyons, March 2, 1862, ADM 128/58, Series 3, TNA.

55. See appendix 1 for full details of Sections 2 and 3 of the Declaration of Paris.

56. Blacker to Sir Alexander Milne, March 12, 1862; Lord Russell to Lord Lyons, April 3, 1862, ADM 128/58, Series 3, TNA.

57. The official title of Sir Alexander Milne's position was "commander in chief, North American and West Indies Station." Louis Blacker to Sir Alexander Milne, March 12, 1862; Lord Russell to Lord Lyons, April 3, 1862, ADM 128/58, Series 3, TNA.

58. William Seward to Lord Lyons, April 9, 1863, *Executive Documents Printed by Order of the House of Representatives, First Session of the 38th Congress, 1863–1864* (Washington, DC: Government Printing Office, 1864), 557–62.

59. *New York Times*, May 23, 1862.

60. Madeline Russell Robinton, *An Introduction to the Papers of the New York Prize Court, 1861–1865*, (New York: Columbia University Press, 1945), 185; *New York Times*, September 22, 1863; Bernath, *Squall across the Atlantic*, 42–44.

61. Samuel Negus, "A Notorious Nest of Offence: Neutrals, Belligerents, and Union Jails in Civil War Blockade Running," *Civil War History* 56, no. 4 (December 2010): 373.

62. Negus, "Notorious Nest of Offence," 385; Foreman, *World on Fire*, 601. Foreman explains that "British prisoners of war in Federal hands were given the option of swearing an oath of allegiance to the United States in exchange for their release [and that] hundreds of British prisoners took advantage of the oath." (*World on Fire*, 601).

63. Mark E. Neely Jr., *The Fate of Liberty: Abraham Lincoln and Civil Liberties* (New York: Oxford University Press, 1991), 139–40.

64. *ORN*, ser. 1, vol. 9, pp. 362–67; Negus, "Notorious Nest of Offence," 377–78.

65. Neely, *Fate of Liberty*, 143–44.

66. Lord Lyons to Lord Russell, January 26, 1864, PRO 30/22/38, TNA.

67. Lord Russell to Lord Lyons, February 20, 1864 PRO 30/22/38, TNA; Lyons to Russell, May 9, May 23, 1864, PRO 32/22/38, TNA.

68. The HMS *Petrel* is sometimes cited in the records as the HMS *Peterel*, but for purposes of simplification we have decided to use the former spelling.

69. Royce Shingleton, *High Seas Confederate: The Life and Times of John Newland Maffitt*, (Columbia: University of South Carolina Press, 1994), 42–47.

70. Foreman, *World on Fire*, 410–11, note 53, p. 872.

71. George Watson to the Admiralty, February 6, 1863, ADM 128/57, Series 3, TNA.

72. Symonds, *Civil War at Sea*, 153–58.

73. George Watson to Admiralty, February 6, 1863; John Francis Ross to Admiral Milne, February 14, 1863, ADM 128/57, Series 3, TNA.

74. Samuel F. DuPont to Gideon Welles, February 9, 1863, *ORN*, ser. 1, vol. 13, pp. 601–2.

75. Alexander Milne to Lord Lyons, February 16, 1863, ADM 128/57, Series 3, TNA. Amanda Foreman notes that Milne informed Admiralty officials in Great Britain, "I cannot trust [Watson] either at Nassau or on the American coast." *World on Fire*, 411.

76. Foreman, *World on Fire*, 792.

77. Foreman, *World on Fire*, 800–804. Roy Jenkins views amicable settlement of the *Alabama* claims as the turning point in the special relationship between Great Britain and the United States. For Jenkins, the *Alabama* settlement "was the greatest nineteenth-century triumph of rational internationalism over short-sighted jingoism . . . [and it] marked the breakpoint between the previous hundred years of Anglo-American strain" and the twentieth-century alliance of the two nations. Jenkins aptly points out that after the *Alabama* settlement, "war between Britain and the United States became almost inconceivable, whereas in the previous hundred years it had been twice a reality and several times a possibility." *Gladstone: A Biography* (New York: Random House, 1995), 356–57.

Chapter 2

1. Craig Symonds, *Lincoln and His Admirals: Abraham Lincoln, the U.S. Navy, and the Civil War* (New York: Oxford University Press, 2008), 40–41.

2. "President Lincoln's Blockade Proclamation," April 19, 1861, *ORN*, ser. 1, vol. 5, p. 620.

3. Symonds, *Lincoln and His Admirals*, 53.

4. "President Lincoln's Blockade Expansion," April 27, 1861, *ORN*, ser. 1, vol. 5, p, 621.

5. For a more detailed discussion of Unionism in the Upper South during the secession crisis and Lincoln's attempts to cultivate it, see Daniel Crofts, *Reluctant Confederates: Upper South Unionists in the Secession Crisis* (Chapel Hill: University of North Carolina Press, 1989). For more information about the political career and moderate politics of John A. Gilmer, see Ezra J. Warner and W. Buck Yearns, *Biographical Register of the Confederate Congress* (Baton Rouge: LSU Press, 1975), 101–2.

6. For the events leading up to secession in North Carolina, see William S. Powell, *North Carolina through Four Centuries* (Chapel Hill: University of North Carolina Press, 1989), 345–48.

7. Bern Anderson, *By Sea and by River: The Naval History of the Civil War* (New York: Alfred A. Knopf, 1962), 9.

8. Gideon Welles to Silas Stringham, May 1, 1861, *ORN*, ser. 1, vol. 5, pp. 619–20.

9. Silas Stringham to Gideon Welles, May 23, 1861, *ORN*, ser. 1, vol. 5, p. 662; Stringham to Welles, May 24, 1861, *ORN*, ser. 1, vol. 5, pp. 664–65; Welles to Stringham, May 28, 1861, *ORN*, ser. 1, vol. 5, pp 677–78.

10. Gideon Welles to Silas Stringham, May 1, 1861, *ORN*, ser. 1, vol. 5, pp. 621–22.

11. Silas Stringham to Gideon Welles, May 30, 1861, *ORN*, ser. 1, vol. 5, p. 682.

12. Silas Stringham to Gideon Welles, September 16, 1861, *ORN*, ser. 1, vol. 6, pp. 216–17; Welles to Stringham, September 18, 1861, *ORN*, ser. 1, vol. 6, pp. 231–32; Symonds, *Lincoln and His Admirals*, 64–65.

13. Silas Stringham to Gideon Welles, May 24, 1861, *ORN*, ser. 1, vol. 5, pp. 664–65; Welles to Stringham, May 28, 1861, *ORN*, ser. 1, vol. 5, pp. 667–78, 701–2.

14. A basic description of the Blockade Strategy Board can be found in James M. Merrill, "Strategy Makers in the Union Navy Department, 1861–1865," *Mid-America: An Historical Review* no. 1 (January 1862: 19–32. However, the most up-to-date treatment of the board is Kevin J. Weddle, "The Blockade Board of 1861 and Union Naval Strategy," *Civil War History* no. 2 (2002): 123–42. The Weddle article provides the most valuable analysis of the Blockade Board's role in the Union war effort, and in the footnotes, Weddle unravels several historical misconceptions about the board.

15. Weddle, "Blockade Board of 1861," 134.

16. Weddle, "Blockade Board of 1861," 135.

17. Blockade Board to Gideon Welles, July 5, 1861, *ORN*, ser. 1, vol. 12, pp. 195–98.

18. Blockade Board to Gideon Welles, July 26, 1861, *ORN*, ser. 1, vol. 12, pp. 201–6; Merrill, "Strategy Makers," 22. For a more detailed discussion of the selection of Port Royal and military action there, see James McPherson, *War on the Waters: The Union and Confederate Navies, 1861–1865* (Chapel Hill: University of North Carolina Press, 2012).

19. Blockade Strategy Board to Gideon Welles, August 9, 1861, *ORN*, ser. 1, vol. 16, p 618–30; Blockade Strategy Board to Welles, September 3, 1861, *ORN*, ser. 1, vol. 16, pp. 651–55.

20. Blockade Board to Gideon Welles, July 16, 1861, *ORN*, ser. 1, vol. 12, pp. 198–201; McPherson, *War on the Waters*, p. 34. For an excellent discussion of the Blockade Board's recommendation on the Outer Banks and North Carolina sounds, see Robert M. Browning Jr., *From Cape Charles to Cape Fear: The North Atlantic Blockading Squadron during the Civil War* (Tuscaloosa: University of Alabama Press, 1993), 7–10. For a brief discussion of the strategic importance of the sounds, also see Merrill, "Strategy Makers," 25.

21. Browning, *From Cape Charles to Cape Fear*, 17–18; Symonds, *Lincoln and His Admirals*, 64; James Russell Soley, *The Blockade and the Cruisers* (New York: Charles Scribner's Sons, 1883), 122–24.
22. Weddle, "Blockade Board of 1861," 142.
23. Gideon Welles to flag officers, January 23,1862, *ORN*, ser. 1, vol. 6, pp. 528–29; Anderson, *By Sea and by River*, 289. Anderson notes that by April 1862 "the Navy had about 300 ships in service," up from 42 when the blockade was declared in 1861 (289).
24. Louis Goldsborough to officers, September 28, 1861, *ORN*, ser. 1, vol. 6, pp. 266–67.
25. Abraham Lincoln, May 12, 1862, *ORN*, ser. 1, vol. 8, p. 21.
26. Gideon Welles to Abraham Lincoln, April 12, 1862, *ORN*, ser. 1, vol. 7, pp. 229–30. For a brief description of nineteenth-century American coal types and their geographic locations, see James Green, *The Devil Is Here in These Hills: West Virginia's Coal Miners and Their Battle for Freedom* (New York: Grove, 2015), 14.
27. For a more detailed discussion of Charleston and blockade-running, see Wise, *Lifeline of the Confederacy*, 121–24.
28. Louis Goldsborough to Gideon Welles, October 4, 1861, *ORN*, ser. 1, vol. 6. p. 286.
29. J. W. Livingston to Silas Stringham, August 15, 1861, *ORN*, ser. 1, vol. 6, pp. 85–86.
30. O. S. Glisson to Louis Goldsborough, April 27, 1862, *ORN*, ser. 1, vol. 7, pp. 284–85; Jas. F. Armstrong to Goldsborough, August 23, 1862, *ORN*, ser. 1, vol. 8, pp. 669, 685; Wise, *Lifeline of the Confederacy*, 242. Wilmington's citizens were not to celebrate the *Kate*'s arrival on August 6, 1862, since the ship brought a scourge of yellow fever that "caused over 1,500 cases . . . killing over 700 . . . over 15 percent of the town's population." Wise, *Lifeline of the Confederacy*, 233, 126–27.
31. Gideon Welles entry for August 30, 1864, *The Civil War Diary of Gideon Welles, Lincoln's Secretary of the Navy*, ed. William E. Gienapp and Erica L. Gienapp (Urbana: University of Illinois Press, 2014), 489.
32. Gideon Welles, entry for August 30, 1864, *The Civil War Diary of Gideon Welles, 489*.
33. W. H. C. Whiting to Stephen Mallory, September 27, 1864, *ORN*, ser. 1, vol. 10, pp. 751–52.
34. A. Ludlow Case to S. P. Lee, March 12, 1863, *ORN*, ser. 1, vol. 8, p. 599; Samuel DuPont to Gideon Welles, May 21, 1863, *ORN*, ser. 1, vol. 14, p. 209; David Dixon Porter to Welles, December 15, 1864, *ORN*, ser. 1, vol. 11, p. 195.
35. T. J. Stiles, *The First Tycoon: The Epic Life of Cornelius Vanderbilt*, (New York: Random House, 2009), 356.

36. Robert W. Daly, "Pay and Prize Money in the Old Navy, 1776–1899," *Proceedings of the U.S. Naval Institute*, 74, no. 8 (August 1948): 546.

37. "An Act for the Government of the Navy of the United States," March 2, 1799, *The Debates and Proceedings in the Congress of the United States*, Sections 5 and 6.

38. "Marchand Report," May 30, 1862, *ORN*, ser. 1, vol. 13, pp. 59–60.

39. Daly, "Pay and Prize Money," 546. For a brief discussion of prize-money incentive and David Dixon Porter's actions off Wilmington, see Chris E. Fonvielle Jr., *The Wilmington Campaign: Last Rays of Departing Hope* (Campbell, CA: Savas, 1997), 93–94. Fonvielle states that Porter claimed $275,000 over a seven-week period in late 1864.

40. Browning, *From Cape Charles to Cape Fear*, 261–64.

41. Various correspondences (unnumbered pages), including between Archibald, Seward, and Lyons, ADM 5/1149, The British National Archives, Kew, (hereafter cited as TNA).

42. S. P. Lee to Welles, January 24, 1863, *ORN*, ser. 1, vol. 8, p. 475; Welles to Lee, January 27, 1863, *ORN*, ser. 1, vol. 8, p. 480.

43. S. P. Lee to O. S. Glisson, July 23, 1864, *ORN*, ser. 1, vol. 10, p. 301; Glisson to Lee, July 25, 1864, *ORN*, ser. 1, vol. 10, p. 303.

44. Gideon Welles to Samuel DuPont, January 25, 1862, *ORN*, ser. 1, vol. 12, p. 522.

45. Samuel DuPont to LeRoy, August 10, 1862, *ORN*, ser. 1, vol. 13, p. 247; also see DuPont's orders to the captain of the USS *Vandalia* for outside blockade service, DuPont to Woolsey, November 17, 1862, *ORN*, ser. 1, vol. 13, p. 452; DuPont to Gideon Welles, June 27, 1862, *ORN*, ser. 1, vol. 13, pp. 134–35.

46. John Dahlgren to Gideon Welles, November 3, 1863, *ORN*, ser. 1, vol. 15, pp. 97–98.

47. Gideon Welles to S. P. Lee, February 27, 1864, *ORN*, ser. 1, vol. 9, p. 507; Welles to Lee, March 19, 1864, *ORN*, ser. 1, vol. 9, pp. 556–57.

48. O. S. Glisson to S. P. Lee, June 27, 1864, *ORN*, ser. 1, vol. 10, pp. 212–13; Lee to Glisson, July 18, 1864, *ORN*, ser. 1, vol. 10, pp. 286–87. For similar instructions to another division leader, see Lee to B. F. Sands, September 18, 1864, *ORN*, ser. 1, vol. 10, p. 467.

49. Samuel DuPont to Drake, June 10, 1863, *ORN*, ser. 1, vol. 14, p. 249; "Dahlgren Order," February 19, 1864, *ORN*, ser. 1, vol. 15, p. 330–31; John Dahlgren to Rowan, February 19, 1864, *ORN*, ser. 1, vol. 15, p. 338; Dahlgren to Rowan, February 25, 1864, *ORN*, ser. 1, vol. 15, pp. 340–41.

50. ADM 128/59, Proceedings of the Federal Cruisers in and About the Bahamas, TNA. See for example Alexander Milne to Lord Lyons, December 16, 1862, pp. 169–75, TNA.

51. FO 881/1163, pp. 17–18, TNA.

52. FO 881/1163, p. 22–41, TNA.

53. J. S. Missroon to Louis Goldsborough, November 16, 1861, *ORN*, ser. 1, vol. 12, p. 348–49; S. F. DuPont to Gideon Welles, December 6, 1861, *ORN*, ser. 1, vol. 12, pp. 384–85; S. F. DuPont to Capt. H. Y. Purriance, December 19, 1861, *ORN*, ser. 1, vol. 12, p. 411.

54. S. F. DuPont to Percival Drayton, March 28, 1862, *ORN*, ser. 1, vol. 12, p. 671–72; Jas. F. Armstrong to Louis Goldsborough, August 27, 1862, *ORN*, ser. 1, vol. 8, p. 685; Pend. Watmough to David D. Porter, November 15, 1864, *ORN*, ser. 1, vol. 11, pp. 66–67.

55. "Dahlgren Report," July 21, 1863, *ORN*, ser. 1, vol. 14, p. 374.

56. "Green Report," September 11, 1863, *ORN*, ser. 1, vol. 14, p. 643; John Dahlgren to C. F. Green, September 15, 1863, *ORN*, ser. 1, vol. 14, p. 648; "Dahlgren Report," September 24, 1863, *ORN*, ser. 1, vol. 14, pp. 671–72.

57. John Dahlgren to Welles, January 7, 1864, *ORN*, ser. 1, vol. 15, pp. 225–26.

58. An investigation found that the USS *Weehawken*'s demise was caused by the crew's failure to properly install gaskets in the bow of the vessel. A storm struck when the he ironclad was loaded with ammunition and riding low in the water. The ship went down by the head, and its pumps, located in the aft section, were of no use to keep it afloat.

59. Browning, *From Cape Charles to Cape Fear*, 242–43.

60. Anderson, *By Sea and by River*, 227–28.

61. Louis Goldsborough to Gideon Welles, November 10, 1861, *ORN*, ser. 1, vol. 6, p. 418; Welles to Goldsborough, November 25, 1861, *ORN*, ser. 1, vol. 6, p. 454.

62. Gideon Welles to Samuel DuPont, January 31, 1862, *ORN*, ser. 1, vol. 12, p. 557–58.

63. Gideon Welles to Samuel DuPont, June 5, 1862, *ORN*, ser. 1, vol. 13, p. 77–78.

64. Wise, *Lifeline of the Confederacy*, 61–62, 67; Gustavus Fox to Louis Goldsborough, March 27, 1862, *ORN*, ser. 1, vol. 7, p. 139; Gideon Welles to squadron commanders, March 28, 1862, *ORN*, ser. 1, vol. 7, p. 175. The blockade-runner *Nashville* underwent two name changes—to *Thomas L. Wragg* and then *Rattlesnake*. The US Navy finally brought the ship to heel on February 28, 1863, and destroyed it—one year to the day after it had run into Beaufort Harbor.

65. Gideon Welles to Samuel DuPont, March 31, 1862, *ORN*, ser. 1, vol. 12, p. 691; DuPont to Welles, April 23, 1862, *ORN*, ser. 1, vol. 12, p. 771–73.

66. Gideon Welles to John P. Hale, May 9, 1862, *ORN*, ser. 1, vol. 13, p. 7–9.

67. Gideon Welles to Edwin Stanton, March 14, 1862, *ORN*, ser. 1, vol. 7, p. 125.

68. John A. Dix to S. P. Lee, October 6, 1862, *ORN*, ser. 1, vol. 8, pp. 29–30; Lee to Dix, October 8, 1862, *ORN*, ser. 1, vol. 8, pp. 30–31; Dix to Lee, October 9, 1862, *ORN*, ser. 1, vol. 8, pp. 32–33; Gideon Welles to Lee, October 13, 1862, *ORN*, ser. 1, vol. 8, p. 35.

69. Gideon Welles to Salmon Chase, October 24, 1862, *ORN*, ser. 1, vol. 8, p. 55; Welles to Edwin Stanton, November 8, 1862, *ORN*, ser. 1, vol. 8, pp. 65–66.

70. "Lincoln Executive Order," November 11, 1862, *ORN*, ser. 1, vol. 8, p. 66.

71. Gideon Welles to S. P. Lee, June 9, 1863, *ORN*, ser. 1, vol. 9, pp. 63–64.

72. Chas. S. Boggs to S. P. Lee, May 28, 1863, *ORN*, ser. 1, vol. 9, pp. 50–1; Lee to Gideon Welles June 6, 1863, *ORN*, ser. 1, vol. 9, p. 64.

73. Lee to Welles, August 7, 1863, *ORN*, ser. 1, vol. 9, pp. 149–50, 183, 230–31.

74. S. P. Lee to Gideon Welles, February 16, 1864, *ORN*, ser. 1, vol. 9, p. 485; Lee to Gustavus Fox, February 20, 1864, *ORN*, ser. 1, vol. 9, pp. 495–97.

75. Gideon Welles to S. P. Lee, April 13, 1864, *ORN*, ser. 1, vol. 9, pp 610–11.

76. Fonvielle, *Wilmington Campaign*, 70–71; Gideon Welles to Abraham Lincoln, October 28, 1864, *ORN*, ser. 1, vol. 11, p. 3.

77. Gideon Welles to Samuel DuPont, January 31, 1863, *ORN*, ser. 1, vol. 13, p. 571; "Porter Report," January 17, 1865, *ORN*, ser. 1, vol. 11, p. 441.

78. Anderson, *By Sea and by River*, 289.

Chapter 3

1. Wise, *Lifeline of the Confederacy*, 107.

2. Roger S. Durham, *High Seas and Yankee Gunboats: A Blockade-Running Adventure from the Diary of James Dickson* (Columbia: University of South Carolina Press, 2005), 1–12. Durham masterfully reconstructs the story of Dickson and Hernandez aboard the *Standard* from Dickson's partial diary. The extant portions of the journal are superb, and Durham fully quotes them, but he excels at filling in the missing information.

3. Durham, *High Seas and Yankee Gunboats*, 34.

4. Durham, *High Seas and Yankee Gunboats*, 44, 51–57.

5. Durham, *High Seas and Yankee Gunboats*, 59, 65, 69.

6. Durham, *High Seas and Yankee Gunboats*, 71, 89, 93, 103–4.

7. Durham, *High Seas and Yankee Gunboats*, 98, 107, 117, 124.

8. Durham, *High Seas and Yankee Gunboats*, 151–54.

9. Marcus Price, "Ships That Tested the Blockade of the Carolina Ports, 1861–1865," *American Neptune* 8 (1948): 199.

10. William Watson, *Adventures of a Blockade Runner; or, Trade in Time of War (London:* T. Fisher Unwin, 1893), 202–3.

11. Watson, *Adventures of a Blockade Runner*, 113.

12. Watson, *Adventures of a Blockade Runner*, 236.

13. Andrew W. Hall, *Civil War Blockade Running on the Texas Coast* (Charleston, SC: History Press, 2014), 39–40. The "one-way" journeys could be in either direction, to or from a key port.

14. "Kennison Report," March 3, 1864, *ORN*, ser. 1, vol. 15, pp. 354–55; Browning, *From Cape Charles to Cape Fear*, 268–69.

15. Jim McNeil, *Masters of the Shoals: Tales of the Cape Fear Pilots Who Ran the Union Blockade* (Cambridge MA: Da Capo, 2003), 4–7.

16. James M. Matthews, ed., *Public Laws of the Confederate States of America, Passed at the First Session of the First Congress; 1862* (Richmond, VA: R. M. Smith Printers, 1862), "An Act to Exempt Certain Persons from Enrollment for Service in the Armies of the Confederate States," 51–52, "An Act to Exempt Certain Persons from Military Duty and to Repeal an Act Entitled 'An Act to Exempt Certain Persons from Enrollment for Service in the Armies of the Confederate States, approved 21st, April 1862," 77–79, "An Act to Organize Forces to Serve During the War," 211–15.

17. Samuel DuPont to Gideon Welles, July 10, 1862, *ORN*, ser. 1, vol. 13, p. 176; S. W. Godon to Welles, October 1, 1862, *ORN*, ser. 1, vol. 13, p. 354.

18. DuPont to Turner, March 24, 1863, *ORN*, ser. 1, vol. 13, pp. 772–73.

19. "Turner Report," May 21, 1863, *ORN*, ser. 1, vol. 14, p. 211; Samuel DuPont to Gideon Welles, June 10, 1863, *ORN*, ser. 1, vol. 14, p. 251.

20. FO 881/1163, Correspondence Respecting the Blockade of the Ports of the Confederate States, Part 2, pp. 44–45, The British National Archives, Kew (hereafter cited as TNA).

21. Silas Stringham to Gideon Welles, May 20, 1861, *ORN*, ser. 1, vol. 5, p. 659.

22. FO 881/1163, p. 22, TNA.

23. FO 881/1163, p. 22, TNA. The *Lion* was found interred at Key West on May 23, so the vessel was apparently recaptured.

24. Various Correspondences, pp. 485–88, ADM 128/58.

25. John Wilkinson, *The Narrative of a Blockade Runner* (Sheldon & Co., New York, 1877), p. 132. Italics are in the original.

26. Chester G. Hearn, *Tracks in the Sea: Matthew Fontaine Maury and the Mapping of the Oceans* (New York: McGraw Hill, 2002).

27. Hearn, *Tracks in the Sea*, 231–39.

28. Ann Blackman, *Wild Rose: The True Story of a Civil War Spy* (New York: Random House, 2005).

29. Blackman, *Wild Rose*, 255.

30. Blackman, *Wild Rose*, 258–65. Blackman notes that there were "eleven blockaders off New Inlet: four near the bar, four in a second line further out, and three outside cruisers. Twelve more warships were guarding the Old Inlet west of Smith Island to catch ships trying to get out that way" (263).

31. Blackman, *Wild Rose*, 271.

32. Blackman, *Wild Rose*, 298–301. Little Rose did not make the return trip to the Confederacy in 1864; otherwise she might have been on the lifeboat as well. When she learned of her mother's death, Little Rose was boarded at a French convent school. The story of Greenhow's gold varies. One version says that the discoverer of Greenhow's body initially buried the gold, then felt guilty and eventually turned it in. Another account says this person patriotically turned in the gold immediately (299–300).

33. Charles S. Davis, *Colin J. McRae: Confederate Financial Agent, Blockade*

Running In the Trans-Mississippi South as Affected by the Confederate Government's Direct European Procurement of Goods (Tuscaloosa, AL: Confederate, 1961; repr., Wilmington, NC, Broadfoot, 2000), 17–26.

34. Davis, *Colin J. McRae*, 27–34; Michael Brem Bonner, *Confederate Political Economy: Creating and Managing a Southern Corporatist Nation, 1861–1865*, (Baton Rouge: LSU Press, 2016), 83–92, 115–22.

35. McRae was probably on board one of the following outbound runs from Mobile: the *General Buckner* on April 20, the *Nita* on April 16, the *Alice* also on April 16, the *Cuba* sometime in April, the *Neptune* also sometime in April, or the *Alice* again sometime in early May. McRae received his appointment for the mission abroad sometime in March 1863, and he arrived in Europe on May 13. As Charles Davis notes, "The exact date of McRae's departure is uncertain. . . . Toward the end of April he had not arrived in Europe and John Slidell, the Confederate commissioner in Paris, wrote to Secretary of State Judah P. Benjamin that something must have happened to him en route" (*Colin J. McRae*, 37). The possible blockade-runners that carried McRae out of Mobile in April and early May can be found in Wise, *Lifeline of the Confederacy*, 267, appendix 14.

36. For more information on McRae's duties and successes in rehabilitating Confederate financial status in Europe, see Davis, *Colin J. McRae*, 51–60. For more information about the blockade-runners owned by the Ordnance Bureau, see Wise, *Lifeline of the Confederacy*, 95–100.

37. Davis, *Colin J. McRae*, 75–86.

38. FO 881/1049, Papers Relating to the Blockade of the Ports of the Confederate States, May 1861 to February 1862, p. 13, TNA; FO 881/1049, pp. 23–24, TNA; FO 881/1049, p. 35, TNA. The *New York Times* referred to Southern newspapers' claims of a paper blockade as an act of "saucy defiance."

39. FO 881/1049, pp. 68–71, TNA; ADM 128/57, Various Reports and Correspondences, pp. 469–74, TNA.

40. FO 881/1049, p. 72, TNA.

41. FO 881/1049, p. 84, TNA.

42. FO 881/1049, Papers Relating to the Blockade of the Ports of the Confederate States, May 1861 to February 1862, pp. 87–88, TNA.

43. FO 881/1049, pp. 94–95, TNA.

44. FO 881/1049, pp. 87–88, TNA.

45. FO 881/1049, "Inclosure 3 in No. 78," p. 97, TNA.

46. FO 881/1049, p. 103, TNA.

47. FO 881/1049, pp. 104–6, TNA.

48. FO 881/1049, pp. 108–9, 120, 135, 141, TNA.

49. FO 881/1049, pp. 108–9, 120, 135, 141, TNA.

50. FO 881/1049, pp. 122–28, TNA.

51. FO 881/1049, pp. 122–28, TNA.

52. FO 881/1049, pp. 120, 132, TNA.

53. FO 881/1049, p. 132, TNA.

54. FO 881/1049, p. 134, TNA.

55. FO 881/1049, p. 140, TNA.

56. FO 881/1049, pp. 133, 136, TNA. One frustrating problem is the lack of detailed cargo manifests for all the blockade-runners. In some cases, these lists either did not exist or were lost to historians. Manifests that did survive provided vague descriptions like "some cotton" or just "cotton." It was not unusual for black-market commodities to be unlisted, and blockade-runners were rarely expected to clear with a customhouse due to the illicit nature of the business. FO 881/1049, p. 143, TNA; FO 881/1049, p. 141, TNA.

57. FO 881/1049, pp. 152–56, TNA.

58. ADM 128/57, p. 29, TNA. The median size was 109 tons, which is significantly larger than the average size indicated in other records. According to other documents, the median size for all recorded vessels during the war was 81 tons. It should be noted, however, that tonnage is not the same as capacity. Schooners could carry a higher percentage of tonnage as cargo, and steamers used about a third or more of their tonnage for boilers and engines.

59. FO 881/1163, Correspondence Respecting the Blockade of the Ports of the Confederate States, Part 2, pp. 1, 4, TNA.

60. FO 881/1163, p. 8, TNA.

61. FO 881/1163, p. 8, TNA.

62. FO 881/1163, pp. 14, 21, TNA.

63. FO 881/1163, p. 12–13, TNA. The alternate spellings "Bayley" and "Bailey" refer to same person. FO 414/26, Correspondence Respecting Interference with Trade between New York and the Bahamas, May 1862 to July 1863, pp. 3–7, TNA.

64. FO 414/26, p. 9, TNA; FO 881/1163, p. 68, TNA.

65. FO 414/26, p. 9, TNA; FO 881/1163, p. 68, TNA.

66. FO 414/26, p. 8, TNA.

67. FO 414/26, pp. 33–34, 36, TNA.

68. FO 414/26, pp. 41–44, TNA.

69. FO 881/1163, pp. 63–64, TNA.

70. FO 881/1281, Correspondence Respecting the "Rappahannock," pp. 12–19, TNA.

71. FO 5/1149, unnumbered pages. A document dated October 3, 1863, shows the horsepower (between 200 and 400) of engines for sale from London to the Confederacy, as well as the price (£48 s10 per horsepower). This record was found on board the blockade-runner *Cornubia*, and the engine design was specified as requested by a "Confederate engineer." It should be noted that

total tonnage does not correlate exactly to cargo capacity, so these figures are the maximum amounts of cargoes that could have been carried through the blockade.

72. S. C. Hawley to William Seward, June 1, 1863, *ORN*, ser. 1, vol. 9, pp. 80–81.

73. Alexander Milne to Glasse, November 30, 1863, ADM 128/60, pp. 865–67, TNA; Milne to Glasse, December 1, 1863, ADM 128/50, pp. 875–78, TNA; Milne to Glasse, December 4, 1863, ADM 128/60, p. 955–57, TNA; Milne to Glasse, December 1, 1863, ADM 128/60, pp. 959–65, TNA.

74. William Seward to Richard Lyons, January 29, 1864, FO 5/1149, unnumbered pages, TNA.

75. Foreman, *World on Fire*, 584.

76. There are numerous biographies of Maffitt and Semmes and countless narratives of the cruises of the *Florida* and *Alabama*. Among the most recent works concerning Raphael Semmes are Stephen Fox's *Wolf of the Deep: Raphael Semmes and the Notorious Confederate Raider CSS Alabama* (2007), Warren Spencer's *Raphael Semmes: The Philosophical Mariner,* and Spencer F. Tucker's *Raphael Semmes and the Alabama* (1998). Biographies of John Newland Maffitt include Edward Boykin's *Sea Devil of the Confederacy: The Story of the Florida and Her Captain John Newland Maffitt* (1959) and Shingleton's *High Seas Confederate* (1994). Summary coverage and context of the raiding careers of the *Florida* and the *Alabama* can be found in Symonds, *Civil War at Sea* (2009) and McPherson, *War on the Waters* (2012). For a more in-depth discussion of the role of Civil War sailors and the story of the *Alabama*, see William Marvel, *The Alabama and the Kearsarge: The Sailor's Civil War* (1996).

77. Shingleton, *High Seas Confederate*, 85. A bonded vessel was released instead of being destroyed, and its owners were obliged to pay the Confederate government after the war for the bonded amount. A bonded ship was essentially spared destruction in exchange for future payment of ransom money.

78. For a full narrative and analysis of the *Alabama*'s impact on the war, see Stephen Fox, *Wolf of the Deep: Raphael Semmes and the Notorious Confederate Raider CSS Alabama,* (New York: Vintage Books, 2007). For a specific account of the *Alabama* sinking the *Hatteras*, see pp. 84–87. Fox claims this battle was "the first time in naval history that a steam warship had sunk another steam warship . . . and in the Civil War, it marked the first (and last) sinking at sea of a Union warship by a Confederate vessel" (87). One can only assume that Fox considers the sinking of the USS *Housatonic* by the CSS *Hunley* in February 1864 to have been in Charleston Harbor, not at sea.

79. Welles, entry for December 29, 1862, *Civil War Diary of Gideon Welles, 109*; Welles to DuPont, January 31, 1863, *ORN*, ser. 1, vol. 13, p. 571.

80. FO 881/1281, p. 19, 22, TNA.

81. Symonds, *Civil War at Sea*, 104; J. Thomas Scharf, *History of the Confederate*

States Navy: From the Organization to the Surrender of Its Last Vessel (1886; repr., New York: Fairfax, 1977), 806–809; Fonvielle, *Wilmington Campaign,* 81–82. Fonvielle asserts that "Whiting was infuriated with the president's logic, and subsequent events proved the general right on both counts. The Federals not only strengthened the blockade of Wilmington but attacked the seaport as well" (82). The *Tallahassee,* renamed the CSS *Olustee,* made another successful foray against Yankee shipping in October before returning to Wilmington, where she was reconverted into a blockade-runner. Jefferson Davis to Zebulon Vance, October 25, 1864, *ORN,* ser. 1, vol. 10, pp. 801–802.

82. For estimates of the commerce raiders' totals, see Shingleton, *High Seas Confederate,* 80; George W. Dalzell, *Flight from the Flag: The Continuing Effect of the Civil War upon the American Carrying Trade* (Chapel Hill: University of North Carolina Press, 1940), 238, 245; Rodney Carlisle, *Rough Waters: Sovereignty and the American Merchant Flag* (Annapolis, MD: Naval Institute Press, 2017), 39–40. Another question that looms for nineteenth-century naval historians is, why did the US merchant marine not rebound after the war? George Dalzell identifies the "flight from the flag" during the Civil War as the catalyst that opened the floodgates of foreign registry in the late nineteenth and early twentieth centuries. Dalzell admits that many of the reasons for foreign registry were economic, like less regulation and cheaper costs, and the Civil War marked a crippling turning point for the American merchant marine. To be specific, Dalzell cites a 1797 law that "denied repatriation" of American ships that adopted a foreign registry. Another factor was a change in typical ship owning. Before the war, shipowners "were owned by large groups of part-owners" each of whom had a share in the vessel's profits. The Civil War witnessed the rise of widespread ship ownership by "the modern industrial and commercial corporation." Dalzell points out the main advantage to the new system: "Investment in shares of stock is simpler, easier, and safer than part ownership of a vessel." Other alleged factors in the decline of the US merchant marine include dilution of labor availability due to military service, cessation of US tariffs for shipbuilders, and the postwar dominance of British iron-hull vessels. (*Flight from the Flag,* 249–56). Historian of the American merchant marine Rodney Carlisle points out that in the postwar decades, "U.S. shipping continued to decline as a percentage of the world trade . . . from about 10 percent in 1870 to just over 3 percent in 1890." Carlisle notes that while American politicians continued to blame British wartime policy for the diminution of the U.S. merchant marine, realists understood that it was the "economic problems and technological developments of the 1870s and 1880s, and gradually, more contemporary concerns with cost and government policy [that] eclipsed the wartime issues" as reasons for foreign registry (*Rough Waters,* 48–51).

Chapter 4

1. Wise, *Lifeline of the Confederacy*, 27.
2. "Introduction," *The Diary of Edmund Ruffin*, ed. with an introduction and notes by William Kauffman Scarborough, vol. 1, *Toward Independence, October, 1856–April, 1861* (Baton Rouge: LSU Press, Baton Rouge, 1972), xv–xlv.
3. "Introduction," *The Diary of Edmund Ruffin, ed.* with an introduction and notes by William Kauffman Scarborough, vol. 1, *Toward Independence, October, 1856–April, 1861* (Baton Rouge: LSU Press, Baton Rouge, 1972), xv–xlv.
4. Edmund Ruffin, entry for April 23, 1861, *The Diary of Edmund Ruffin*, ed. with an introduction and notes by William Kauffman Scarborough, vol. 2, *The Years of Hope, April, 1861—June, 1863* (Baton Rouge: LSU Press, 1976), 7, 17.
5. Ruffin, entry for June 3, 1861, *Diary of Edmund Ruffin*, 2: 40, 137; Edmund Ruffin, entry for October 13, 1863, *The Diary of Edmund Ruffin*, ed. with an introduction and notes by William Kauffman Scarborough, vol. 3, *A Dream Shattered, June, 1863—June, 1865* (Baton Rouge: LSU Press, 1989), 186.
6. Ruffin, entries for January 6 and 10, 1862, April 1862, and October 1862, *Diary of Edmund Ruffin, 2:* 210, 233, 276, 462, 590; Ruffin, entry for January 17, 1864, *Diary of Edmund Ruffin*, 3: 309.
7. Ruffin, entries for January 6 and 10, 1862, April 1862, October 1862, January 1863, *Diary of Edmund Ruffin*, 2:210, 233, 276, 462, 590; Ruffin, entry for January 17, 1864, *Diary of Edmund Ruffin*, 3:309.
8. Emma Holmes, *The Diary of Miss Emma Holmes, 1861–1866*, ed. with an introduction by John F. Marszalek (Baton Rouge: LSU Press, 1979), 45–47, 93, 181.
9. Holmes, *The Diary of Miss Emma Holmes, 1861–1866*, 45–47, 93, 181.
10. Mary Chesnut, *Mary Chesnut's Civil War*, ed. C. Vann Woodward (New Haven: Yale University Press, 1981), xxx–xlv.
11. Chesnut, entries for July 16, August 8, 1861, *Mary Chesnut's Civil War*, 101, 134.
12. Chesnut, entries for September 19, October 13, November 16, December 13, 1861, *Mary Chesnut's Civil War*, 197, 215, 237, 262.
13. Chesnut, entry for March 12, 1862, *Mary Chesnut's Civil War*, 306.
14. Chesnut, entries for March 14, 1862, November 5, 1864, *Mary Chesnut's Civil War*, 2, 308, 486.
15. Catherine Ann Devereux Edmondston. *"Journal of a Secesh Lady": The Diary of Catherine Ann Devereux Edmondston* ed. Beth Gilbert Crabtree and James W. Patton (Raleigh: Division of Archives and History, North Carolina Department of Cultural Resources, 1979), 75–6.
16. Edmondston, *Journal of a Secesh Lady*, 84, 97, 145. Edmondston was well versed in the legal blockade arguments regarding the Declaration of Paris. In

August she opined, "[The Union] blockade was by no means an effective one, & we [are] looking in good faith to Europe that she would insist on the observation of the treaty of Paris, which declares that a blockade to be binding shall be effective" (84).

17. Edmondston, *Journal of a Secesh Lady*, 220.

18. John Beauchamp Jones, *A Rebel War Clerk's Diary*, ed. Howard Swiggett (New York: Old Hickory Bookshop, 1935), 1: 26, 44, 47, 101–2.

19. Jones, *A Rebel War Clerk's Diary*, 1: 165, 239, 280 and 2: 18, 94.

20. Jones, *A Rebel War Clerk's Diary*, 2: 374.

21. Ella Gertrude Clanton Thomas, *The Secret Eye: The Journal of Ella Gertrude Clanton Thomas, 1848–1889*, ed. Virginia Ingraham Burr, introduction by Nell Irvin Painter (Chapel Hill: University of North Carolina Press, Chapel Hill, 1990), 185, 188, 220, 233, 257.

22. Emma LeConte, *When the World Ended: The Diary of Emma LeConte*, ed. Earl Schenk Miers (New York: Oxford University Press, 1957), 12, 75, 90.

23. Edmondston, *Journal of a Secesh Lady*, 56, 140.

24. Symonds, *Civil War at Sea*, 41.

25. Edwin B. Coddington, "The Civil War Blockade Reconsidered," in *Essays in History and International Relations in Honor of George Hubbard Blakeslee*, ed. Dwight E. Lee and George E. Reynolds (Worcester, MA: Clark University Press, 1949), 290.

26. Marcus Price, "Blockade Running as a Business in South Carolina during the War between the States, 1861–1865," *American Neptune* 9 (January 1949): 53.

27. James M. McPherson, *Battle Cry of Freedom: The Civil War Era* (New York: Oxford University Press, 1988), 381.

28. C. L. Webster, III. *Entrepôt: Government Imports into the Confederate States* (Roseville, MN: Edinborough, 2010), 45.

29. The table was calculated by taking aggregate totals from the Price and Wise data. Please see appendix 4 concerning methodology for more details about how this data set was constructed.

30. Coddington, "Civil War Blockade Reconsidered," 300.

31. Coddington, "Civil War Blockade Reconsidered," 302, 305.

32. McPherson, *Battle Cry of Freedom*, 382; Eugene Lerner, "The Monetary and Fiscal Programs of the Confederate Government, 1861–1865," *Journal of Political Economy*, 62, no. 6 (December 1954): 506–7.

33. Eugene Lerner, "The Monetary and Fiscal Programs of the Confederate Government, 1861–1865," *Journal of Political Economy*, 62, no. 6 (December 1954): 506–7; Eugene Lerner, "Money, Prices, and Wages in the Confederacy, 1861–1865," *Journal of Political Economy*, 63, no. 1 (February 1955): 26–28, 40. For criticism of Memminger's policies, see Douglas B. Ball, *Financial Failure and Confederate Defeat* (Urbana: University of Illinois Press, 1991). Lerner is

a bit easier on Memminger and tends to see a reluctant Confederate Congress as the primary obstacle to sound financial policy. For detailed Confederate inflation statistics, see Roger L. Ransom, "The Historical Statistics of the Confederacy," in *Historical Statistics of the United States: Earliest Times to the Present*, ed. Susan Carter et al. (New York: Cambridge University Press, 2006), vol. 5, part E, pp. 773–805.

34. Ella Lonn, *Salt as a Factor in the Confederacy* (1933; repr., Tuscaloosa: University of Alabama Press, 1965), 14–15.

35. Anderson, *By Sea and by River*, 303.

Chapter 5

1. McPherson, *Battle Cry of Freedom*, 382.

2. David G. Surdam, *Northern Naval Superiority and the Economics of the American Civil War* (Columbia: University of South Carolina Press, 2001), 3–4.

3. Surdam, *Northern Naval Superiority*, 207–9.

4. S. P. Lee to Gideon Welles, July 1, 1864, *ORN*, ser. 1, vol. 10, p. 221–22.

5. S. P. Lee to Gideon Welles, August, 6, 1864, *ORN*, ser. 1, vol. 10, p. 338–39.

6. *The Statutes at Large of the Provisional Government of the Confederate States of America*, ed. James Muscoe Matthews (Richmond, VA: R. M. Smith, printed to Congress, 1864), 213. Great Britain negated Confederate letters of marque for privateers when it refused to accept captured prizes in British ports. If Confederate privateers were to be rewarded for their efforts, they would have to take their prizes back into a Confederate port. This British policy undermined the profit motive for would-be rebel privateers and meant the Confederate policy resulted in very little harm to Union shipping.

7. Confederate diplomats to Lord Russell, November 21, 1862, *ORN*, ser. 2, vol. 3, p. 299–301.

8. James Mason to Lord Russell, July 7, 1862, *ORN*, ser. 2, vol. 3, p. 495–96.

9. Jefferson Davis, *The Rise and Fall of the Confederate Government*, (New York: D. Appleton, 1881), 371–3.

10. Samuel DuPont to Gideon Welles, August 28, 1862, *ORN*, ser. 1, vol. 13, pp. 287–88.

11. See chapter 3, "The Impact of the Blockade," in Richard E. Beringer, Herman Hattaway, Archer Jones, and William N. Still Jr., et al., *Why the South Lost the Civil War* (Athens: University of Georgia Press, 1986), 56–59. This chapter was most likely written by William Still, since he was the expert on naval history among the authors. See also Owsley, *King Cotton Diplomacy*, 250–91.

12. Wise, *Lifeline of the Confederacy*, 226. Wise uses a detailed statistical study to support his analysis of material ineffectiveness, so this interpretation could be described as a hybrid between statistical and material ineffectiveness.

13. Browning, *From Cape Charles to Cape Fear*, 142, 156.

14. Browning, *From Cape Charles to Cape Fear*, 197, 264, 268.

15. Browning, *From Cape Charles to Cape Fear*, 306.

16. Owsley, *King Cotton Diplomacy*, 285.

17. Price, "Ships That Tested the Blockade of the Carolina Ports"; Price, "Blockade Running as a Business in South Carolina"; Marcus Price, "Ships That Tested the Blockade of the Gulf Ports, 1861–1865," *American Neptune* 11 (1951); Marcus Price, "Ships That Tested the Blockade of the Gulf Ports, 1861–1865," *American Neptune* 12 (1952); Marcus Price, "Ships That Tested the Blockade of the Georgia and East Florida Ports, 1861–1865," *American Neptune* 15 (1955).

18. Ideally, it would be possible to construct a data set containing all the inter- and intracoastal vessels that traveled between Southern ports from 1861 to 1865. However, this is probably impossible since these smaller boats were typically not registering in customshouses. In essence, the inter- and intra-coastal ships are a "known unknown" of wartime maritime traffic. We did not count these vessels' port visits—when we could track them—as successful blockade runs.

19. Wise, *Lifeline of the Confederacy*, 5, 227–328.

20. Each year from 1861 to 1863 has at least one ninety-two day phase, and 1864 has two ninety-two day phases to account for there being a February 29—1864 was a leap year.

21. Statistics compiled from the Marcus Price / Stephen Wise data. Chart 1 is a visual reflection of Table 1 and is also the product of the Price / Wise data sets.

22. Note that Table 2 has more data than Table 1, which includes only phases one through twelve. Table 2 also includes the preliminary and final phases.

23. Statistics compiled from Marcus Price / Stephen Wise data sets.

24. Statistics compiled from Marcus Price / Stephen Wise data sets.

25. The four out of five statistic represents one-way attempts and means that each steam-powered blockade-runner, on average, made two full round trips before being captured or destroyed. Statistics compiled from Marcus Price / Stephen Wise data sets.

26. Anderson, *By Sea and by River*, 228.

Conclusion

1. Wise, *Lifeline of the Confederacy*, 3.

WORKS CITED

Published Primary Sources

Allen, Charles Maxwell. *Dispatches from Bermuda: The Civil War Letters of Charles Maxwell Allen, United States Consul at Bermuda, 1861–1888.* Edited by Glen N. Wilche. Kent, OH: Kent State University Press, 2008.

Barrett, John G., and Buck Yearns, eds. *The North Carolina Civil War Documentary.* Chapel Hill: University of North Carolina Press, 1980.

Chesnut, Mary. *Mary Chesnut's Civil War.* Edited by C. Vann Woodward. New Have, CT: Yale University Press, 1981.

The Congressional Globe: A Century of Lawmaking for a New Nation; US Congressional Documents and Debates, 1774–1875.

Conventions and Declarations between the Powers Concerning War, Arbitration and Neutrality. The Hague, Netherlands: Martinus Nijhoff, 1915.

Dahlgren, John A. *Memoir of John A. Dahlgren, Rear-Admiral United States Navy.* Boston: James R. Osgood, 1882.

Davis, Jefferson. *The Rise and Fall of the Confederate Government.* 2 vols. New York: D. Appleton, 1881.

Edmonston, Catherine Ann Devereux. *"Journal of a Secesh Lady": The Diary of Catherine Ann Devereux Edmondston, 1860–1866.* Edited by Beth Gilbert Crabtree and James W. Patton. Raleigh: Division of Archives and History, North Carolina Department of Cultural Resources, 1979.

Executive Documents Printed by Order of the House of Representatives, First Session of the 38th Congress, 1863–1864. Washington, DC: Government Printing Office, 1864.

Hansard, *House of Commons Debates.* 1837.

Holmes, Emma. *The Diary of Miss Emma Holmes, 1861–1866.* Edited with an introduction and notes by John F. Marszalek. Baton Rouge: LSU Press, 1979.

LeConte, Emma. *When the World Ended: The Diary of Emma LeConte.* Edited by Earl Schenk Miers. New York: Oxford University Press, 1957.

Marchand, John B. *The Journals of John B. Marchand, U.S. Navy, 1861–1862.* Edited with commentary by Craig L. Symonds. Newport, RI: Naval War College Press, 1976.

Morley, John. *Life of Cobden.* London: Thomas Nelson, 1903.

Niche, Glen N., ed. *Dispatches from Bermuda: The Civil War Letters of Charles Maxwell Allen, United States Consul at Bermuda, 1861–1888.* Kent, OH: Kent State University Press, 2008.

Ruffin, Edmund. *The Diary of Edmund Ruffin*. Edited with an introduction and notes by William Kauffman Scarborough. Vol. 1, *Toward Independence: October, 1856–April, 1861*. Baton Rouge: LSU Press, 1972.

———. *The Diary of Edmund Ruffin*. Edited with an introduction and notes by William Kauffman Scarborough. Vol. 2, *The Years of Hope: April, 1861–June, 1863*. Baton Rouge: LSU Press, 1976.

———. *The Diary of Edmund Ruffin*. Edited with an introduction and notes by William Kauffman Scarborough. Vol. 3, *A Dream Shattered: June, 1863–June, 1865*. Baton Rouge: LSU Press, 1989.

Russell, William Howard. *My Diary North and South*. Edited by Eugene H. Berwanger. New York: Alfred A. Knopf, 1988.

Stephens, James P. edited by Jack L. Dickinson. *"If I Should Fall in Battle": The Civil War Diary of James P. Stephens*. Huntington, WV: John Deaver Drinko Academy for American Political Institution and Civic Culture, Marshall University, 2003.Thomas, Ella Gertrude Clanton. *The Secret Eye: The Journal of Ella Gertrude Clanton Thomas, 1848–1889*. Edited by Virginia Ingraham Burr. Introduction by Nell Irvin Painter, Chapel Hill: University of North Carolina Press, 1990.

United States War Department. *Official Records of the Union and Confederate Navies in the War of the Rebellion*. Washington, DC: Government Printing Office, 1899.

Vance, Zebulon. *The Papers of Zebulon Baird Vance*. Edited by Joe A. Mobley. Assisted by Anne Miller and Kenrick Simpson. Vol. 3, *1864–1865*. Raleigh: Office of Archives and History, North Carolina Department of Cultural Resources, 2013.

———. *The Papers of Zebulon Baird Vance*. Edited by Joe A. Mobley. Vol. 2, *1863*. Raleigh: Division of Archives and History, North Carolina Department of Cultural Resources, 1995.

Vandiver, Frank, ed. *Confederate Blockade Running Through Bermuda, 1861–1865: Letters and Cargo Manifests*. Austin: University of Texas Press, 1947.

Watson, William. *Adventures of a Blockade Runner; or, Trade in Time of War*. London: T. Fisher Unwin, 1893.

Welles, Gideon. *Diary of Gideon Welles: Secretary of the Navy under Lincoln and Johnson*. Vol. 1, *1861-March 1864*. New York: W. W. Norton, 1960.

Wilkinson, John. *The Narrative of a Blockade Runner*. New York: Sheldon, 1877.

Wixson, Neal E., ed. *From Civility to Survival: Richmond Ladies during the Civil War*. Bloomington, INL iUniverse, 2012.

Newspapers

New York Times

Secondary Sources

Anderson, Bern. *By Sea and by River: The Naval History of the Civil War.* New York: Alfred A. Knopf, 1962.

Bauer, K. Jack. *Surfboats and Horse Marines: U.S. Operations in the Mexican War, 1846–1848.* Annapolis, MD: United States Naval Institute Press, 1969.

Beckert, Sven. *Empire of Cotton: A Global History.* New York: Alfred A. Knopf, 2014.

Beringer, Richard E., Herman Hattaway, Archer Jones, and William N. Still Jr. *Why the South Lost the Civil War.* Athens: University of Georgia Press, 1986.

Bernath, Stuart L. *Squall across the Atlantic: American Civil War Prize Cases and Diplomacy.* Berkeley: University of California Press, 1970.

Berwanger, Eugene H. *The British Foreign Service and the American Civil War.* Lexington: University Press of Kentucky, 1994.

Blackman, Ann. *Wild Rose: The True Story of a Civil War Spy.* New York: Random House, 2005.

Bonner, Michael Brem. *Confederate Political Economy: Creating and Managing a Southern Corporatist Nation.* Baton Rouge: LSU Press, 2016.

Boykin, Edward. *Sea Devil of the Confederacy: The Story of the Florida and Her Captain, John Newland Maffitt.* New York: Funk and Wagnalls, 1959.

Browning, Robert M., Jr. *From Cape Charles to Cape Fear: The North Atlantic Blockading Squadron during the Civil War.* Tuscaloosa: University of Alabama Press, 1993.

———. *Success Is All That Was Expected: The South Atlantic Blockading Squadron during the Civil War.* Washington, DC. Brassey's, 2002.

Carlin, Colin. *Captain James Carlin, Anglo-American Blockade Runner.* Columbia: University of South Carolina Press, 2017.

Carlisle, Rodney. *Rough Waters: Sovereignty and the American Merchant Flag.* Annapolis, MD: Naval Institute Press, 2017.

Cochran, Hamilton. *Blockade Runners of the Confederacy.* Indianapolis: Bobbs-Merrill, 1958.

Dalzell, George W. *The Flight from the Flag: The Continuing Effect of the Civil War upon the American Carrying Trade.* Chapel Hill: University of North Carolina Press, 1940.

Davis, Charles S. *Colin J. McRae: Confederate Financial Agent, Blockade Running in the Trans-Mississippi South as Affected by the Confederate Government's Direct European Procurement of Goods.* Tuscaloosa, AL: Confederate, 1961. Reprint. Wilmington, NC: Broadfoot, 2000.

Davis, Lance E., and Stanley L. Engerman. *Naval Blockades in Peace and War: An Economic History since 1750.* Cambridge: Cambridge University Press, 2006.

Dickey, Christopher. *Our Man in Charleston: Britain's Secret Agent in the Civil War South.* New York: Crown, 2015.

Dougherty, Kevin. *Strangling the Confederacy: Coastal Operations of the American Civil War.* Philadelphia: Casemate, 2010.

Doyle, Don H. *The Cause of All Nations: An International History of the American Civil War.* New York: Basic Books, 2015.

Durham, Roger S. *High Seas and Yankee Gunboats: A Blockade-Running Adventure from the Diary of James Dickson.* Columbia: University of South Carolina Press, 2005.

Durkin, Joseph T. *Confederate Navy Chief: Stephen R. Mallory.* Columbia: University of South Carolina Press, 1954.

Foreman, Amanda. *A World on Fire: Britain's Crucial Role in the American Civil War.* New York: Random House, 2010.

Fox, Stephen. *Wolf of the Deep: Raphael Semmes and the Notorious Confederate Raider CSS* Alabama. New York: Vintage Books, 2007.

Hall, Andrew W. *Civil War Blockade Running on the Texas Coast.* Charleston, SC: History Press, 2014.

Hearn, Chester G. *Tracks in the Sea: Matthew Fontaine Maury and the Mapping of the Oceans.* New York: McGraw Hill, 2002.

Hickey, Donald R. *The War of 1812: A Forgotten Conflict.* Urbana: University of Illinois Press, 2012.

Jenkins, Roy. *Gladstone: A Biography.* New York: Random House, 1995.

Jones, Wilbur Devereux. *The American Problem in British Diplomacy, 1841–1861.* London: Macmillan, 1974.

Leigh, Philip. *Trading with the Enemy: The Covert Economy during the American Civil War.* Yardley, PA: Westholme, 2014.

Lonn, Ella. *Salt as a Factor in the Confederacy.* 1933 Reprint. Tuscaloosa: University of Alabama Press, 1965.

McNeil, Jim. *Masters of the Shoals: Tales of the Cape Fear Pilots Who Ran the Union Blockade.* Cambridge, MA: Da Capo, 2003.

McPherson, James M. *War on the Waters: The Union and Confederate Navies, 1861–1865.* Chapel Hill: University of North Carolina Press, 2012.

Moore, R. Scott. *The Civil War on the Atlantic Coast, 1861–1865.* Washington, DC: Center of Military History, US Army, 2015.

Neely, Mark E., Jr. *The Fate of Liberty: Abraham Lincoln and Civil Liberties.* New York: Oxford University Press, 1991.

Owsley, Frank L. *King Cotton Diplomacy: Foreign Relations of the Confederate States of America.* Chicago: University of Chicago Press, 1931.

Rees, Sian. *Sweet Water and Bitter: The Ships That Stopped the Slave Trade.* Durham: University of New Hampshire Press, 2011.

Ridley, Jasper. *Lord Palmerston.* New York: E. P. Dutton, 1970.

Robinton, Madeline Russell. *An Introduction to the Papers of the New York Prize Court, 1861–1865.* New York: Columbia University Press, 1945.

Scharf, J. Thomas. *History of the Confederate States Navy: From Its Organization to the Surrender of Its Last Vessel.* 1886 Reprint. New York: Fairfax, 1977.

Shingleton, Royce. *High Seas Confederate: The Life and Times of John Newland Maffitt.* Columbia: University of South Carolina Press, 1994.

Smith, Andrew F. *Starving the South: How the North Won the Civil War.* New York: St. Martin's, 2011.

Soley, James Russell. *The Blockade and the Cruisers.* New York: Charles Scribner's Sons, 1883.

Stern, Phillip Van Doren. *Secret Missions of the Civil War.* New York: Bonanza Books, 1959.

Stiles, T. J. *The First Tycoon: The Epic Life of Cornelius Vanderbilt.* New York: Random House, 2009.

Still, William N., Jr. *Iron Afloat: The Story of the Confederate Armorclads.* Nashville, TN: Vanderbilt University Press, 1971.

Surdam, David G. *Northern Naval Superiority and the Economics of the American Civil War.* Columbia: University of South Carolina Press, 2001.

Symonds, Craig. *The Civil War at Sea.* Oxford: Oxford University Press, 2009.

———. *Confederate Admiral: The Life and Wars of Franklin Buchanan.* Annapolis, MD: Naval Institute Press, 1999.

———. *Lincoln and His Admirals: Abraham Lincoln, the US Navy, and the Civil War.* New York: Oxford University Press, 2008.

Taylor, A. J. P. *The Struggle for Mastery in Europe, 1848–1918.* Oxford: Oxford University Press, 1954.

———. *The Trouble Makers: Dissent over Foreign Policy.* Bloomington: Indiana University Press, 1958.

Webster, C. L., III. *Entrepôt: Government Imports into the Confederate States.* Roseville, MN: Edinborough, 2010.

Wills, Mary Alice. *The Confederate Blockade of Washington, D.C., 1861–1862.* Parsons, WV: McClain, 1975.

Wise, Stephen R. *Lifeline of the Confederacy: Blockade Running during the Civil War.* Columbia: University of South Carolina Press, 1988.

Wright, Gavin. *The Political Economy of the Cotton South: Households, Markets, and Wealth in the Nineteenth Century.* New York: W.W. Norton, 1978.

Articles

Bailey, Frank E. "The Economics of British Foreign Policy, 1825–1850." *Journal of Modern History* 12, no. 4 (December 1940).

Bonner, Michael Brem, and Peter McCord. "Reassessment of the Union Blockade's Effectiveness in the Civil War." *North Carolina Historical Review* 88, no. 4 (October 2011).

Daly, Robert W. "Pay and Prize Money in the Old Navy, 1776–1899." *Proceedings of the U.S. Naval Institute* 74, no. 8 (August 1948).

Hetherington, Bruce W., and Peter J. Kower. "A Reexamination of Lebergott's Paradox about Blockade Running during the American Civil War." *Journal of Economic History* 69, no. 2 (June 2009).

Lebergott, Stanley. "Through the Blockade: The Profitability and Extent of Cotton Smuggling, 1861–1865." *Journal of Economic History* 41, no. 4 (December 1981).

———. "Why the South Lost: Commercial Purpose in the Confederacy, 1861–1865." *Journal of American History* 70, no. 1 (June 1983).

May, Robert E., "The Irony of Confederate Diplomacy: Visions of Empire, the Monroe Doctrine, and the Quest for Nationhood." *Journal of Southern History* 83, no. 1 (February 2017).

Merrill, James M. "Strategy Makers in the Union Navy Department, 1861–1865." *Mid-America: An Historical Review* 44 (January 1962).

Negus, Samuel, "A Notorious Nest of Offence: Neutrals, Belligerents, and Union Jails in Civil War Blockade Running." *Civil War History* 56, no. 4 (December 2010).

Paulin, Charles Oscar. "A Half Century of Naval Administration in America, 1861–1911." *United States Naval Institute Proceedings* 39, no. 1 (March 1913).

Price, Marcus. "Blockade Running as a Business in South Carolina during the War between the States, 1861–1865." *American Neptune* 9 (1949).

———. "Ships That Tested the Blockade of the Carolina Ports, 1861–1865." American Neptune 8 (1948).

———. "Ships That Tested the Blockade of the Georgia and East Florida Ports, 1861–1865." American Neptune 15 (1955).

———. "Ships That Tested the Blockade of the Gulf Ports, 1861–1865." American Neptune 11 (1951).

———. "Ships That Tested the Blockade of the Gulf Ports, 1861–1865." American Neptune 12 (1952).

Weddle, Kevin J. "The Blockade Board of 1861 and Union Naval Strategy." *Civil War History* 48, no. 2 (2002).

INDEX

Adams, Francis, 22
Adams, John, 10
adaptation effect, 146
Agrippina (ship), 116
Alliance (ship), 106–7
Anaconda Plan, 2, 53, 58, 166
Anderson, Bern, 75, 142, 162
Antonica, 35
Archibald, Edward, 109
Arkansas, allegiance of, 46
Armstrong, J. F., 62–63
Army Corps of Engineers, 61
assumption, pitfall of, 151
Atkinson, John, 32
Atlantic Seaboard, bases on, 55
Austria, as signatory, 13

Bache, Alexander, 54
Bahamas, 27, 37, 96, 102, 113–14, 115, 117–18, 167; geography of, 71
Baja California, 11
Bald Head Island, 61
Baltimore, prize court in, 66
Bancroft, George, 11
Banshee (blockade-runner), 118–19
Barnard, J. G., 54
Bauer, K. Jack, 11
Bayley, C. J., 113
Beaufort, North Carolina, 59, 76, 106; port, 107; prize court in, 66; runs into, 106
Beckert, Sven, 21
belligerent rights, 23–26, 42
Benjamin, Judah P., 16, 20

Bermuda, 99; reporting on blockade-runners in, 102
Black Belt plantations, 100
Black Sea, 13
Blacker, Louis, 28–29
Blackman, Ann, 98
Blanch, Captain, 86–87
blockade: defining, 14; international law, 13; as naval strategy, 10; opinions on, 18; paper blockade, 4, 19–20, 76, 80, 103, 109; principles of, 10–11; proclaiming, 12; setting standards for, 10–11; speculation about, 16. *See also* Union blockade
blockade, psychology of: blockade commentary, 134; Confederate social psyche, 135; contributory effectiveness, 140–43; cumulative psychological toll, 136; ersatz measures, 134; psycho-historiographic effect, 139–44; shipping deterrent, 138–39; Southerners and, 126–37. *See also* effectiveness, evaluating
Blockade and the Cruisers, The (Soley), 152
blockade diplomacy, 104, 110, 115, 128; capturing British nationals, 34; elimination of privateering, 33–34; friendly intimidation, 113–14; HMS *Petrel* episode, 36–40; imprisoning Northern subjects, 36; *Labuan* (ship), affair of, 27–33; and secession crisis, 14–19; silent consent, 119; stakes of, 128; start of, 19–27; *Vixen* affair, 12–13